COMPUTE!'s First Book of
COMMODORE

COMPUTE! Publications,Inc.
One of the ABC Publishing Companies

Greensboro, North Carolina

Commodore 64 is a trademark of Commodore Electronics, Ltd.

The following article was originally published in *COMPUTE!* Magazine, copyright 1982, Small System Services, Inc.:
"Commodore 64 Memory Map" (October)
The following articles were originally published in *COMPUTE!* Magazine, copyright 1983, Small System Services, Inc.:
"Commodore 64 Architecture" (January)
"All About WAIT Instruction" (January)
"REM Revealed" (January)
"Perfect INPUTs" (January)
"Joysticks and Sprites" (February)
"Data Storage" (March)
"The Confusing Catalog" (March)
"Automatic Program Selector" (March)
"Data Searcher" (June)
"Soft-16" (June)
The following articles were originally published in *COMPUTE!* Magazine, copyright 1983, COMPUTE! Publications, Inc.:
"Backup 1540/1541 Disks" (July)
"Programmer's Alarm Clock" (July)
The following article was originally published in *COMPUTE!'s Gazette*, copyright 1983, COMPUTE! Publications, Inc.:
"Alfabug" (July)
The following article was originally published in *COMPUTE!* Magazine, copyright 1983, Jim Butterfield:
"Commodore 64 Video — A Guided Tour, Parts I-VII"

Printed in the United States of America

ISBN 0-942386-20-5

10 9 8 7 6 5 4 3

COMPUTE! Publications, Inc. Post Office Box 5406, Greensboro, NC 27403, (919) 275-9809, is a subsidiary of American Broadcasting Companies, Inc. and is not associated with any manufacturer of personal computers. Commodore 64 is a trademark of Commodore Electronics, Ltd.

Contents

Foreword

The Commodore 64 computer was introduced in the fall of 1982, and immediately became the first choice of hundreds of thousands of new and experienced computer users. Its music, sound, and graphics capabilities are remarkable, and its price tag brought it within the reach of many first time buyers.

COMPUTE! Books is ready to help you make the most of it. *COMPUTE!'s First Book of Commodore 64* offers something for computer users at every level of expertise, from the beginner to the expert. And as you gain experience and move from one level to the next, you'll find that this book can provide the key to each level of computer knowledge.

For beginners, the "Starting Out" section offers an introduction to the Commodore 64 and the step-by-step creation of a simple program.

If you're interested in graphics, Jim Butterfield's seven-part "Commodore 64 Video" is the ideal introduction.

Do you use joysticks, printers, disks, cassettes? There are articles and programs to help you.

To learn your computer from the inside out, the "Memory" section shows you where everything is — and provides "A Window on Memory" which lets you scroll through all 64K and see what is happening to memory while the computer is running.

And if you program in machine language, this book includes a complete monitor, "Micromon-64," and a complete assembler program, written in BASIC.

Of the articles in this book which originally appeared in *COMPUTE!* Magazine or *COMPUTE!'s Gazette for Commodore*, many have been enhanced since their original publication. Many other articles and programs, however, are appearing here for the first time anywhere.

Chapter 1

Starting Out

More Than Just Another Computer

Sheldon Leemon

Don't let its outward resemblance to the VIC fool you. Inside, the Commodore 64 is full of brand-new technology. While it retains certain features of older Commodore computers, the 64 extends many of those features and at the same time introduces new ones.

The New Chip

Let's start with the microprocessor, the "computer on a chip" that forms the heart of the system. Every Commodore machine from the original PET through the VIC has been built around the 6502 chip. The 64, however, uses a 6510 microprocessor. This chip uses the same machine instructions as the 6502, which aids in software compatibility, but adds a built-in Input/Output (I/O) Port. The 64 uses this port to manage addressing space.

As its name indicates, the 64 comes with 64K RAM standard. But it also has an 8K BASIC Interpreter ROM, an 8K Operating System Kernal ROM, a 4K Character Generator ROM, a 6581 Sound Interface Device (SID), a 6566 Video Interface Controller (VIC-II), and two 6526 Complex Interface Adapter chips, which along with the other I/O chips require 4K of addressing space for their hardware registers. That adds up to 88K, 24K more than the 6510 chip can address at once.

In order to allocate resources, the I/O port allows the user to determine which segments of RAM and ROM will be addressed at any one time. The standard configuration allocates 40K of consecutive RAM for BASIC programming (about 2K of which is taken up by screen memory and system workspace); 8K to the BASIC ROM; 4K for addressing graphics, sound, and I/O chips; 8K for the Operating System Kernal ROM, which includes the screen editor and housekeeping software; with 4K of spare RAM

3

left over for "safe" memory, which can be used for machine language programs, an I/O buffer, etc.

This default memory allocation can be easily changed by the user to one of seven other possible memory maps. Any of the programs in ROM may be switched out and replaced by RAM. That means a program like a word processor, which needs as large a storage area as possible, could simply switch out the BASIC ROM and gain access to 8K more RAM space. As a matter of fact, all 64K of RAM could be used at once (although some portion would have to be devoted to I/O driver routines, like a screen editor, and the I/O devices would have to be switched back in for communication with peripherals).

Memory addressing space can be allocated not only between internal RAM and ROM, but between external ROM cartridges as well. These cartridges (which are *not* compatible with those designed for the VIC) can hold up to 16K of ROM and can be made to operate either in place of the BASIC ROM or along with it to extend its set of commands.

The Same BASIC

The BASIC used in the 64 is the familiar Commodore BASIC 2, and the Operating System Kernal is generally patterned after its predecessors. This somewhat represents a compromise. On the one hand, it allows a high degree of compatibility with the large body of software currently available for Commodore computers.

Most of the nongraphics type of software, including much business and educational software, can easily be converted, and indeed much of it already has been converted for use on the 64. In fact, Commodore offers a PET emulator program which will allow the user to run a very high percentage of PET programs on the 64 virtually unchanged.

It would, however, have been nice to have software built-in that was better adapted to the tremendous new graphics and sound capabilities of this computer. As it stands, the user must PEEK and POKE quite a bit more than a user-friendly system should require. It is some consolation, however, that the system ROMs can be easily switched out and a whole new Operating System loaded in from disk, should an easier method for using 64 graphics and sound be developed in the future.

Better Graphics

What makes the 64's color graphics so extraordinary is a separate integrated circuit chip which processes the video display information. Just as the VIC has its Video Interface Controller chip (for which it was named), the 64 has a VIC, too — or to be more exact, a VIC-II. The 6566 video chip supports a wide range of character graphics, bitmapped graphics, and sprite graphics. Let's examine what each of these types of graphics has to offer.

Character Graphics

Character graphics includes the ordinary text characters that appear on the screen when you turn the computer on. The text display consists of 25 lines, each having 40 characters. These characters are formed from data stored in the Character Generator ROM, which holds the two standard Commodore character sets, regular and inverse video. One set contains uppercase letters and graphics characters, and the other has both upper- and lowercase.

However, the user is not limited to the standard character set stored in ROM. User-defined characters, up to 256 at any one time, may be displayed from RAM, allowing the programmer to display foreign language alphabets, math symbols, or custom graphics characters. Like the VIC, one area of memory on the 64 is set aside for the characters to be displayed, while a separate area holds the color information for each character. This means that the user can individually select one of 16 different foreground colors for each of the 1000 characters that appears on the screen.

Besides the standard character display, there are two other more specialized text modes. The first is a *multicolor character mode*, similar to those found on the VIC and the Atari computers. In this mode, each character is made up of eight rows, each four dots across. The color of each dot may be selected from one of two color registers or from the value stored in color memory for that particular character, so that each character may display up to three colors at once, in addition to the background color. Although the standard character ROM is not set up to accommodate such characters, by using custom graphics characters the programmer can take advantage of this feature to create colorful graphics displays that are easily animated.

To aid in this animation, the 64 has fine-scrolling registers, which allow both the horizontal and vertical position of characters to be changed one increment at a time, so that they may be moved smoothly across the screen. In order to create a "buffer" area for new information to enter the screen as the old information scrolls off it, the screen size may be shrunk to 24 rows of 38 characters each.

One interesting feature of this mode is that when it is
enabled, only those characters whose color codes are above a certain number will be displayed as multicolored. All other characters will be displayed normally. Thus, multicolor characters may
be mixed freely with normal, high-resolution characters on the
same screen.

The other special mode is the *extended background color mode*.
When this mode is enabled, only 64 characters may be displayed
at any one time, but the user not only can choose the foreground
color for each letter but may select the background color from one
of four color registers as well. These registers may be set to any of
the 16 colors available on the 64. This allows the screen to be di-
vided into different colored "windows," for a split-screen display,
for example. Extended-color mode cannot be combined with
multicolor mode or bitmap mode.

Bitmap Graphics

Bitmap graphics enables the high-resolution plotting of 320 dots
horizontally by 200 dots vertically. As on the VIC, the display
data, or bitmap, is set up in the same format as character graphics.
Each byte of information has eight bits, each of which represents a
horizontal dot. Each group of eight bytes has its rows of dots
stacked one on top of the other, so that the groups of eight bytes
form an 8 x 8 grid. This makes plotting individual points a little
more difficult than a sequential arrangement would, but it also
makes it easier to intermix character data into a bitmap display.

As in the character modes, the foreground color of each 8 x 8
grid may be individually selected. Bitmap mode requires 8K of
memory for screen data and another 1K for a color memory. The
multicolor option is also available in bitmap mode. Although the
resolution is reduced to 160 dots horizontally, this mode offers the
widest variety of color selection, as it allows each dot within a 4 x 8
grid to be one of three individually selectable colors.

Sprite Graphics

Sprite graphics is a feature which aids in the animation of
graphics characters, or *sprites*. It really comprises a completely
separate system for displaying graphics, in addition to the more
normal character or bitmap graphics. A sprite is a special graphics
character whose shape is defined by 63 bytes of data, laid out in a
24 x 21 dot array. This means that each sprite is approximately
three text characters wide by two-and-a-half characters tall. Up to

eight of these sprites may be displayed on any horizontal line.

Sprites have many interesting attributes that make them useful in games and animation. The 16K display area of memory can hold up to 256 blocks of 64 bytes of sprite data. The shape to be displayed is indicated by a register which points to the block number to be used. Changing this number instantly changes the shape of the sprite. This makes animation as easy as stepping through a number of shapes. Each sprite has an individual color register, so that its color may be chosen from one of the 16 standard colors. A multicolor sprite mode, similar to multicolor character and bitmap modes, is available. It reduces the horizontal resolution to 12 dots across, but allows each sprite to display two colors from shared multicolor registers, as well as its unique sprite color. Horizontal and vertical placement of sprites is accomplished by changing the value of the X and Y position registers. Movement will occur instantly upon such a change. Each sprite may be enlarged to double size in either the horizontal or vertical plane, or both at once. When a sprite is moved to a spot on the screen already occupied by regular graphics, a priority register determines which will be displayed. Thus, each sprite may be selected to move either *in front of* or *behind* other screen graphics. There is also a system of *collision detection* to let the user know when a sprite is positioned in the same spot as character or bitmap graphics, or when two sprites overlap. By checking these registers, a game program, for example, can tell when an explosion is in order.

More Features!

Much more could be said about the VIC-II chip. For instance, though it can address only 16K of memory at a time, any of four banks of 16K can be selected. Within a 16K bank, the placement of the screen display may be easily selected, allowing two or more screen areas to be set up in memory at once and rapidly alternated, a procedure known as *page flipping*. Even if the 16K bank chosen is one in which the 6510 addresses ROM memory, the VIC-II can address the RAM which shares its memory space, thus allowing the same memory location to do double duty. Likewise, the VIC-II can address the character ROM as if it were in RAM, even though the 6510 cannot tell that it is there. The VIC-II also provides support for input from a light pen. Of great interest to machine language programmers is the system of raster interrupts. The VIC-II can generate an interrupt request in synchronization with the raster scan display. This means that the more advanced programmer can change any of the VIC registers partway down the screen, so that two or more character sets can be displayed on different parts of the screen simultaneously, or that the same sprite can appear at two different vertical locations at once, thereby increasing the total number of sprites that can be shown.

A Music Chip: SID

Owners of the 64 will be glad to discover that their VIC has a brother, SID (Sound Interface Device). SID is a musician on a chip, capable of easily producing sounds more often associated with expensive keyboard synthesizers than with home computers. SID provides a wide range of controls over three musical voices, including high-resolution control over pitch (frequency), tone color (timbre), and dynamics (volume). It can even be used to filter external signals that are fed into its audio input! Although briefly explaining these features is no substitute for hearing the effects they produce, it may give you some idea of the range of sounds available.

The frequency of each voice is controlled by a 16-bit register, which means that the pitch can be changed in 65536 steps, covering over eight octaves. While pitch is a concept most of us readily understand, there are other, more subtle sound components which SID can control: One of these is *waveform*. Each voice can be set to one of four waveforms. The Triangle waveform output is low in harmonics and has a mellow, flute-like quality. The Sawtooth waveform is rich in even and odd harmonics and has a bright, brassy quality. The Pulse waveform has a harmonic content that can be adjusted by the Pulse Width registers and can produce tone qualities ranging from bright, hollow square waves to a nasal, reedy pulse. And the Noise waveform produces a random signal which can be varied from a low rumbling to hissing white noise. This waveform is good for creating explosions, wind, snare drums, engine noises, etc.

Another important control is the volume shaping of the Attack/Decay/Sustain/Release (ADSR) registers. These registers control the sound *envelope*. This term describes how the sounds produced by different types of instruments build to peak (attack), drop to an intermediate level (decay), hold that level for a time (sustain), and finally fade away (release). Each type of instrument has its own distinct pattern. When a drum is hit, the sound reaches full volume and decays rapidly to zero volume, while on string instruments the note may be sustained for a long time. The ADSR controls of the SID chip allow it not only to imitate the sounds of a wide range of instruments, but to synthesize patterns not found on any existing musical instrument.

There are a number of other controls as well. A Sync control synchronizes the fundamental frequency of two oscillators, pro- ducing "hard sync" effects. A Ring Modulation control allows the creation of bell or gong sounds. Individually selected Highpass, Lowpass, and Bandpass filters are available for all three voices and can be used singly or in combination.

Though not sound related, this chip also controls the reading of paddle controllers.

If reading about SID's capabilities doesn't excite you, hearing them certainly will. The only drawback to all of this power is that there are no BASIC commands to allow easy access to 64 sound. After setting up volume and ADSR levels, each note will require that you POKE at a minimum two frequency bytes and one wave- form byte.

Communicating with the Outside

To round out its complement of support chips, the 64 has two 6526 Complex Interface Adapter (CIA) chips. These chips each have two 8-bit I/O ports, which are used for reading the keyboard and joystick ports, as well as for communicating with external parallel and serial devices over the User Port and the Serial Bus. In addition, each has two independent, linkable 16-bit interval timers, which can also count external pulses or measure fre- quency, pulse width, and delay times of external signals. Each chip also has a 24-hour, time-of-day clock with programmable alarm.

The 64 can use the same 1541 disk drive and 1525 printer as the VIC, or with an IEEE cartridge it can use the same wide range of dot-matrix and letter-quality printers, and floppy and hard- disk systems available for the CBM line.

A lot of software is available for the 64, and many vendors of Commodore software have made their offerings 64-compatible. Major producers of arcade-type games have 64 translations com- pleted or in the works. Commodore itself already has or is ready- ing a number of arcade games for release, as well as utilities such as the VSP cartridge to add graphics and sound commands to BASIC. The best news of all is that most software for the 64 is be- ing priced well below comparable titles for the older CBM line.

1 Starting Out

This stands to reason, for even with 64K of RAM and full-blown color graphics and sound capabilities, the Commodore 64 is one of the least expensive computers currently on the market. With its introduction, the group of people who can afford to own a powerful computer has suddenly grown much, much larger.

Making the Computer Do What You Want

Orson Scott Card

Just how do you write a program? Here is an organized method of design-ing and writing a program from the idea to the finished product. Along the way, both beginners and intermediate programmers will learn some new techniques — and a great deal about 64 sound.

What's the hardest thing about programming?

It's not really that hard to learn the commands and what they do. The words are mostly English, and the rules pretty much make sense. You had a much harder time with high school Span-ish or French than you'll ever have learning 64 BASIC.

But when you sit down to write your first serious program, you might run right into a brick wall.

Where do you start? What do you say? With foreign language study you had dialogues to teach you speech patterns, but you don't have any memorized dialogues to teach you that you begin with "Buenos días, Señor 64." You don't have a friendly partner who is willing to try to understand what you're saying despite your accent. The computer won't prompt you and say, "OK, you've given me the variables. Now you need to start a loop." The structure, the shape of the program, depends entirely on you. And if the computer doesn't understand you, too bad.

A Program from the Ground Up

One of the best ways to learn programming techniques is to do it with someone else who explains what each line or technique is for. That's what the rest of this article is for. I'll create a program, a simple utility, and describe what I'm doing as I do it. Now, I'm not an expert on the 64 or any other computer, but I have written a few fairly complex programs that actually worked, and some things I've picked up might be useful to you.

11

Designing the Program

As long as you're going to create a program, you might as well create something useful. One of the most interesting features of the 64 is the way it controls and produces sound. More than any other home computer, this one puts the power of a synthesizer into your hands. Unfortunately, the sound commands aren't very easy to use — it takes a lot of different commands to make even the simplest sounds. So this program will be a simple utility to allow you to test sounds, changing them as much as you want, until you find the right one.

The first step in programming is to decide what you want the program to do. Here's a list of features I think this sound utility ought to include:

1. The sound should repeat, over and over, while users can change the sound right from the keyboard.

2. The computer should report to the users all the numbers needed to exactly reproduce the sounds that they hear.

3. Users should be able to change all the features of the sound: waveform, pulse width, pitch, attack, decay, sustain, release, and duration.

4. Users should be able to do all this whether they understand anything about sound or not — in other words, their ears should tell them what they're doing, leaving them free to experiment.

5. Almost as important as what the program *will* do is what the program *won't* do. It won't use more than one voice at a time. It won't allow the creation of tunes. It won't directly store the sound parameters on tape or disk or list them to a printer. And it won't be fast. All those features, if we had them, would make a fantastic program, but we're after something simple right now.

A Few Words on 64 Sound

The best way for you to learn what the different sound features of the 64 do is to have you type in this program, RUN it, and hear what each different effect sounds like.

But the numbers in this program won't make any sense to you without a basic understanding of what the 64 is doing to create sound. There are eight locations in memory that you need to change in order to produce a sound for one voice. In this utility program, I'm going to assign the address of each of these locations to a variable name, so let's use the variable names from the start:

P1 and P2. These are the "high frequency byte" and "low frequency byte." The addresses for voice 1 are 54273 (P1) and 54272 (P2). What they control is the pitch of voice 1 — how high or low the note is on the musical scale. The higher the number, the higher the note. P1 is the broad control, like the channel selector on your TV. P2 is fine tuning.

VL. This is the general volume setting for all three voices in the 64. It can be set from 0 to 15: 0 is off; 15 is maximum. We are going to set it once, at the beginning of the program, and leave it alone — there are much better volume controls later in the program. The address is 54296.

AD. Attack and decay are the first two parts of the sound envelope, often referred to as ADSR envelope — Attack/Decay/Sustain/Release. Attack is how quickly the sound gets to full volume. Decay is how quickly it drops off. Sustain is how loud it is through the rest of the note. Release is how long it takes for the sound to die away when the note is stopped. I won't even attempt to describe the effects of different sound envelopes to you — the program will do it much better.

Attack and decay are controlled from the same location in memory: 54277. There are 15 possible levels for attack, and 15 possible levels for decay. And there are eight bits in the number stored at 54277. Attack is controlled by the four highest bits (the "high nybble"), and decay by the four lowest. If you don't know what bits are, don't worry. It's enough to know that the meaningful values for attack are multiples of 16, from 16 to 240, while the meaningful values for decay are the numbers from 1 to 15. To set up both attack and decay, you choose the numbers you want for each, add them together, and POKE them in. In other words,

POKE AD,ATTACK+DECAY

SR. The same system works for sustain and release. Sustain uses the high nybble and release uses the low nybble. The location in memory is 54278.

WF. Waveform is controlled at 54276. There are four options, represented by the numbers 17, 33, 65, and 129. The lowest number is a fairly pure tone; the highest is noise. You have to hear the others.

SW. The square waveform, number 65, has another significant controlling number, the pulse width, controlled at locations 54274 and 54275. In our program, we'll store 8 in 54275 and allow the user to modify the number at SW.

Organizing the Program

All the program really has to do is find out what values the user
wants to use and POKE them into the right memory locations.
This is the point where careful programming makes the difference between useful programs and confusing software that is
more trouble than it's worth.

For instance, we could simply have a program like this:

```
10 POKE 54296,15
20 FOR I=54272 TO 54278:INPUT N:POKE I,N:
   NEXT I
30 FOR I=1 TO 250: NEXT I:POKE 54276,254:
   GOTO 20
```

There it is. A complete program. Nothing could be simpler. RUN
it, and it will prompt you to put in a number. It will take each
memory address in numerical order, take whatever you type in,
and make the sound. Then it will ask you for another.

Sounds great — until you try to use it. Then you have to remember the right order for the numbers you type in. If you make
a mistake, there's no way of checking to see what you did wrong.
If you forget where you are, you might as well press RUN/STOP
and start over.

This is not what you would call "user-friendly." One mistake
and the whole thing crashes down around your ears. You can't
tell what's going on, it makes each sound only once, and even if
you *do* produce a sound you like, there's no guarantee that you
can remember how to make it again!

User-friendly programming. The principles of user-friendly
programming are simple enough:

1. Tell users what they need to do.
2. Protect them from mistakes.
3. Do something useful.
4. Tell them what they did.

When users sit down to run your program, they shouldn't
face a blank screen with a single question mark on it. They should
have a clear explanation of what to do. If they push the wrong
button or enter the wrong value, it shouldn't hurt a thing. And
when they get a result — in this case, a sound — they should hear
it over and over; and while it is playing they should *see* the
numbers that are being POKEd for each function, so that they can
jot them down and use them later in a program.

Most of the numbers to be POKEd have only a few valid choices. Why should the user have to remember what those choices are? Instead of using raw INPUT statements, let's create some *toggles*, so that by pushing a single button, the user can switch from one option to another. For instance, with WF (waveform) the only valid numbers are 17, 33, 65, and 129. In our program, the space bar will be the toggle. Each time the user presses the space bar, the program will POKE the next higher value into WF. If the last value was 129, then pressing the space bar will make the program start over at 17.

Let's think through how we would like the program to work — from the user's point of view. Let's say you sit down at the computer, load the program from tape or disk, and type RUN. The screen should display a menu of choices — what result will come from pushing a certain key.

Keyboard use. The keys we'll use will be the function keys on the right side of the keyboard, in combination with the shift key. We can also use the cursor keys (CRSR left/right and CRSR up/down), the space bar, the RETURN key, and perhaps the up-arrow key.

Why these keys, instead of letter keys? As long as the choices are fairly few, the function keys and the major, powerful keys on the keyboard like RETURN, the space bar, SHIFT, COMMODORE, and the cursor keys are the most memorable. If there are eight or fewer choices, the joystick is even better.

If you have large numbers of functions, however, the letter keys might be best, especially if you can choose letter keys that help the user remember what the function is — *W* for waveform, for instance, *A* for attack, *D* for decay, and so on. (If you prefer that method, you'll have no trouble altering this program to fit your needs.)

Communication

There are two displays this program will need. First, there should be a continuous display of what key to press in order to change each value. Second, there should be a display showing what values are being POKEd to make the sound the user is hearing. This display needs to be updated every time a value is changed.

Menus. The display of optional choices and how to select them is the *menu*. Especially when your program uses toggles, there must be a display to show what the toggles are. A simple program, in which there are only a few choices, usually gets by with a simple menu — all the possible choices displayed at once.

Really complex programs, like word-processing programs, use *nested* menus. This means that they are given one menu of a few choices. Then, when they make a choice, a new menu is displayed showing further options. Think of it as a shopping mall. There are many stores to choose from when you first come in. Once you choose a store — department store, for instance — you have many departments to choose from. And once you choose a department, you still have many items on racks or shelves to select from. Figure 1 is a diagram of nested menus.

Another menu concept is *chained* menus. After you make a choice at your first menu, you are presented with a second menu that was not affected in any way by the first choice. A third, fourth, and fifth menu may follow in order. Think of it as going along a cafeteria line. You can select from the salad display, but then you must move on to the vegetables, and then the main courses, and then the beverages, always in the same order. Initialization routines to set up complex software usually use chained menus. Figure 2 is a diagram of chained menus.

Figure 1. Nested Menus

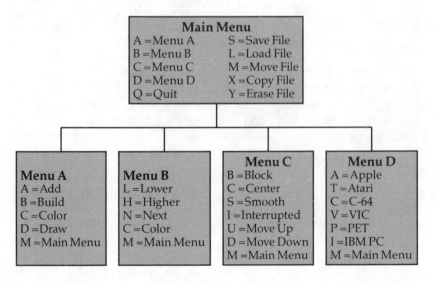

Figure 2. Chained Menus

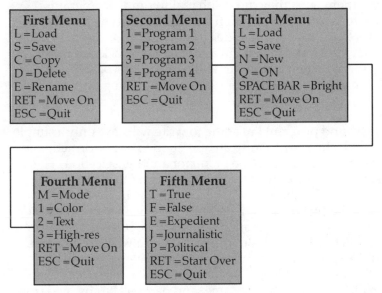

First Menu	Second Menu	Third Menu
L =Load	1 =Program 1	L =Load
S =Save	2 =Program 2	S =Save
C =Copy	3 =Program 3	N =New
D =Delete	4 =Program 4	Q =ON
E =Rename	RET =Move On	SPACE BAR =Bright
RET =Move On	ESC =Quit	RET =Move On
ESC =Quit		ESC =Quit

Fourth Menu	Fifth Menu
M =Mode	T =True
1 =Color	F =False
2 =Text	E =Expedient
3 =High-res	J =Journalistic
RET =Move On	P =Political
ESC =Quit	RET =Start Over
	ESC =Quit

You can see that your choice of simple, nested, or chained menus depends on the needs of the program.

If your program has only a few choices and will return to the main program after completing each chosen task, then a simple menu is all you will need.

If your program has many, many choices, you will probably want to group the choices into meaningful categories. A main menu will let users choose a category, and the menu for that category will let them choose which specific item they want. A benefit of the nested menus is that you can use the same toggles in each different menu, but the *meaning* of each toggle will be changed.

If your program goes through a setup phase, or always does things in a certain order, then you'll want to progress from step to step, offering users certain choices at each step, and then proceeding to the next step. If the choices at each step of a chained menu system are similar, it's a good idea to have the toggles carry similar meanings. For instance, if several menus have the option "Enter a new filename," then it's a good idea to have the same key activate that choice each time. If *E* chooses that option on the first menu, but *F* is the toggle for that choice on the next, the user will have a perfect right to be annoyed at you.

Feedback. Just as important as telling users what they can do is telling them what they did. With really complex programs, where after a setup the program will take some time performing several actions, it's not a bad idea to stop and show users exactly what they chose and give them a chance to go back and make changes. And when a program will perform irrevocable operations, like wiping out a disk or permanently changing a data file, it isn't optional any more — you *must* give them a chance to double-check.

The sound program I'm going to write will have only a simple menu. Each choice will cause an operation to be performed, and the program will return to the menu for another selection. There is no setup, and we don't have enough choices to justify nesting.

And as for feedback, it will be a simple matter to maintain a display of the current selections being POKEd in to create the current sound. Each time a change is made, the "current selections" display will be refreshed. But the menu will always be the same — it should be printed once and stay on the screen. It would be a waste of time to print it again and again. That means that part of the screen will always be the same, and part will be changed from time to time. Since we have so few choices, it will be a simple matter to keep all the information on the same screen display.

I wouldn't be surprised if a third of the program ended up being devoted to displays. They're so vital to making a program usable that it's rarely a good idea to scrimp in that area.

Plan for Revision

Every program, no matter how useful, is going to be changed someday. Even if you think it's perfect for your needs, someone else might use it and want to make an alteration. It helps you and it helps future adapters if you plan your program so that it's easy to figure out what's going on in it. There are some habits that are almost universal.

For instance, most programmers begin their program with *assignment of variables.* Even though the variable won't be used until later, if every variable in a program is assigned right at the beginning, it's far easier to make sure you don't use the same name twice to mean different things, or assign a variable to carry a value that is already held by another variable.

Most programmers also put their *initialization* steps into one area of the program, so it's easy to follow the initial setup.

Programs that involve repeated user input are usually constructed around a *main loop,* which gets information from the user over and over again and then branches to subroutines in order to carry out the user's commands.

And, finally, most programs have an escape sequence, so that when the user chooses to quit the program, the operating system of the computer is restored to normal before the program ends.

Outlining the Program

If you take computer programming classes, you will probably learn a complex system of diagramming programs, with squares, circles, diamonds, and other shapes carrying definite meanings. Most of the time, though, I find that a simpler format is good enough for what I'm doing.

What shape should the program take?

1. Assigning Variables

Here are the first two lines of our program:

```
1Ø  P1=54273:P2=54272:VL=54296:AD=54277:S
    R=54278:WF=54276:SW=54274
2Ø  SC=653:KD=197
```

The variables in line 10 should look familiar — they assign the addresses of the sound memory locations to the variables that we already discussed.

Keyboard codes. However, line 20 has a few new things. SC, with the value 653, is the location that the operating system uses to store the SHIFT and COMMODORE key values. If the value at 653 is zero, neither key is pressed. If the value is 1, the SHIFT key is pressed. If the value is 2, the COMMODORE key is pressed.

KD, with the value 197, is the location where the operating system stores the code for the key that is currently being pressed. This is *not* the ASCII code, and it is not the internal character code — it is a keyboard code that reports on the *key,* not the character. The operating system takes the information at 197 and combines it with the information at 653 in order to translate the keyboard code into ASCII and internal character codes.

Something you might want to try right now is a simple program that will let you see the code for individual keys. Just type this in without a line number, in direct mode. When you press the RETURN key, the program will run.

```
FOR I=0 TO 10000:PRINT PEEK(197),PEEK(653
  ):NEXT I
```

As long as you aren't pressing any key, the screen will report values of 64 and 0. Pressing keys will change the values. Notice that a regular key will return the same code number whether the SHIFT key is pressed or not. Press the function and cursor keys — they return the lowest numbers of all, and their codes are all in sequence. That will be convenient for us later.

2. Initialization

The values of the variables assigned so far will never change — they are permanent. Now, however, we begin to initialize variables that *will* change. We initialize them so that when the program begins, it will immediately start creating a sound, and so that each variable holds a valid value. This will enable our change routines to work properly from the start.

```
25 POKE 54275,8:POKE VL,15
30 S1=22:S2=53:ATTACK=16:DECAY=8:SUSTAIN
   =16:RELEASE=8:SQUARE=128
35 WAVE=35:DUR=100:OFF=254:TEN=10
```

Line 25 POKEs 54275 with the value 8. This is part of the pulse width assignment, but we won't be changing it in our program. The same with the volume assignment, POKE VL,15. This sets the volume at its loudest. The ADSR envelope will make particular changes within the range of possible volumes, however, so you'll almost never want to set your volume at anything less.

Line 30 initializes the variables that will change. S1 and S2 are the pitch values that will be POKEd into locations P1 and P2. ATTACK is the attack value, and it will be added to DECAY to be POKEd into address AD. SUSTAIN and RELEASE will be added together to be POKEd into SR. SQUARE is the square wave pulse width, and it will be POKEd into location SW.

WAVE is the value of the waveform, and it will be POKEd into WF to start the sound. OFF will also be POKEd into WF, but only at the end of the sound, to turn it off. The value of OFF will always be 254. DUR is the duration of the timing loop. It will not be POKEd anywhere; it will be used as the counter in a FOR-NEXT loop to decide how long each note will last.

Line 35 has a variable named TEN. This is a toggle that will have a value of either 10 or 1. Our program will check the value of

TEN to see whether to change pitch values by ones or tens. This is because there are 255 possible values for each of the two pitches, and cycling through those values one at a time will get awfully tedious, unless there's a way to do it faster. Our program will let the user choose between fast (by 10) and slow (by 1) stepping through the pitches.

Notice that I have chosen to use variable names that mean something — ATTACK, WAVE, DECAY, DUR, TEN. The computer doesn't care. It only pays attention to the first two characters of the variable name — ATTACK looks just like ATTILA and ATROCIOUS to the computer. The reason for using whole words is that it's much easier for you to remember what the variable names are while you're programming, and it's easier for someone coming afterward to figure out what each variable stands for. Just be careful that you don't accidentally give two variables names that the computer thinks are the same. If, instead of S1 and S2, we had used SOUND1 and SOUND2, the computer would see only SO and treat them as if they were the same variable. We definitely wouldn't get the results we planned on.

3. Menu and Current Value Display

Putting up the display. The last step in initialization is putting up the display — the menu and the feedback. We'll do it this way:

```
40 GOSUB 300
```

With this GOSUB, the program will jump to line 300, which begins a routine that puts up the menu and the display of values currently being POKEd. How did I choose line 300? Because I knew I wanted the main loop to begin at line 100 and figured that it would finish well before 300. I like to begin my main subroutines on even-hundred lines — it's easier to find them again that way.

As long as we're planning the display subroutine, let's do it now.

```
300 PRINT CHR$(147)"F1/2{6 SPACES}= HIGH
    FRE DOWN/UP"
310 PRINT "F3/4{6 SPACES}= LOW FRE DOWN/
    UP"
320 PRINT "F5/6{6 SPACES}= ATTACK/DECAY"
330 PRINT "F7/8{6 SPACES}= SUSTAIN/RELEA
    SE"
```

```
340 PRINT "SPACE BAR = CHANGE WAVEFORM"
350 PRINT "CRSR U/D{2 SPACES}= DURATION
    MORE/LESS"
355 PRINT "CRSR L/R{2 SPACES}= SQUARE WA
    VE WIDTH"
360 PRINT "UP-ARROW{2 SPACES}= PITCH INT
    ERVAL TOGGLE":PRINT "RETURN
    {4 SPACES}= STOP"
365 POKE 214,10:POKE 211,0:PRINT
370 PRINT "HIGH FRE="STR$(S1)"{2 SPACES}
    "TAB(20)"LOW FRE="STR$(S2)"
    {2 SPACES}"
380 PRINT "ATTACK="STR$(ATTACK)" "TAB(20
    );"DECAY="STR$(DECAY)" "
390 PRINT "SUSTAIN="STR$(SUSTAIN)" "TAB(
    20);"RELEASE="STR$(RELEASE)" "
400 PRINT "WAVEFORM="STR$(WAVE)" "TAB(20
    )"DUR="STR$(DUR)" "
410 PRINT "SQUAREWAVE WIDTH="STR$(SQUARE
    )" ":RETURN
```

Lines 300 through 360 show all the possible choices. But first, in line 300, the statement PRINT CHR$(147) clears the screen.

What do those cryptic menu entries mean? F1/2 means that pressing F1 (function key 1) will give you the first result, and F2 (F1 shifted) will give you the second result. The first result is high frequency down; shifted, it is high frequency up. F5/6 means that pressing F5, unshifted, will change the attack; pressing F6, shifted, will change the decay.

The layout is reasonably consistent. Whenever a choice includes a down/up option, the unshifted key means down and the shifted key means up. The ADSR envelope choices are together, in their proper order — attack, decay, sustain, release — and one key always controls both halves of a two-nybble choice. The space bar is used to change the waveform, which has the largest single effect on the sound. The up/down cursor key controls, not the quality of the sound, but its duration; the left/right cursor key controls the most rarely used function, the pulse width of the square wave. The up-arrow key controls the TEN toggle. And the RETURN key allows the user to stop the program.

Why provide a key to stop the program? All the user needs to do is press RUN/STOP and the program will end, won't it? Yes, but RUN/STOP won't turn off the sound! If you happen to press it during the middle of a note, the note will keep on sounding forever. Pressing RETURN will provide an orderly, *quiet* end for the program.

Positioning the cursor. Line 365 is the line that enables us to leave the menu on the screen without ever having to print it again, even though we will be updating the rest of the display with every change. If we wanted to start in the upper-left-hand corner each time, we could replace line 365 with PRINT CHR$(147). But we don't want to wipe out the menu. So instead we will tell the cursor to PRINT everything that follows starting at line 10, column zero. POKEing 10 into location 214 tells the operating system to begin the next PRINT statement on that line; POKEing a 0 into location 211 tells the operating system to skip that many spaces before beginning the PRINT. Once you get the whole program typed in and saved, you may want to change these values and see what it does to the display.

Skipping over spaces on a line. Lines 370 through 410 display the current values. Since certain values belong together — the two pitches, attack and decay, sustain and release — it made sense to lay out this display with two items on a line. However, since the length of each entry will change, it wouldn't work to simply type in a certain number of spaces, the way we did in the menu to skip from the left-hand column to the right-hand column. After all, sometimes the value of S1 will have three digits, and sometimes only one — as the value changed, the right-hand column would keep shifting.

So instead, we use the TAB function. Instead of printing blank spaces between one entry and the next, the TAB function skips over a number of columns and begins PRINTing everything after it in the column specified in parentheses. On our display, we will begin each second entry at the twentieth column — TAB(20). Everything *before* the TAB column will be left alone.

Leading and trailing spaces. There's another problem with displaying numbers that change, however. The 64 automatically skips a space before and after a number whenever you PRINT a variable. The leading space leaves room for the minus sign before negative numbers. The trailing space is provided so that if you print several variables in a row, you can see where one leaves off and the next begins. The trouble is, we don't *want* those spaces this time. Because of skipping a space after the number, when we

23

change the value of WAVE from 129 to 17, it will look like we
changed it from 129 to 179. The 9 will be left hanging.

And it doesn't help just to put a blank space — " " — after the
variable name. That blank space will simply begin *after* the trailing space. The 9 will still be left hanging.

The STR$ solution. The solution, then, is to print the vari-
ables, not as numerical variables, but as string variables. And 64
BASIC has a built-in function, STR$, that does it very nicely. In-
stead of PRINT WAVE, we say PRINT STR$(WAVE). What STR$
does is evaluate the value of WAVE and turn it into the ASCII
string that expresses that value. It's a trivial difference to human
beings — it comes out looking like the same number to us. But to
the computer, they are not the same thing at all.

One result of that difference is that the computer *doesn't* skip
leading and trailing spaces when it PRINTs strings. When we
change the value of WAVE from 129 to 17 in the statement

```
PRINT "WAVEFORM="STR$(WAVE)"{2 SPACES}"
```

the result, on our screen, is not 129 followed by 179; it is 129 followed by 17, which is exactly what we want.

Double use of a subroutine. Line 410 ends with the RETURN
statement, which causes the program to jump back to the statement after the GOSUB in line 40. You may wonder why the menu
(lines 300-360), which is printed only once, is included as part of
the subroutine that prints the current value display (lines
365-410), which will be updated and rePRINTed often.

It didn't have to be that way. I could have put the menu between lines 40 and 100 and included only 365-410 in the subroutine. I did it to show you a technique that you may want to use.
Later in the program, we will reuse that subroutine, but not in a
statement that says GOSUB 300. Instead, the statement will say
GOSUB 365. It will begin executing the subroutine at line 365,
which positions the cursor, and then flow through to line 410,
which RETURNs.

When you have a routine that sometimes includes several
statements and sometimes doesn't, one of the simplest things to
do is group those statements at the beginning of the subroutine,
and then sometimes use an entry point before those statements,
and sometimes use an entry point after them.

There are dangers, though, to having a subroutine do double
duty. Once again, we need to think of revisions. What if you were

doing revisions in a part of the program that entered the subroutine at line 300, and you discovered something you wanted to add to the subroutine. If the program were very complex, or you hadn't worked on it in a long time, you might forget that other parts of the program also enter the subroutine at 365. Suppose that you then made a change at line 380 that will work just fine for the routines that enter at 300 — but ruin everything for the routines that enter at 365.

In a small program like this one, that sort of thing is pretty unlikely, and multiple entry points can save time; but the *safest* thing is to create each subroutine with one and only one entry point and one and only one RETURN point. This is one of the principles of "structured" programming.

4. The Main Loop
Here is the main loop of the program, the things that will be repeated, over and over, until the program is ended:

```
100 SH=PEEK(SC):KEY=PEEK(KD):IF KEY<>64
    THEN GOSUB 500:GOSUB 365
105 IF KEY=255 THEN 200
110 POKE P1,S1:POKE P2,S2
120 POKE AD,ATTACK+DECAY:POKE SR,SUSTAIN
    +RELEASE:POKE WF,WAVE:POKE SW,SQUARE
130 FOR I=0 TO DUR:NEXT I
140 POKE WF,WAVE AND OFF
150 FOR I=0 TO 75:NEXT I
160 GOTO 100
```

Read the keyboard. Line 100 finds out what key, if any, the user has pressed. The computer finds out the value stored at SC and assigns it to the variable SH. This will be a 1 if the SHIFT key is pressed, 2 if the COMMODORE key is pressed, or a 0 if neither is pressed. Then KD is PEEKed and the value is placed in KEY, which tells which key has been pressed.

If KEY does not contain a 64, then a key has been pressed, and we will want the program to do certain things. First, the program will jump to the subroutine at 500. This is the Change Value Subroutine that finds out *which* key was pressed and makes changes accordingly. Then the program will GOSUB to 365 and update the current value display — this is the second entry point to that subroutine, which you've already seen.

Everything after THEN. Remember that everything that appears on a line after the THEN statement will be executed if the condition is true, and *none* of it will be executed if the statement is false. In other words, if KEY equals 64 (meaning that no key was pressed), the program jumps right to line 105, ignoring everything else on line 100.

Internal flag. Line 105 is deceptive. It looks as though it is doing part of the job that the subroutine at 500 will do — checking to see what key was pressed. Actually, however, the keyboard cannot possibly return a value of 255. The only way that KEY can equal 255 is if the program changes it to 255. This serves as a *flag*. There is only one way that KEY can ever equal 255, so testing for 255 finds out if that condition has been met. If that flag is set, then the program will branch to line 200 — and line 200 ends the program!

Making the sound. Lines 110 and 120 actually make the sound. Line 110 POKEs the correct values into the frequency control locations. Line 120 POKEs the correct values into the ADSR and waveform locations. Every time this loop repeats, this action is performed and a sound begins, whether the values have been *changed* or not. This is why the sound repeats over and over, regardless of whether the user presses a key.

Repeating without waiting. This is why we wrote the program to get the user's choices by reading KD and SC rather than using INPUT statements. When you use an INPUT statement, the program stops and *waits* until the user enters something, then presses RETURN. That would make it difficult to make the sound repeat over and over.

The disadvantage of reading KD and SC, however, is that there is no regular mathematical relationship between the keyboard codes and the characters they stand for. If you actually had to be able to understand all the possible combinations of SHIFT, CONTROL, and keys using the keyboard codes, your program would be terribly slow and unwieldy. This method works best when only a few keys are meaningful, and it's important not to stop and wait for input.

Delay loops. Line 130 and line 150 are both delay loops, or empty loops. They make the computer do nothing over and over again, for as long as we tell it to. The loop in 130 decides how long the sound will last, and its duration is controlled by the value of the variable DUR. If DUR is a low number, the sound will be short; if it is a high number, the sound will be long. The user can change this value while the program is running.

The loop in line 150, however, is a constant length. This is because it is the time *between* notes. Why have any delay at all? Because the release step in the ADSR envelope happens *after* the note ends — it decides how quickly the sound dies down at the end of the note. If we went straight from the end of one sound to start a new one, there wouldn't be time for the user to hear the effect of using different release values.

Notice that both empty loops use the same counter variable, I. This works fine because the one loop closes before the next begins. However, if you nest two loops, one *inside* the other, you must use different counter variables or the program will become completely confused.

Turning off the sound. Line 140 POKEs the value of OFF into location WF. This turns off the sound we just produced. Why do we AND the value of OFF with the value of WAVE? To turn off the

Figure 3. Bitwise AND

Bits On and Off								Decimal Number
1	1	1	1	1	1	1	0	254
								AND
0	0	0	1	0	0	0	1	17
left on				turned off				result
0	0	0	1	0	0	0	0	16

Notice that ANDing any number with 254 will turn off only the rightmost (least significant) bit. All other on bits will stay on.

sound, we must make the least significant (lowest-numbered) bit at WF be a 0. We could just POKE a 0 into WF, but that is like using a sledgehammer to push a needle.

What does AND do? When you use AND with a number instead of a logical expression ("bitwise AND" instead of "logical" or "Boolean AND"), the computer compares the bits in both numbers. Any bit that is on (has a value of 1) in *both* numbers will be on (1) in the result. But any number that is off (0) in *either* number will be off (0) in the result. OFF has a value of 254, and in the number 254 every single bit is on *except* the least significant bit. Therefore, no matter what the other number is, that least significant bit will be a 0 in the result. Any other bit that is on, however, will stay on, because it will find a match in the number 254. Figure 3 shows how bitwise AND works in the expression WAVE AND OFF.

Close the loop. Line 160 closes the main loop by sending the program back to 100. It will keep doing this forever if the user never ends the program. That's why a loop made with a GOTO is called an endless loop.

5. Exit Routine

Line 200 is very simple — it exits from the program. But it does it cleanly. First, you can get to this line only when the sound is off. Every time through the main loop, the sound is off after line 140 and does not turn on again until the loop repeats and reaches line 110. The command that can send us to the exit routine is in line 105. Therefore, you can only reach this routine when the sound is off.

```
200 POKE 198,0:END
```

What is POKE 198,0 doing? Every time you press a key on the 64, the value of the key you pressed is automatically put into a keyboard buffer. This happens even during a program like this one, where we aren't accessing the keyboard buffer. Location 198 contains the number of characters stored in the buffer. If we didn't POKE a 0 there, the values of the keys you had last pressed would be stored there, and when the program ended, those characters would be printed on the screen. It wouldn't cause any harm, but it looks funny and forces the user to move down a line or erase those characters. So POKE 198,0 just tidies up a bit at the end of the program.

6. Evaluate KEY

In lines 500 through 530, the program evaluates the value of KEY and SH and figures out what subroutine to branch to.

```
500 IF KEY=1 THEN KEY=255:RETURN
505 IF KEY=54 THEN TEN=1-9*(TEN<>10)
510 IF KEY=60 THEN 600
520 IF KEY<2 OR KEY>7 THEN RETURN
530 KEY=KEY-1:ON KEY GOSUB 540,550,560,5
    70,580,590:RETURN
```

Exit flag set. Line 500 checks to see if RETURN was pressed. If so, it changes KEY to 255 and RETURNs. But why not just end the program right at line 500? We could enter this line:

```
500 IF KEY=1 THEN POKE 198,0:END
```

That line would work just fine. The program would end, and because we can't reach line 500 unless the sound is off, we would be ending very neatly. If you use this line, you can delete line 105 and line 200. The program is shorter and runs faster.

I simply have a personal aversion to ending programs in the middle of an unresolved subroutine. We executed a GOSUB to get to line 500, and I don't like to end unless the program has executed a RETURN. It's just a quirk of mine. I like to be neat. This is the sort of thing that programmers do because they feel like it. That's why if you assign two programmers to do the identical task, they will come back with very different programs. People do things differently.

Toggling TEN. Line 505 checks to see if the key pressed was the up-arrow key. If it was, then TEN will be changed. If it was 1, it will become 10; if it was 10, it will become 1.

Look carefully at the expression after the equal sign (=) in line 505. Let's evaluate that expression the way the computer would, and see what's going on.

We start inside the parentheses, with the expression TEN <> 10. If this expression is false, then it will return a value of 0. If it is true, it will return a value of -1. This is very important! True expressions equal negative one (-1), and false expressions equal zero (0). Knowing this can help you make your programs run faster, with fewer IF statements. In this case, if TEN does *not* equal 10, then the expression is true, and returns a value of -1. If TEN *does* equal 10, then the expression is false, and returns a value of 0.

The next step is to multiply the result of TEN <> 10 by 9. If the expression was false, or 0, then the result of this operation is 0. If it was true, then the result is -9.

Now we *subtract* that value from 1. If the value was 0, then
1 - 0 = 1. TEN will equal 1. If the value was -9, then 1- (-9) is the same
thing as 1 + 9, or 10.

See how it worked? If TEN was already equal to 10, then it
will end up equal to 1. If TEN was already equal to 1, then it will
end up equal to 10. We are simply switching back and forth.

Another way of doing this would have taken two lines and
two IF statements. Please *don't* enter these lines — they're just an
example:

```
505 IF KEY=54 AND TEN=1 THEN TEN=10:GOTO
    510
506 IF KEY=54 AND TEN=10 THEN TEN=1
```

Why is the GOTO statement at the end of line 505? Remember
that at the end of the operation in line 505, TEN will be equal to 10
no matter what. If it wasn't already equal to 10, the line changed it.
Then, if it goes right on to 506, TEN will be changed right back to
1. From then on, TEN would always be 1, regardless of whether
the user tried to toggle the value or not. We would add a GOTO at
the end of 505, so that if the value was *changed* in line 505, it will
skip over 506 and not get changed back.

The way we have it in the program, with a single line, is much
better.

Line 510 checks to see if the space bar was pressed. If it was,
the program jumps to line 600.

Then, in line 520, the program checks to see if the value of
KEY is between 2 and 7. If it isn't, the program RETURNs from the
subroutine and does nothing more. This means that if the user
presses a key that means nothing, the program will simply ignore
it and go back to the main loop.

Setting up a valid ON statement. A quirk of the keyboard
code is very helpful to us right now. It just happens that the two
cursor keys and the four function keys are all in numerical order,
from 2 to 7. And it also happens that an ON statement is the
simplest way to have multiple branches.

We have six possible branches. ON evaluates the expression
that follows it. If the expression has a value of 1, the program will
branch to the first line number following the expression. If ON
finds a value of 2, it will branch to the second line number, and
so on.

But ON is very fussy. It stops the program with an error statement if the expression is not an integer, if it is not a positive num-

ber, if it is a zero, or if there is no line number to correspond with the value. In order to use ON effectively, you have to keep tight control of the expression following ON.

In our program, it's easy. We have already screened out every possible value of KEY except the numbers from 2 to 7. Now all we do is subtract 1 from KEY, and it will consist of a number from 1 to 6. If we make sure we have six line numbers following the GOSUB command, we're safe. We just have to make sure that the line numbers are the right ones, and the rest of our choices are taken care of. (By the way, KEY =KEY-1 isn't really necessary. The statement could begin 530 ON KEY-1 GOSUB … and it would work just as well. Better, in fact, because it would take up less space and run a bit faster.)

7. Value Change Subroutines

Lines 540 and 545 change the value of SQUARE. Lines 550 and 555 control RELEASE and SUSTAIN, depending on whether the SHIFT key is pressed. Line 560 controls S1, and 570 controls S2. Lines 580 and 585 change the values of DECAY and ATTACK. 590 and 595 control DUR. 600 and 610 control WAVE.

```
540 SQUARE=SQUARE-TEN+2*TEN*ABS(SH=1)
545 SQUARE=SQUARE-256*(ABS(SQUARE>255)-A
    BS(SQUARE<0)):RETURN
550 IF SH=1 THEN RELEASE=RELEASE+1-15*AB
    S(RELEASE=15):RETURN
555 SUSTAIN=SUSTAIN+16-240*ABS(SUSTAIN=2
    40):RETURN
560 S1=S1-TEN+2*TEN*ABS(SH=1):S1=S1-256*
    (ABS(S1>255)-ABS(S1<0)):RETURN
570 S2=S2-TEN+2*TEN*ABS(SH=1):S2=S2-256*
    (ABS(S2>255)-ABS(S2<0)):RETURN
580 IF SH=1 THEN DECAY=DECAY+1-15*ABS(DE
    CAY=15):RETURN
585 ATTACK=ATTACK+16-240*ABS(ATTACK=240)
    :RETURN
590 DUR=DUR-25*(ABS(SH=0)-ABS(SH=1)):IF
    DUR<25 THEN DUR=25
595 RETURN
600 WAVE=WAVE+16*(INT(WAVE/16)):IF WAVE>
    129 THEN WAVE=17
610 RETURN
```

1 Starting Out

The best way to figure out what is going on in each of these lines is to carry out the operations exactly the way the computer does — the way we did when we evaluated line 505. Always execute the expression inside the innermost parentheses first. Always multiply and divide before adding and subtracting.

There are several things you want to look for. First, wherever the value of SH is tested or used, the program is deciding how to act depending on whether the SHIFT key is pressed or not. A similar test occurs wherever you see the program testing to see if a value is greater than 255 or less than 0. Since numbers outside the range of 0 to 255 cannot be POKEd, it is essential that they be changed to legal numbers. The simplest method is subtracting 256 from numbers greater than 255, and adding 256 to numbers less than 0.

Second, notice how TEN and other numbers are used to see to it that only the correct values result from the operations. ATTACK, for instance, in line 585, can only end up with a value that is a multiple of 16. The program sees to this by adding 16 to the old value of ATTACK. This works every time except when ATTACK had a previous value of 240 — then the new value is 256, which is not a legal value. So whenever ATTACK *starts out* (before adding 16) at 240, the program adds 16 but then subtracts 240, resulting in a value of 16 for ATTACK. From there, the cycle begins again.

Third, notice the use of the ABS function. Remember that when an expression is true, it returns a value of -1. But it is often more useful to turn this into a positive number. There are several ways to do it. One is simply to put a minus sign in front of the expression: -(-1) is equal to positive 1. Another way is to subtract the true expression in a situation where you really want to add it. But I prefer to use ABS, because it's foolproof. If a number is positive or zero, ABS leaves it alone. If a number is negative, however, ABS turns it positive.

In all of these, keep in mind the fact that if the expression is *false*, its value is 0. So if you add or subtract the result of the expression, a false will have no effect. But if you *multiply* the result of an expression, a false will always give you a zero product.

Notice that lines 595 and 610 consist of a single RETURN statement. Why weren't these RETURNs put on the end of the line before, the way it is done in 570 and 580 and others? Because both of these lines end with an IF statement, so that a RETURN on the same line would be executed only if the condition is true.

So even if there were a RETURN on the end of the line, the program would still need to have a RETURN on the next line to end the subroutine in case the result is false. Since nothing else but the RETURN will happen on that line, why type in an extra RETURN? The one will be enough to end each subroutine.

However, in cases like 550 and 555, where we never want *both* lines to execute, we need to have a RETURN at the end of each line so it can't "fall through" and execute the wrong line. Perhaps the easiest way to see the result of allowing the program to fall through is to remove one of the RETURNs and then see what happens to the values when you press the keys — you get more than you bargained for.

Does this seem like an awful lot to think about every time you program? Actually, you have to make about as many decisions whenever you drive a car. It's just a matter of habit. Once you're used to thinking this way, it won't occur to you that you're even doing something difficult. And it won't be very long before you look back at this program and think, "Is this *all*?"

Well, it isn't all — it never is. Because once you're comfortable with my version of the program, you'll start to think of features you want to add and slow places that you can speed up. It wouldn't be hard to have three voices going at once and to use the COMMODORE key to cycle from one voice to the next. Or to make the screen change colors every time the waveform is changed. Or to allow direct keyboard entry of certain pitches instead of having to rotate through them 1 or 10 values at a time. When you start customizing programs like that, you've got it.

The following program repeats what has been given, in parts, throughout this chapter.

64 Sound

```
10 P1=54273:P2=54272:VL=54296:AD=54277:S
   R=54278:WF=54276:SW=54274
20 SC=653:KD=197
25 POKE 54275,8:POKE VL,15
30 S1=22:S2=53:ATTACK=16:DECAY=8:SUSTAIN
   =16:RELEASE=8:SQUARE=128
35 WAVE=35:DUR=100:OFF=254:TEN=10
40 GOSUB 300
100 SH=PEEK(SC):KEY=PEEK(KD):IF KEY<>64
    THEN GOSUB 500:GOSUB 365
105 IF KEY=255 THEN 200
110 POKE P1,S1:POKE P2,S2
```

```
120 POKE AD,ATTACK+DECAY:POKE SR,SUSTAIN
    +RELEASE:POKE WF,WAVE:POKE SW,SQUARE
130 FOR I=0 TO DUR:NEXT I
140 POKE WF,WAVE AND OFF
150 FOR I=0 TO 75:NEXT I
160 GOTO 100
200 POKE 198,0:END
300 PRINT CHR$(147)"F1/2{6 SPACES}= HIGH
     FRE DOWN/UP"
310 PRINT "F3/4{6 SPACES}= LOW FRE DOWN/
    UP"
320 PRINT "F5/6{6 SPACES}= ATTACK/DECAY"
330 PRINT "F7/8{6 SPACES}= SUSTAIN/RELEA
    SE"
340 PRINT "SPACE BAR = CHANGE WAVEFORM"
350 PRINT "CRSR U/D{2 SPACES}= DURATION
    MORE/LESS"
355 PRINT "CRSR L/R{2 SPACES}= SQUARE WA
    VE WIDTH"
360 PRINT "UP-ARROW{2 SPACES}= PITCH INT
    ERVAL TOGGLE":PRINT "RETURN
    {4 SPACES}= STOP"
365 POKE 214,10:POKE 211,0:PRINT
370 PRINT "HIGH FRE="STR$(S1)"{2 SPACES}
    "TAB(20)"LOW FRE="STR$(S2)"
    {2 SPACES}"
380 PRINT "ATTACK="STR$(ATTACK)" "TAB(20
    );"DECAY="STR$(DECAY)" "
390 PRINT "SUSTAIN="STR$(SUSTAIN)" "TAB(
    20);"RELEASE="STR$(RELEASE)" "
400 PRINT "WAVEFORM="STR$(WAVE)" "TAB(20
    )"DUR="STR$(DUR)" "
410 PRINT "SQUAREWAVE WIDTH="STR$(SQUARE
    )" ":RETURN
500 IF KEY=1 THEN KEY=255:RETURN
505 IF KEY=54 THEN TEN=1-9*(TEN<>10)
510 IF KEY=60 THEN 600
520 IF KEY<2 OR KEY>7 THEN RETURN
530 KEY=KEY-1:ON KEY GOSUB 540,550,560,5
    70,580,590:RETURN
540 SQUARE=SQUARE-TEN+2*TEN*ABS(SH=1)
545 SQUARE=SQUARE-256*(ABS(SQUARE>255)-A
    BS(SQUARE<0)):RETURN
550 IF SH=1 THEN RELEASE=RELEASE+1-15*AB
    S(RELEASE=15):RETURN
555 SUSTAIN=SUSTAIN+16-240*ABS(SUSTAIN=2
    40):RETURN
560 S1=S1-TEN+2*TEN*ABS(SH=1):S1=S1-256*
    (ABS(S1>255)-ABS(S1<0)):RETURN
```

```
570 S2=S2-TEN+2*TEN*ABS(SH=1):S2=S2-256*
    (ABS(S2>255)-ABS(S2<0)):RETURN
580 IF SH=1 THEN DECAY=DECAY+1-15*ABS(DE
    CAY=15):RETURN
585 ATTACK=ATTACK+16-240*ABS(ATTACK=240)
    :RETURN
590 DUR=DUR-25*(ABS(SH=0)-ABS(SH=1)):IF
    DUR<25 THEN DUR=25
595 RETURN
600 WAVE=WAVE+16*(INT(WAVE/16)):IF WAVE>
    129 THEN WAVE=17
610 RETURN
```

Chapter 2

BASIC Programming

All About the WAIT Instruction

Louis F. Sander and Doug Ferguson

WAIT is one of Commodore BASIC's most mysterious instructions — seldom seen in programs, rarely mentioned in magazines, and nearly impossible to understand in manuals. To find out how helpful it can be for all kinds of applications (program debugging, single-stepping, even a superior form of the common pause GET K$: IF K$=""THEN), read on.

WAIT allows a BASIC program to communicate with hardware and with certain software external to itself. It causes the computer to suspend all apparent activity on receipt of a signal from the keyboard, an external device, or the computer's internal timers. Normal activity resumes when the signal is removed. Thus, WAIT provides a simple means of pausing until a key is pressed, an interval ends, or contacts open or close. We'll soon get to some useful examples.

When executed, WAIT examines a selected memory location and halts the program if the location contains a specified "trigger value." The program continues if, or as soon as, any other value appears in the selected location. Optionally, WAIT can be made to ignore some of the bits in the location it is testing.

In other words, WAIT halts a program if, and for as long as, selected bits in a chosen location have one specific pattern. Note carefully: the program waits *if* a specific pattern exists, not *for* a specific pattern to appear.

WAIT's format is:

WAIT ADDR, MASK, TRIG

ADDR, MASK, and TRIG can be any numeric constants, expressions, or variables in the range 0-65535 for ADDR, and 0-255 for MASK and TRIG. TRIG and its leading comma may be left out of the statement if desired, in which case TRIG defaults to zero.

Technically speaking, the WAIT statement reads the status of memory location ADDR, exclusive-ORs it with TRIG, then ANDs the result with MASK, repeating these steps until a nonzero result is obtained. *Practically* speaking, few human minds can *follow* such logic, let alone comprehend its effect on their programs. If you prefer simplicity, think of WAIT as saying this: "Pause if the MASK bits in the contents of ADDR are the same as those in TRIG. Otherwise, continue." But let's illustrate some of its specific uses.

ADDR is the address of the memory location to be tested. WAIT halts the program if ADDR contains a preselected trigger value, resuming execution if and when ADDR's contents change. It follows that ADDR must be a location whose contents can change independently of the program, or there will be no way to resume program execution. Relatively few memory locations meet this criterion — mainly they are associated with the keyboard, the user and serial ports, and the computer's internal timers. Table 1 is a partial listing of such locations.

Table 1. Some Useful Memory Locations

Memory Location	Contents
162	Increments every jiffy (1/60 second).
161	Increments every 256 jiffies (4.2 seconds).
160	Increments every 65536 jiffies (18.2 minutes). Zeroing TI$ zeros all three clock locations.
197	Unique value for the key pressed at the current jiffy. No key = 64.
653	Status of SHIFT key. Up =0, Down =1.
198	Number of characters in the keyboard buffer (0 to 9).

MASK determines whether WAIT tests all, or only some, of the bits in ADDR. If a given bit in MASK is set to one, the corresponding bit in ADDR will be tested. Otherwise, the bit will be ignored. If the entire contents of ADDR are to be tested, MASK must equal 255; any lower number will cause WAIT to ignore one or more bits. The various powers of two are often used in MASK to monitor a single bit for a one or a zero. Zero is a legal value for MASK, but should never be used, since it always causes an endless halt. (Any number AND zero equals zero.)

TRIG is the value that triggers a halt. If WAIT is executed when ADDR contains TRIG, the program will stop until TRIG is replaced by another value. Of course, if MASK is blocking out one or more bits, any number whose unblocked bits are identical to those in TRIG will have the same effect as TRIG and will cause the program to halt. TRIG's default value is zero, so when TRIG is omitted from the WAIT statement, a halt occurs whenever all the unblocked bits are zero.

WAIT has three other notable properties. First, just as PRINT can be abbreviated as "?", WAIT can be abbreviated as "W shifted A". You can use this property to save keystrokes and line space. Second, the STOP key will not terminate a WAIT. That can only be done by satisfying the logical conditions in the argument or by using the RUN/STOP-RESTORE combination. So as soon as you put a WAIT statement into a program, SAVE a copy on tape or disk; that will save *you* if you've made an error. Finally, WAIT does not affect the jiffy clock — TI and TI$ continue counting during WAITs, even though the computer and the STOP key are ostensibly dead. So by using the memory locations of the jiffy clock, you can precisely control WAIT's pauses.

Real World Applications

End-of-the-program questions are well suited for the WAIT command. To replay or not to replay is hardly a menu of choices. With WAIT, the computer "waits" for the replay signal. Even if the player wants to quit, he can always RUN/STOP-RESTORE or turn off the power.

Try these three short demos to see the possibilities.

```
10 FOR X=1 TO 20:NEXT X:REM KILL SOME TI
   ME
20 WAIT 197,64,64:REM WAITS FOR YOU TO P
   RESS A KEY TO MOVE ON
30 PRINT "YOU PRESSED A KEY!!!THANKS"
40 POKE 198,0:REM CLEARS THE KEYBOARD BU
   FFER


10 REM WHEN YOU RUN THIS SHORT PROGRAM H
   OLD THE <RETURN> KEY DOWN TO WAIT
20 WAIT 197,64:REM WAITS FOR YOU TO TAKE
    YOUR FINGER OFF THE KEYBOARD
30 PRINT "YOU TOOK YOUR FINGER OFF THE K
   EYBOARD"
40 POKE 198,0:REM CLEARS THE KEYBOARD BU
   FFER
```

41

```
6000 PRINT "YOU WIN!!":PRINT "PRESS FIRE
     -BUTTON TO PLAY AGAIN"
6010 WAIT 145,16:REM IN CASE BUTTON IS A
     LSO USED IN THE GAME ITSELF
6020 WAIT 145,16,16
6030 PRINT:RUN
6040 REM PRESS STOP/RUN AND RESTORE TO S
     TOP THIS DEMO
```

Here is a table showing the specific test values for the joysticks.

Table 2. Joystick Test Values

	Joystick 1	Joystick 2
FIRE	WAIT 145,16,16	56464,16,16
LEFT	WAIT 145,4,4	56464,4,4
DOWN	WAIT 145,2,2	56464,2,2
UP	WAIT 145,1,1	56464,1,1
RIGHT	WAIT 145,8,8	56464,8,8
ANY	WAIT 145,31,31	56464,31,31

This table assumes you want to test if the joystick is *pressed* a certain way. If you want to test that a certain position is *not pressed*, just leave off the last number.

Tracing with WAIT

Another way to use WAIT is in FOR/NEXT loops in either program or direct mode. For example, to examine the contents of the ROM memory containing BASIC, type in the following program:

```
100 FOR X=10 * 4096 TO X + 8191: PRINT X
    ,PEEK(X)
110 WAIT 197,64
120 NEXT
```

or the direct statement:

```
FOR X = 10*4096 TO X+8191: PRINT X,PEEK(X
    ): WAIT 197,64: NEXT
```

A list of memory addresses and contents will begin to scroll by. To stop printing, press any key (except RESTORE, SHIFT, CTRL, or the COMMODORE key). Printing resumes when the key is released. If the WAIT is changed to WAIT 653,1,1, the

SHIFT key alone becomes the control key. This has the advantage of providing a "hands off" pause by using the SHIFT LOCK key.

It is also possible to single-step (go through a program line by line) using the WAIT command. Simply change the WAIT to

WAIT 197,64: WAIT 197,64,64

for "any key" control or

WAIT 653,1,1: WAIT 653,1

for SHIFT key control, although the SHIFT LOCK is of no consequence when single-stepping.

Escape from examining memory by hitting the RUN/STOP key.

There are, of course, many other ways to use the WAIT command. A good way to learn is to experiment. The information contained here should be only a beginning.

REM Revealed

John L. Darling

Did you know that you can prevent someone from easily LISTing your program? This is one of several hidden secrets of the REM statement. Did you ever try putting shifted or reverse video characters behind a REM? The results you get when you LIST may come as a surprise. Try these experiments to learn about the tricks you can play with REMs.

There are quite a few hidden surprises in the REM statement. Many are just plain fun, but a few can be put to good use. Let's go exploring.

The REM statement was designed to provide a way to add remarks or comments in a program. During execution of the program, all the characters on a line following the REM are ignored. Thus, the only time the remarks are seen is when the program is LISTed.

Also note that, for program operation, it doesn't make any difference whether the characters following the REM are enclosed in quote marks or not, but it sure can change the results you get when you LIST the program. First, let's look at the REM when quotes are not used. The results you get when the program is LISTed will be determined by the following rules:

1. Nonshifted characters appear as typed in.
2. Shifted characters are converted to BASIC commands if the ASCII code for the character is equivalent to a BASIC command token.
3. Reverse fields are stripped from any character.

Before we examine these rules, you should put your computer into lowercase mode by hitting the shift-COMMODORE key. It is easier to discuss upper- and lowercase letters than it is to describe graphic symbols. Reverse video characters are turned on with CTRL-9 and turned off with CTRL-0.

To illustrate these rules, type in the following four lines and then LIST.

```
10 rem a b c d e f
20 rem A B C D E F
30 rem {RVS}a b c d e f{OFF}
40 rem {RVS}A B C D E F{OFF}

list

10 rem a b c d e f
20 rem atn peek len str$ val asc
30 rem a b c d e f
40 rem atn peek len str$ val asc
```

Line 10 demonstrates Rule 1. All the characters are LISTed just as they were entered. This is the normal effect that we're all used to.

Line 20 doesn't look much like the original, does it? It illustrates Rule 2: the shifted letters are interpreted as BASIC command tokens.

Lines 30 and 40 show Rule 3 in action. They look just like lines 10 and 20 because the reverse field was stripped when the lines were entered.

LIST Blocking

Now we get to the question of how to prevent someone from easily LISTing your program. Let's examine Rule 2 a little more closely. Certain characters become "tokens" which cause unusual effects. One will cause the LIST operation to terminate with a "syntax error" message when it is encountered. These tokens are equivalent to a shifted-L.

This can be verified by the following line.

10 rem L

When you attempt to list the line, the result will be:

10 rem
?syntax error
ready.

Up to now, it's just been fun, but there is a reason you might want to use this line. If this special REM line is the first line in a program, it prevents a normal LISTing. Let's assume that the first line in a large program is line 100. Inserting this special REM line ahead of the program causes the LIST operation to terminate as soon as it encounters the special shifted character. However, LIST

45

100- will allow the program to be displayed normally.

Consider the following situation. A quiz program has the answers in DATA statements at the end of the program listing. Inserting the special REM line just ahead of these DATA statements will prevent the answers from being displayed during a LIST. Don't forget that REM statements are ignored during program execution, so they won't affect the actual program operation.

Quote Mode

Now, let's examine the quote mode. A new set of rules applies when the REM characters are enclosed in quotes:

1. Shifted and nonshifted characters LIST as they were typed in.

2. Reverse video characters are preserved when inside quotes (they are not stripped, as is the case in the nonquote mode).

3. Some reverse video characters and combinations of characters behave as print control commands when LISTed.

Rules 1 and 2 produce results that you would normally expect during the LIST operation. They LIST exactly as typed in. No examples are provided for these rules, but try a few experiments to verify this for yourself.

Here are some interesting examples of Rule 3 in action. (The comments in brackets are the resultant action produced during LIST.)

```
rem "▨          [insert]
rem "▨          [return]
rem "▨          [shifted return] = *
rem "▨▨         * + [home]
rem "▨▨         * + [clear screen]
rem "▨▨         * + [cursor down]
rem "▨▨         * + [cursor up]
rem "▨▨         * + [cursor right]
rem "▨▨         * + [cursor left]
```

When these characters are inside a REM" statement, strange things are going to happen.

To enter the following tests, first type the line number, the REM, the quote symbol, and then RETURN. Next, edit the line by positioning the cursor past the quote mark, press the RVS ON key (CTRL-9) and then the letters. This allows you to put the reverse video characters on the screen line.

```
10 rem"help !████
```

```
list
```

```
10 rem"he
```

The four reverse *t* characters achieve the same thing that
would occur if the DEL key was pressed during an edit operation,
deleting the last four characters. Adding more reverse *t* characters
(15 total) on the rest line will cause the entire line to disappear *after*
it is LISTed on the screen.

Notice that many of the cursor controls shown require the M
(shifted RETURN) character to be the first character. This is important, for without the shifted RETURN most of the cursor controls or special control codes will not be executed. As soon as this
character is encountered, a shifted RETURN will be generated.
All characters following the shifted-M will be printed as if they
were in a PRINT statement, rather than in a REM. Consequently,
if any of these characters are cursor controls, they will produce a
cursor control action as if they were inside the quotes following a
PRINT statement.

If the reverse *t*'s in the previous example were replaced with
reverse MS characters, then the LIST operation would list that
line up to the ! and then the cursor will go to the top of the screen
since MS is interpreted as a HOME command. If this was listed to
a Commodore printer and the paging mode was on, the printer
would eject a page after LISTing that line.

A Program Within a Program

Let's try one final example to illustrate how the reverse field
shifted-M works in combination with other characters. To avoid
errors, here is a complete key sequence that will produce the following line:

```
1,0,SPACE,R,E,M,",",DEL,RVS,SHIFT-M,
SHIFT-S,Q,Q,Q,Q,OFF,I,SPACE,T,H,I,N,K,
SPACE,I,SPACE,A,M,SPACE,S,RVS,Q,OFF,I
RVS,Q,OFF,C,RVS,Q,OFF,K,RVS,S,OFF,",
SHIFT-L
```

```
10 rem "█████████i think i am s█i█c█k█"
     L
```

Can you guess the results? If you type the line correctly, the following will happen after you LIST:

1. 10 REM" will be printed.

2. A CLEAR SCREEN will be printed, blanking the screen and also the previous 10 REM".

3. Four cursor-downs will be printed.

4. The message I THINK I AM SICK will be printed with the I,C,K characters on different lines.

5. A cursor-home will occur.

6. "@ will be printed on the top line followed by a ?SYNTAX ERROR message on the next line. (Note that the special shifted character is no longer enclosed in quotes.)

7. Finally, the READY message will appear with the cursor above the I THINK I AM S line.

The above line could be inserted in most programs, and it will not affect the program execution performance in the least. You just can't get a normal LISTing of the program.

There are a lot more combinations to try, so have fun. It's like having a program inside another program. The second program requires a LIST command for execution instead of a RUN command.

From IFs to ANDs

Stephen D. Eitelman

Presented here are some efficient ways to program for joysticks.

The *Commodore 64 User's Guide* is strangely lacking in information on programming the joysticks. In "Commodore 64 Memory Map" (see Chapter 7), Jim Butterfield shows the memory locations for the joysticks: 56320 and 56321. With this data, a simple program PEEK to the appropriate location should permit a determination of the memory contents versus stick direction. With a joystick plugged into port 1 (plug in the joystick with the power *off* for safety), try this program:

```
10 PRINT PEEK (56321)
20 GOTO 10
```

Line 10 prints the contents of memory location 56321. Line 20 creates an endless loop to allow viewing of different joystick positions just by moving the joystick. When the program is RUN, a column of 255s scrolling upward should appear. Now move the joystick to the north (up). The number should now read 254. Moving the joystick to the northeast should produce 246. Table 1 gives the values produced at each joystick position.

Table 1. Joystick Port 1 — Memory Location 56321

Position	Memory Contents	Position	Memory Contents
Center	255	South	253
North	254	Southwest	249
Northeast	246	West	251
East	247	Northwest	250
Southeast	245	Fire Button	239

A similar table can be generated for port 2. Plug a joystick into port 2, change the memory location in line 10 from 56321 to 56320, and RUN the program. Going around the compass again produces the data as indicated in Table 2.

Table 2. Joystick Port 2 — Memory Location 56320

Position	Memory Contents	Position	Memory Contents
Center	127	South	125
North	126	Southwest	121
Northeast	118	West	123
East	119	Northwest	122
Southeast	117	Fire Button	111

The 64 Sketchpad

With this data, a simple program can be written that moves a graphics symbol around the screen under control of the joystick (Program 1). (Be sure to save this program; we will use it again later.) Pressing the fire button clears the screen and starts a "fresh page." The lines in this program perform the following actions:

Line	Action
5	Clear screen.
7	Brown border: black background.
10	Variable JM (Joystick Memory) set for port 2.
20	Set Screen Location and Screen Color to center of screen.
30,40	Put a ball in center and color it green.
50,60	Set variables for No Joystick and directions using Table 2.
70-150	Test JM for direction, set X and Y increment.
155	If Fire Button pressed, erase and start over.
160	No motion; start JM test sequence again.
170	Set new SL.
175,177	Keep SL within limits of screen memory.
180	Set new SC.
185,187	Keep SC within limits of screen color memory.
190	Draw a ball at new SL.
200	Color ball green at new SL.
205	Slow it all down.
210	Begin another loop to find next location.

There's an Even Better Way!

Lines 50-155, while pretty straightforward, seem unnecessarily long. Jim Butterfield gives a better way in an article entitled "VIC Sticks" in *COMPUTE!'s Second Book of VIC*. Although this article deals (very properly) with VIC-20 joystick programming, there are some valuable lessons worth investigating for applicability to the 64 joysticks. The first is that horizontal and vertical increments can be generated in one-line statements using the SGN function and some logic if the directions have nonoverlapping binary values. The second lesson is that diagonals are the sum of the vertical and horizontal values on either side, so that it is unnecessary to treat diagonals separately. The third lesson is that the binary values of joystick directions are inverted (bits are set to zero instead of one when a given direction switch is activated). Butterfield inverts the values with the logical NOT statement to convert to "positive" logic. To see if these tricks will work with the 64, try the following modification to the short program at the beginning of this chapter (joystick in port 2):

```
10 PRINT (NOT PEEK(56320))+128
20 GOTO 20
```

The addition of 128 in line 10 is a "fudge factor" to force the joystick center position to be zero after the inversion. Going around the compass again produces results very similar to those for the VIC-20 as seen in Table 3.

Table 3. Joystick Port 2 — Memory Location 56320

Position	Inverted Memory Contents +128
Center	0
North	1
South	2
West	4
East	8
Fire Button	16
Northeast (=N +E)	9
Southeast (=S +E)	10
Southwest (=S +W)	6
Northwest (=N +W)	5

From this table, you can see that the major points of the compass have nonoverlapping binary values and that the diagonals are the sum of the vertical and horizontal values on either side. Thus it should be possible to adapt Butterfield's one-line VIC horizontal and vertical incrementers to the 64.

> Direction D =(NOT PEEK(56320)) +128
> Horizontal H =East - West; H =0, +1, -1 only
>   H =SGN(D AND 8)-SGN(D AND 4)
> Vertical   V =-North +South; V =0, +1, -1 only
>   V =SGN(D AND 2)-SGN(D AND 1)

Saving Memory

Our sketchpad program can now be shortened considerably with this far more elegant approach. First eliminate lines 50-160 inclusive from Program 1. Then add the following lines:

```
50 D=(NOT PEEK(56320))+128:REM INVERT DI
   RECTION BYTES
55 IF D=16 THEN 5:REM FIRE BUTTON.START
   OVER
60 H=SGN(D AND 8)-SGN(D AND 4)
70 V=SGN(D AND 2)-SGN(D AND 1)
```

In lines 170 and 180, substitute H for X and V for Y. The program should perform the same as before with a net saving of nine lines.

A similar investigation for port 1 reveals that the inverted directions are the same as for port 2. The only difference is in the PEEK statement. Substitute the following:

```
D=(NOT PEEK(56321))+256
```

Now the Sketchpad program will work for port 1. The Modified Sketchpad is Program 2.

Program 1. 64 Sketchpad

```
5 PRINT "{CLR}"
7 POKE53280,9:POKE53281,0
10 JM=56320:REM JOYSTICK MEMORY,PORT 2
20 SL=1524:SC=55796:REM SCREEN LOCATION
   & PIXEL COLOR. START IN MID SCREEN
30 POKE SL,81:REM BALL IN MIDDLE OF SCRE
   EN
40 POKE SC,5:REM GREEN BALL
50 NJ=127:N=126:NE=118:E=119:SE=117
60 S=125:SW=121:W=123:NW=122:FB=111
70 IF PEEK(JM)=NJ THEN X=0:Y=0
80 IF PEEK(JM)=N THEN X=0:Y=-1
90 IF PEEK (JM)=NE THEN X=1:Y=-1
100 IF PEEK (JM)=E THEN X=1:Y=0
110 IF PEEK (JM)=SE THEN X=1:Y=1
120 IF PEEK (JM)=S THEN X=0:Y=1
130 IF PEEK (JM)=SW THEN X=-1:Y=1
140 IF PEEK (JM)=W THEN X=-1:Y=0
150 IF PEEK (JM)=NW THEN X=-1:Y=-1
155 IF PEEK(JM)=FB THEN GOTO 5
160 IF X=0 AND Y=0 THEN 70:REM NO MOTION
170 SL=SL+X+40*Y:REM NEW LOCATION
```

```
175 IF SL>=2023 THEN SL=2023
177 IF SL<=1024 THEN SL=1024
180 SC=SC+X+40*Y:REM COLOR @ NEW LOC'N
185 IF SC>=56295 THEN SC=56295
187 IF SC<=55296 THEN SC=55296
190 POKE SL,81:REM BALL @ NEW LOC'N
200 POKE SC,5:REM GREEN BALL
205 FOR DL= 1 TO 50:NEXT DL:REM DELAY
210 GOTO 70:REM DO NEXT BALL LOCATION
220 END
```

Program 2. Modified Sketchpad

```
5 PRINT "{CLR}"
7 POKE53280,9:POKE53281,0
10 JM=56320:REM JOYSTICK MEMORY,PORT 2
20 SL=1524:SC=55796:REM SCREEN LOCATION
   & PIXEL COLOR. START IN MID SCREEN
30 POKE SL,81:REM BALL IN MIDDLE OF SCRE
   EN
40 POKE SC,5:REM GREEN BALL
50 D=(NOT PEEK(56320))+128:REM INVERT DI
   RECTION BYTES
55 IF D=16 THEN 5:REM FIRE BUTTON.START
   OVER
60 H=SGN(D AND 8)-SGN(D AND 4)
70 V=SGN(D AND 2)-SGN(D AND 1)
170 SL=SL+H+40*V:REM NEW LOCATION
175 IF SL>=2023 THEN SL=2023
177 IF SL<=1024 THEN SL=1024
180 SC=SC+H+40*V:REM COLOR @ NEW LOC'N
185 IF SC>=56295 THEN SC=56295
187 IF SC<=55296 THEN SC=55296
190 POKE SL,81:REM BALL @ NEW LOC'N
200 POKE SC,5:REM GREEN BALL
205 FOR DL= 1 TO 50:NEXT DL:REM DELAY
210 GOTO 50:REM DO NEXT BALL LOCATION
220 END
```

Menumaker

Richard L. Witkover

This easy-to-use utility will help you create attractive, well-formatted display screens.

Your newest programming masterpiece is finally done. Itching to show it off, you find someone to try it out on. Eagerly, you seat him at the terminal and stand back anticipating his reaction. He glances at the screen, looks at the keyboard, looks at the screen again, and then just sits. Finally, he asks, "What am I supposed to do?"

"Oh," you say, "just hit RETURN to activate the laser discombobulator, and use the I, J, K, and M keys to control up or down and right or left. The %-key creates a new Zippity and —." By this time your victim's eyes are glassy, but he recovers enough to say, "Let me know when you finish it; I'll try it then."

Crestfallen, you are about to say, "It *is* finished," but catch yourself and only mumble, "Yeah, I've got to add a few extra messages." You sulk for a while but finally have to admit that even though your new program is the greatest game in the world, it is no good unless people know how to play it.

The second act of this little scenario shows the programmer busily typing in a few options such as "… which do you choose, 1, 2, or 3?" We have all done this as beginners, but you can be sure that the pros would never be satisfied with that.

The Menu

The answer, of course, is a simple, informational display on the screen. "Menumaker" is a utility that will print a display starting at any row or column, or will center the text by row, column, or both. After the longest line, the program will print a dash. All shorter lines will be filled with dashes to this point. The last column is used to draw an array of cursor boxes which, along with the flashing cursor, will move. To allow only a single key to control its motion, the cursor has a wraparound feature. Selection is made by moving the cursor to the row desired by means of the cursor UP/DN key (either way), then hitting any key to select the row on which the cursor sits. Finally, to dress up the display, Menumaker draws a round-cornered box around the whole menu.

Menumaker is presented here as a self-contained program that you can use to try different layouts to find the one which best suits the application. The program was written in four parts using GOSUBs to produce the entire display. In this way the parts can be fitted into your own programs as needed. For example, you may wish to place some instructions in one section of the screen and draw a box around them. No user selection is involved, so the cursor portion of the program isn't needed.

The Program

Part 1 extends through line 290. It sets up the various constants and gets the input values of RI$, CI$, and TE$, which set the positioning of the rows, the columns, and the text lines, respectively. The variables RI$ and CI$ are tested to see if the automatic centering option was chosen, and if not, whether the numerical values are within the allowed ranges. These are set by the screen character limits with allowances for the borders of the box, the dash, and cursor array.

The text input is obtained by lines 170-195, checking that the maximum character count isn't exceeded. Each line is ended with a carriage return until a null line ends the loop. As each line is read in, its length is measured and the largest count is retained as LW% in line 194.

If the centered option is selected, lines 205-240 will compute the cursor column number and the text starting column number.

Part 2, lines 320 to 370, prints the text on the screen, and Part 3, lines 510 to 680, draws the bordering box. The final part, lines 800-920, is the cursor routine.

Putting It All Together

Now that you have Menumaker, how can you put it to work? The straightforward way is to just type it in as needed, leaving out all the REMs but making sure that all of the required input variables are satisfied. These are defined in the leader block preceding each subroutine.

There are many frills or variations which could be used with Menumaker. For example, you could make the cursor a different color. How about changing the color of the selected text line to highlight the choice? Just making the box different in color from the text will add a bit of pizazz. You could use a joystick to move the cursor or just use the fire button. The variations are endless, so have some fun and dress up your programs while you make them easier to use with Menumaker.

Menumaker

```
7 REM{11 SPACES}MENUMAKER
8 REM{2 SPACES}THIS PROGRAM DISPLAYS UP
  TO 22
9 REM{2 SPACES}LINES OF UP TO 35 CHARACT
  ERS.
10 REM THE CHOICE IS MADE BY MOVING THE
11 REM CURSOR VERTICALLY (WITH WRAP-
12 REM AROUND) ALONG AN ARRAY IN THE
13 REM LAST COLUMN. HITTING ANY KEY BUT
14 REM THE UP/DN CURSOR WILL ENCODE THE
15 REM THE ROW #.A BOX IS DRAWN AROUND
16 REM THE MENU. THE TOP LEFT-HAND CHAR
17 REM INSIDE THE BOX CAN BE LOCATED
18 REM SPECIFICALLY OR THE BOX CAN BE
19 REM CENTERED IN ROW AND/OR COLUMN.
20 REM*******************************
40 REM *******************************
41 REM
42 REM{4 SPACES}THE FOLLOWING ARE COMPUT
   ER
43 REM{7 SPACES}DEPENDENT CONSTANTS:
44 REM
45 REM{7 SPACES}CM=40{2 SPACES}:MAX # CO
   LS
46 REM{7 SPACES}RM=24{2 SPACES}:MAX # RO
   WS
47 REM{6 SPACES}SC%=1024:ST OF C-64 SCRE
   EN
48 REM{7 SPACES}PN=87{2 SPACES}:NORMAL C
   URSOR POKE
49 REM{7 SPACES}PR=215 :REV CURSOR POKE
50 REM{7 SPACES}CR=119 :NORMAL CURSOR CH
   R$
52 REM
53 REM{2 SPACES}CHANGE AS NEEDED FOR COM
   PUTERS
54 REM{2 SPACES}OTHER THAN THE COMMODORE
   64.
55 REM
56 REM*******************************
57 REM
```

```
60 CM=40:RM=24:SC%=1024:PN=87:PR=215:CR=
   119
69 REM********************************
70 REM
71 REM{5 SPACES}PARAMETER INPUT ROUTINE
72 REM
73 REM{7 SPACES}REQUIRED INPUTS ARE:
74 REM
75 REM{6 SPACES}RI$=STARTING TEXT ROW
76 REM{6 SPACES}CI$=STARTING TEXT COL
77 REM{6 SPACES}TE$=UP TO 22 TEXT LINES
78 REM
79 REM ROUTINE ACCEPTS A NUMBER FOR RI$
80 REM AND CI$, OR 'C',IN WHICH CASE IT
81 REM WILL CENTERS ROWS AND/OR COLS.
82 REM
83 REM TEXT STRINGS CAN BE A MAX OF 35
84 REM CHARACTERS,EACH LINE ENDING WITH
85 REM A CARRAIGE RETURN. TEXT ENTRY
86 REM ENDS WITH A NULL LINE.
87 REM
88 REM********************************
89 REM
90 REM{2 SPACES}THE FOLLOWING ARE SCREEN
   CHAR
91 REM{2 SPACES}CODES FOR THE C-64:
92 REM{8 SPACES}ER$=ERASE SCREEN
93 REM{8 SPACES}CD$=CURSOR DOWN
94 REM{8 SPACES}CL$=CURSOR LEFT
95 REM{8 SPACES}RO$=REVERSE ON
96 REM{8 SPACES}HO$=HOME
97 REM********************************
98 ER$=CHR$(147):CD$=CHR$(17):CL$=CHR$(1
   57):RO$=CHR$(18):HO$=CHR$(19)
100 DIM TE$(22)
105 PRINTER$;CD$;CD$;"ENTER ROW AND COLU
    MN OF START OF TEXT"
110 PRINT"{7 SPACES}FOR CENTERED TEXT EN
    TER 'C'"
115 INPUT"{2 DOWN}{8 SPACES}ROW,COL=";RI
    $,CI$
120 LW%=0:CS%=0
125 IFCI$="C"THEN140
130 CS%=VAL(CI$)
135 IFCS%<1ORCS%>(CM-5)THEN INPUT"{RVS}C
    OL# INVALID- ENTER COL#";CI$:GOTO125
140 IF RI$="C"THEN LM=RM-2:GOTO160
145 RT%=VAL(RI$)
```

```
150 IFRT%<1 OR RT%>RM-2THEN INPUT"{RVS}R
    OW# INVALID- ENTER ROW #";RI$:GOTO14
    Ø
155 LM=RM-1-RT%
160 PRINTCD$;CD$;" ENTER UPTO"LM;"LINES
    ENDING EACH WITH A"
165 PRINT" CARRAIGE RETURN. EXIT WITH A
    NULL LINE"
170 FOR NL=1TO LM
175 PRINT"LINE #";NL;:INPUTTE$(NL)
180 IF TE$(NL)=""THEN200
185 L=LEN(TE$(NL)):CL=CM-4-CS%
190 IFL>CLTHEN PRINTTAB(1Ø);"{RVS}TOO MA
    NY CHAR, MAX="CL:TE$(NL)="":GOTO175
194 IF LW%<L THENLW%=L
195 NEXT NL
200 LW%=LW%+2:NL=NL-1
205 IFRI$="C"THENRT%=INT(RM-NL)/2+1
225 IFCI$="C"THEN235
230 C%=CS%+LW%-1:GOTO240
235 C%=INT(CM+LW%)/2-1:CS%=C%-LW%+1
240 S%=SC%+C%+CM*RT%
250 GOSUB 320:REM TEXT TYPE-OUT
260 GOSUB 500:REM DRAW THE BOX
270 GOSUB 719:REM MAKE THE CURSOR
280 PRINT"{HOME}{3 SPACES}THE ROW IS =";
    R%
290 END
300 REM*****************************
301 REM
302 REM{5 SPACES}TEXT TYPE-OUT ROUTINE
303 REM
304 REM{6 SPACES}REQUIRED INPUTS ARE:
305 REM
306 REM{6 SPACES}RT%=TOP ROW #
307 REM{6 SPACES}NL =# LINES OF TEXT
308 REM{6 SPACES}TE$=TEXT LINE ARRAY
309 REM
310 REM*****************************
320 IFRT%=1THENLF$="":GOTO34Ø
330 LF$="":FORI=1TORT%-1:LF$=LF$+CD$:NEX
    T
340 PRINT ER$;LF$
350 FORI=1TONL:ND$="":NC=LW%-LEN(TE$(I))
    -1:FORN=1TONC:ND$=ND$+"*":NEXT
360 PRINT TAB(CS%);TE$(I)+ND$:NEXTI
370 RETURN
400 REM*****************************
401 REM
```

```
402 REM ROUTINE TO MAKE ROUND CORNERED
403 REM BOXES WITH TOP LEFT-HAND CORNER
404 REM OF INTERIOR AT DESIRED ROW AND
405 REM COLUMN.
406 REM
407 REM{3 SPACES}WHEN USED AS MERGED COD
    E
408 REM{3 SPACES}THE REQUIRED INPUTS ARE
    :
409 REM
410 REM{4 SPACES}RT%=# OF TOP INSIDE ROW
411 REM{4 SPACES}NL =# OF INSIDE LINES
412 REM{4 SPACES}LW%=# OF INSIDE CHAR -1
413 REM{4 SPACES}CS%=# OF LEFT INSIDE CO
    L
414 REM
415 REM{4 SPACES}LT$=LEFT-TOP CHR$
416 REM{4 SPACES}RT$=RIGHT-TOP CHR$
417 REM{4 SPACES}SD$=SIDE CHR$
418 REM{4 SPACES}DA$=DASH CHR$
419 REM{4 SPACES}LB$=LEFT-BOT CHR$
420 REM{4 SPACES}RB$=RIGHT-BOT CHR$
421 REM
422 REM*******************************
500 REM THE FOLLOWING ARE FOR THE C-64
510 LT$=CHR$(117):RT$=CHR$(105)
520 RB$=CHR$(107):LB$=CHR$(106)
530 DA$=CHR$(99):SD$=CHR$(125)
540 IF CS%<>0THENBL%=CS%:GOTO560
550 BL%=INT(CM-LW%)/2
560 BR%=BL%+LW%
570 PRINTHO$;
580 LF$=CHR$(0):LN$=CHR$(0)
590 IF RT%<=1THEN610
600 FORA=1TORT%-1:LF$=LF$+"{DOWN}":NEXT
610 FORA=1TOLW%:LN$=LN$+DA$:NEXT
620 PRINTLF$;
630 PRINTTAB(BL%-1);LT$;LN$;RT$
640 FORA=1TONL
650 PRINTTAB(BL%-1)SD$;TAB(BR%);SD$
660 NEXTA
670 PRINTTAB(BL%-1);LB$;LN$;RB$
680 RETURN
700 REM*******************************
701 REM
702 REM ROUTINE TO PUT ON CURSOR ARRAY
703 REM WITH FLASHING CURSOR. CURSOR UP
704 REM /DOWN KEY IS USED TO MOVE WITH
705 REM WRAP-AROUND. HIT ON ANY OTHER
```

```
706 REM KEY EXITS ROUTINE WITH R%=ROW
707 REM OF CURSOR.
708 REM
709 REM
710 REM{4 SPACES}THE REQUIRED INPUTS ARE
    :
711 REM
712 REM{6 SPACES}RT%=TOP ROW #
713 REM{6 SPACES}NL =# OF ROWS
714 REM{6 SPACES}LW%=COL#-1 OF CURSOR
715 REM{6 SPACES}CS%=COL# OF 1ST CHAR
716 REM{6 SPACES}S% =CURSOR SCREEN LOC
717 REM
718 REM*******************************
719 REM
800 RB%=NL+RT%-1:LF$=CHR$(0)
810 IF RT%=1THEN830
820 FORA=1TORT%-1:LF$=LF$+CD$:NEXT
830 PRINTHO$;LF$
840 FORI=1TONL:PRINTTAB(C%);CHR$(CR);"
    {OFF}":NEXT
850 R%=RT%
860 POKES%,PN:FORI=1TO50:NEXT
870 POKES%,PR:FORI=1TO50:NEXT
880 GETB$:IFB$=""THEN860
890 IFB$<>CHR$(145)THEN930
900 POKE S%,PN
910 IFR%>RT%THENR%=R%-1:S%=SC%+C%+R%*CM:
    GOTO980
920 S%=SC%+C%+RB%*CM:GOTO980
930 IFB$<>CD$THENRETURN
950 POKE S%,PN
960 IFR%<RB%THENR%=R%+1:S%=SC%+C%+R%*CM:
    GOTO980
970 S%=SC%+C%+RT%*CM
980 R%=INT((S%-SC%)/CM):GOTO860
```

Data Storage

Ron Gunn

Data storage can be the most perplexing aspect of programming for the novice. Here are some practical tips which just might save you days of experimentation.

Types of Data

Commodore computers use three kinds of variables, and it is the values stored in variables that you will be dealing with when you save and recall data. The first of these is floating point, represented by a variable like A or A(X). The second is integer, represented by a variable like A% or A%(X).

The third is the string variable, represented by A$ or A$(X). Any of these varieties can be single: A; or may have subscripts: A(X); A(X,Y); or A(X,Y,Z). Part of your sense of power in computing comes when you realize just how much data you can pack and organize into those multiple-subscripted arrays.

When you are putting data out on tape or disk and expecting to read it back in, you must remember two things: 1. The three variable types are different and are not interchangeable. 2. They are put onto the recording medium in series without any identification and must therefore be read back in, in exactly the same sequence, to be recovered.

Only the data is recorded, not the variable names themselves. You can send it onto the tape as A, and can call it B when reading it back in. That is fair. But if you read data back as B% or B$, you will get an error message. Some error messages are really undeserved, as you know. This one is deserved. Don't mix your data types — integer to integer, string to string, and so on.

A Caution about String Variables

String variables, however, are a special case. Let's see why. In Commodore BASIC, unlike some other versions, there is a default value for variables. It is set when the machine is turned on or when an array is dimensioned. The value is zero.

When you write string variables to tape, however, this default value of zero is not a legitimate representation of anything. A string "0" would be ASCII 48, but that is not what is there. What is there is a binary, octal, decimal, hex 0 — which, in the special language of strings, represents a null. Neither the cassette nor the disk will accept null strings. Result: input rejects it and the data isn't transferred.

The cure is logical, once it is pointed out: load all string variables, including string arrays, with a string variable that the tape or disk can recognize. Example: you have dimensioned a string array A$(20) that may not be filled from your program when you want to save it. Right after the DIMension statement, do the following:

```
11000 DIM A$(20)
11010 FOR I=0 TO 20:A$(I)="X":NEXT
```

The array has now been loaded with a recognizable string ("X") and can be saved. All unused parts of it will be saved as X and will not confuse things later.

Saving Simple Variables

When the sequence used in saving data is also followed in loading data, then the right variables get put back where they belong, and the transfer proceeds smoothly. You can safely use the following procedure, and it will work very well indeed on cassette:

```
12000 OPEN 2,1,1:REM WRITE
12010 PRINT#2,A;",";B%;",";C$
12020 REM WHAT IS THIS?
```

You should be surprised by line 12010. First the variables are mixed, but that *is* OK as long as they are brought back in in the same order. A floating point, an integer, and a string can be safely handled on the same line. You can't just have your other program trying to bring in a string when a number is next in line to come off the tape.

Second, what is all that between the variables? It is instructions to the computer about what to put on the tape record. Semicolons suppress "carriage returns," but commas are put in to allow the beginning and end of each separate item of information to be established. These are *delimiters*. They are like walls to make sure that two items are separated. (A *carriage return* is like moving the paper up one line when you hit the RETURN key on a normal typewriter. Each time you use a PRINT statement in BASIC, it is followed by a carriage return unless you put a semicolon after it.)

Let's Put It on a Disk
So far we've zeroed in on cassette data operations. What about the same thing on disk? (Skip this section if you are concerned now just about cassette data.)

```
12000 DO$="1:SCORE,S,W"
12010 OPEN 2,8,9,DO$
12020 PRINT#2,A;",";B%;",";C$;CHR$(13);
```

In line 12000, a record is defined as associated with disk unit 1: it is to be called SCORE and is identified as Sequential. This will be a Write operation. A later Read operation will be needed to bring it back in. In line 12010, file 2 is opened to unit 8 (the disk) with a secondary address of 9. Use 9 for a disk secondary address unless you specifically want something else. It works. The last part of the file opening statement is the DO$ that was defined in line 12000.

Line 12020 contains all of the variables and delimiters used in the cassette statement, with one addition: a carriage return CHR$(13) has been added to the disk statement. Note that it is surrounded by semicolons so no line feeds will be slipped in. You want a CHR$(13), not a CHR$(13) CHR$(10), there to keep the records straight.

Saving Array Variables
While it is clear that mixing variable types on a single line is OK as long as they are recovered in that same order, this does not seem to be true if an array is involved. The following is not recommended:

```
13000 FOR I=0 TO 20
13010 PRINT#2,A(I)
13020 PRINT#2,B$(I)
13030 NEXT
```

For reliable records, just don't mix string and numerical variables in a FOR/NEXT loop when saving data. Use an entirely separate loop to handle the strings. Any potential savings by avoiding the use of another separate loop to handle the strings can be costly. This works reliably:

```
13000 FOR I=0 TO 20
13010 PRINT#2,A(I)
13020 NEXT
13030 FOR I=0 TO 20
13040 PRINT#2,B$(I)
13050 NEXT
```

If this were a disk operation, each PRINT #2 statement would end
with:

   ;CHR$(13);

A Practical Application

Now let's define and then write a minor cassette or disk data *tour-
de-force* program. Let's say you need to input two arrays that contain names and scores for a tournament. NT$ is the name of the
tournament, TP the number of tournament players, N$(TP) their
names, and S(TP) their scores. We are reading data:

```
15000 OPEN 1,1
15010 INPUT#1,NT$,TP
15020 CLOSE 1
15030 DIM N$(TP),S(TP)
15040 OPEN 1,1
15050 FOR I=0 TO TP
15060 INPUT#1,N$(I)
15070 NEXT
15080 FOR I=0 TO TP
15090 INPUT#1,S(I)
15100 NEXT
```

At 15010 the name and size are brought in on the same line.
That's OK. They were put on the record earlier using the necessary delimiters. The file is then closed to bring all of the information in from the buffer.

At 15030, TP is used to dimension the necessary arrays to
hold the data. Then, using loops, the data for names and then for
scores is brought in separately. So, we have stuck to our principles. Single-line data is mixed because it will mix. Array data is
not mixed even though it seems compellingly simple to do so.

Not that we referred to both cassette and disk in this program. The only difference between input of cassette data and input of disk data is the opening statements (i.e., OPEN 1,8 instead
of OPEN 1,1). It is actually practical to have independent opening

statements, but then GOSUB to the same input loop subroutine
for both cassette and disk. When you are reading data back in,
there are no forced delimiters and no fancy manipulation of the
line feeds. You can easily make your program read either cassette
or disk data with negligible extra programming or complexity.

The Commodore cassette and disk are amazingly reliable in
handling data. I once tried saving and then reloading .5 mega-
bytes (500,000 characters) in the same program, and no errors
occurred.

Chapter 3

Commodore 64 Video

An Introduction to the 6566 Video Chip

Jim Butterfield

Before setting off on our expedition, we need to establish a few landmarks which will place the chip within the Commodore 64 architecture.

Memory and Video

The 6566 chip relates to memory in two ways. First, the chip's control registers are accessible in addresses 53248 to 53294 or, if you'd rather, hexadecimal D000 to D02E. We'll change these registers if we want to change the behavior of the chip.

The chip itself looks directly into memory as it generates video. It is usually looking for at least two things: what characters to display and how to display them. It finds what characters to display in an area called "screen memory," or, more formally, the "video matrix." It finds out how to display the characters by looking at the Character Generator table, or the Character Base.

Since the chip generates a lot of video, it looks at memory a great deal. Most of the time, it can do this without interfering with the processor's use of memory; but every five hundred microseconds or so, it needs to stop the processor briefly in order to get extra information. This doesn't hurt anything: the pause is so short that we don't lose much processing time.

But occasionally, the microprocessor is engaged in timing a critical event and does not want to be interrupted. In this case, it shuts off the 6566 chip until the delicate work is over. Ever wondered why the screen blanks when you read or write cassette tape? To give the computer an extra edge while timing tape, that's why.

Charting the 64

When the video chip goes to memory for its information, it has a

69

special problem: it can reach only 16K of memory. That's OK for most work. For example, the screen (or video matrix) is usually located at 1024 to 2023 (hex 0400 to 07E7), so we'll use it there. But if we wanted to move screen memory to a new location, say 33792, we would need to work out some details, since the chip would not normally be able to reach addresses so high in memory.

We are given some help in doing this by the 64 architecture itself. There are two control lines called VA15 and VA14 which allow us to select which block of 16K memory we want the video chip to use. Note that once we've selected a block, the chip must get all its information from that block: we can't mix and match.

The control lines are available in address 56576 (hex DD00) as the two low-order bits. The memory maps you get are:

• **POKE 56576,4** the chip sees RAM from 49152 to 65535. There's no Character Generator; you'll have to make your own.

• **POKE 56576,5** the chip sees RAM from 32768 to 36863 and from 40960 to 49151. The ROM Character Generator is in the slot from 36864 to 40959.

• **POKE 56576,6** the chip sees RAM from 16384 to 32767. No Character Generator.

• **POKE 56576,7** the chip sees RAM from 0 to 4095, and from 8192 to 16383. The ROM Character Generator is in the slot from 4096 to 8191. This is the normal Commodore 64 setup.

Also note that the chip never has access to RAM at addresses 4096 to 8191 and 36864 to 40959. You will not be able to put screen memory or sprites there.

Be careful with these. If you move the chip's memory area, you'd better be sure to move the screen. For example, try the following:

```
POKE 648,132:POKE56576,5
```

You'll find yourself transferred to a new, alternate screen. The new screen will be "dirty" — it hasn't been cleaned up. Typing a screen clear will make things look neat, and you may then play around with an apparently normal machine. When you're finished, turn the power off for a moment to restore your machine to the standard configuration.

The Chip: Video Control

Now for the 6566 chip itself. We'll go through the registers, but not in strict numeric order.

Location 53265 (hex D011) is an important control location. It contains many functions; its normal value is 27 decimal.

Values from 24 to 31 control the vertical positioning of the characters on the screen. Try this:

```
FOR J=24 TO 31:POKE 53265,J:NEXT J
```

You'll see the screen move vertically, leaving an empty spot near the top. POKE 53265 back to 27.

If we subtract 8 from the value in location 53265, the screen will lose a line: instead of 25 lines we'll have only 24. The best way to see this is to clear the screen, write TOP on the top line, BOTTOM on the bottom line (don't press RETURN!), and then move the cursor to about the middle of the screen and type:

```
POKE 53265,19
```

You'll see the top and bottom trimmed to half a line each.

Think about using these two features together. If we have a screen full of information, we would normally scroll when we wanted to write more — the characters would jump up a line. But if we can switch to 24 lines, slide the characters up gently, and then switch back to 25 lines, we'd have a smooth scroll.

POKE 53265 back to 27

If we subtract 16 from this location, we'll blank the screen. This will give the processor a little more accuracy in timing. In fact, this POKE is the key to allowing us to LOAD a program from an old-style 1540 disk unit. If the disk hasn't been modified, it will deliver bits slightly too fast for the computer. But we can bridge the gap with POKE 53265,11:LOAD and the loading will take place successfully. When the load is complete, we can get the screen back with POKE 53265,27.

High Resolution

The next control bit — value 32 — switches the display to pure bits. No more characters; the screen will be purely pixels as we switch to high-resolution mode. We'll use a lot of memory for this one: memory to feed the screen will be 8000 bytes.

High resolution needs to be carefully set up, but let's plunge right into it. Type POKE 53265,59 and you'll see an intricate pattern on the screen. What you are looking at now is a bitmap of RAM memory addresses 0 to 4096, plus the Character Generator area. The top of the screen will twinkle a little. Some of the page zero values change constantly — things like the realtime clock and the interrupt values.

In the bottom half of the screen, we'll see the Character Generator itself. Oddly enough, the characters are readable. That's because of the way high-resolution bitmapping works: each sequence of eight consecutive bytes maps into a character space, not across the screen, as you might think.

Now we're going to play around a little. First, clear the screen. Surprise! It doesn't clear, but the colors change. That's because screen memory, into which we are typing, holds color information for the high-resolution screen. Now, we'll clean out a band of hi-res data by typing in a BASIC line. We must do this "blind"; the screen won't help us. Type:

```
FOR J=3200 TO 3519:POKE J,0:NEXT J
```

If you've typed correctly, you'll see a blank band across the screen. Don't worry about the color change as you type. Now we'll enter (blind again):

```
FOR J=3204TO3519 STEP 8:POKE J,255:NEXT J
```

You should see a high-resolution line drawn across the screen.

That's all the high-resolution fun we're going to have this session, but you may be starting to get an idea of what's going on. Turn off the power, and let's look at other things.

Extended Color

If we add 64 to the contents of 53265, we'll invoke the extended color mode. This will allow us to choose both background and foreground colors for each character. Normally, we may choose only the foreground: the background stays the same throughout the screen. You lose some colors, but get better combinations.

Try POKE 53265,91. Nothing happens, except that the cursor disappears, or at least becomes less visible. Why? We've traded the screen reverse feature for a new background color. Try typing characters in reverse font, and see what happens. Try choosing some of the specialized colors — the ones you generate with the

COMMODORE key rather than CTRL. See how you like the effect. Think how you might be able to use it.

Extended color is purely a screen display phenomenon. POKE 53265,27 will bring all the characters you have typed back to their normal appearance.

Table 1.
6566 Video Chip:
Control and Miscellaneous Registers

D011	Extended Color Mode	Bit Map	Display Enable	Row Select	Y-Scroll	53265
D012	Raster Register					53266
D013	Light Pen Input					53267
D014						53268
D016	unused	Reset	Multi-Color	Col Select	X-Scroll	53270

D018	Screen				Character Base			unused	53272
	VM13	VM12	VM11	VM10	CB13	CB12	CB11		
D019	IRQ	unused			Interrupt Sense				53273
					LP	SSC	SBC	RST	
D01A	unused				Light Pen	Interrupt Enable Collision with		Raster	53274
						Sprite	Back		

Color Registers

D020	unused	Exterior	53280
D021	unused	Background #0	53281
D022	unused	Background #1	53282
D023	unused	Background #2	53283
D024	unused	Background #3	53284
D025	unused	Sprite Multicolor #0	53285
D026	unused	Sprite Multicolor #1	53286

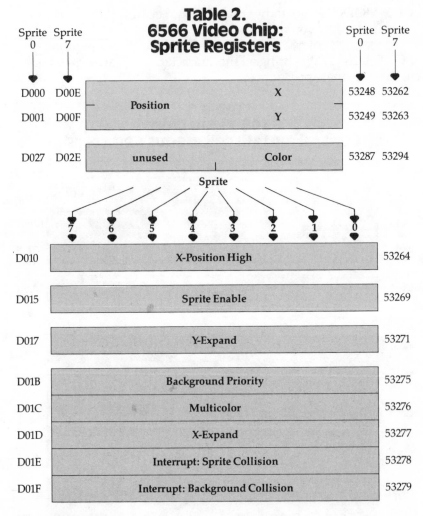

Table 2.
6566 Video Chip:
Sprite Registers

	Sprite 0	Sprite 7				Sprite 0	Sprite 7
Position	D000	D00E	X			53248	53262
	D001	D00F	Y			53249	53263
	D027	D02E	unused	Color		53287	53294
X-Position High	D010					53264	
Sprite Enable	D015					53269	
Y-Expand	D017					53271	
Background Priority	D01B					53275	
Multicolor	D01C					53276	
X-Expand	D01D					53277	
Interrupt: Sprite Collision	D01E					53278	
Interrupt: Background Collision	D01F					53279	

The High Bit

There's one more bit in location 53265, the one we would get if we added 128. Don't do this now: this bit is part of a value we'll discuss later: the "raster value." You won't use this one out of BASIC, but it can be handy at machine language speeds.

There's Much More

We've done a lot of things so far, using only one control location. It's a big chip. It will take a lot of time to digest all its possibilities. It's fun, and it can create remarkable effects.

The 6566 Video Chip —

The Raster Register, Interrupts, Color and More.

Jim Butterfield

In the introduction we began touring the 6566 chip, which gives the Commodore 64 its video. We saw the variety of important controls that we can reach in location 53265: vertical screen positioning, screen blank, bitmapping, and extended color. There's a second control location, at 53270 (hexadecimal D016); let's look at it.

The first thing we should note about this location is that the two high bits are not used. That means that we can usefully POKE only values from 0 to 63 in there. It happens that if we PEEK 53270, we'll probably see a number that is 192 too big; if you want to see the working value, use PEEK(53270) AND 63, which will throw away the unused part of the number.

We saw a vertical fine scroll in location 53265. Location 53270 has a horizontal fine scroll that works exactly the same way. Type:

```
FOR J= 8 TO 15:POKE 53270,J:NEXT J
```

You'll see the screen characters slide over horizontally. As with the vertical fine scroll, we also have facilities for trimming the size of the screen. Restore the screen to its original form with POKE 53270,8. Then shrink the screen by typing POKE 53270,0. You'll see a character disappear from each end. In other words, you now have a 38-character screen instead of 40 characters. Don't forget that fine scroll and shrink can be used effectively together.

If you add 16 to the contents of 53270, you'll switch to multi-color mode. This is not the same as extended color which we discussed previously. Multicolor allows *selected* characters to be shown on the screen in a combination of colors. Extended color allows screen background and foreground to be set individually for each character.

If you're familiar with the VIC-20, you'll find that setting the multicolor mode makes the Commodore 64 behave in the same way. Here's the trick: we invoke multicolor on an individual character by giving that character a color value greater than 7. This way, the regular colors (red, blue, black) behave normally, but the new pastels (gray, light red) switch to multicolor mode.

You'll need to create a new character base to exploit the advantages of multicolor, since the old characters weren't drawn with color in mind. However, we can get a quick idea of the feature by invoking it: POKE 53270,24 sets up multicolor; the screen characters may turn a little muddy, but don't worry about them. Set a primary color such as cyan and type a line. Normal, right?

Next, set up one of the alternate colors (hold down the COMMODORE key and press a key from 1 to 8). Type some more; you'll get multicolor characters. They won't make much sense, since the Character Generator isn't building the colors suitably; but you can see that something new is going on.

Adding 32 to the contents of 53270 gives chip reset. You won't want to do this very often — it's done on your behalf when you turn the power on. If you do use chip reset, remember that to make it work, you must turn reset on and then off again. POKE 53270,32:POKE 53270,8 will clear you out of multicolor mode.

Setting Screen and Characters
Location 53272 sets the location of screen RAM (the video matrix) and the Character Generator (the Character Base). Don't forget that they must be in the same 16K block, as determined by the low bits of address 56576.

You can get the BASIC address of screen RAM in this way: take the contents of 53272 and divide by 16; then throw away the remainder and multiply by 1024, and you have the screen address. You can get the BASIC address of the Character Base in this way: take the contents of 53272 and divide by 16. Then take the remainder, subtracting one if it's odd, and multiply by 1024; that's the Character Base address. Both addresses will need to be adjusted to allow for the 16K quadrant we have selected.

If we are in bitmap mode, we get the Character Base address in a slightly different way. If we divide the contents of 53272 by 16, take the remainder and divide by 8, discarding the remainder, and finally, multiply by 8192, we will have the bit image; it should be either 0 or 8192.

How does this work out in the standard Commodore 64? We may PEEK 53272 and see a value of 21. That means the screen is at INT(21/16)* 1024, or address 1024. Right on target. The character matrix works out: the remainder of 21/16 is 5, so drop one for the odd number, giving 4; multiply by 1024 to get address 4096. In the introduction I indicated that RAM was replaced by the Character Generator ROM at this video chip address. And when we flipped to bitmapping in the last episode, we still got remainder 5; divide by 8, giving 0, then multiply by 8192 — you still get 01 high-resolution screen from address 0.

If you'd like to try your hand at the arithmetic, flip to upper-/lowercase mode (hold down SHIFT and press the COM-MODORE key) and see what addresses have changed. Or if you'd rather, try typing in FOR J =1 TO 100:POKE 53272,21:POKE 53272,23:NEXT J and watch the action.

The Raster Register

Location 53266 (hex D012) and the high bit of the previous location are not of much use to the BASIC programmer, but can be very valuable to the machine language beginner. Here's the idea: by looking at these locations, you can tell exactly where the screen is being scanned at that moment. This allows you to change the screen as it's being scanned. Halfway down, you could switch from characters to bitmap, or change to multicolor, or move a sprite that has already been displayed.

If you're really interested in machine language, you may want to take an extra step: instead of watching where the screen is, you can leave the message "Wake me when you get to scan line 100." ML beginners will recognize this as an interrupt request. How do you set the identity of the desired scan line? By placing it into the same locations, that's how. We have a dual function here: when we read, we recall the scan location; when we write, we store an interrupt value.

Light Pen

Locations 53267 and 53268 (hex D013 and D014) are the light pen registers. An Atari-style light pen can be plugged into the joystick port number one; if it sees a suitable signal from the screen, the X and Y values will be latched into these registers. The light pen can be used on an interrupt basis: we can "stop the music" and get immediate action if we choose to set things up that way.

This is the second time we've mentioned interrupts; perhaps we'd better discuss them a little more closely.

Interrupts

Interrupts are for machine language experts — things happen too fast for BASIC to cope in this area. There are four types of interrupts: raster, light pen, and two kinds of sprite collision. (We'll talk about sprites in the next section.) We may use all of them or none; and even when these signals are not used for interrupt, we can check them.

Location 53273 (hex D019) tells us which of the four events has occurred. We don't need to make the interrupts "live"; they will signal us anytime the particular event happens. The weights are as follows:

1 (bit 0) — the raster has matched the preset line value;

2 (bit 1) — a sprite has collided with the screen background;

4 (bit 2) — a sprite has collided with another sprite;

8 (bit 3) — the light pen has sensed a signal;

128 (bit 7) — one of the above has triggered a live interrupt.

Once any of the above takes place, the bit will remain stuck on until you turn it off. How do you turn it off? This may sound goofy, but you turn an interrupt signal off by trying to turn it on. Hmmm, let me try that again. Suppose that we have both a raster and a light pen signal; we'll see a value of 9 (8 +1) in the interrupt register. Now suppose further that we are ready to handle the light pen, so we want to turn its signal off. We do this by storing 8 into location 53273. Huh? Wouldn't that turn it on? Nope, it turns it off, and leaves the other bit alone. So after storing 8, we look at the register again, and (you guessed it) we see a value of 1 there. Honest.

Location 53274 (hex D01A) is the interrupt enable register: it sets the above signals for "live interrupt." Select bits 0 to 3 corresponding to the interrupts you want. Whatever live interrupt you select will now trigger a processor interrupt and also light up that high bit of 53273. Don't forget to shut the interrupt flag off when you service the interrupt, using the method indicated in the previous paragraph. Otherwise, when you finish the job and return from the interrupt (with RTI), it will reinterrupt you all over again.

A Little Color

Some of the colors we have mentioned and some we have yet to discuss are neatly stored in addresses 53280 to 53286 (hex D020 to D026). We may store only values 0 to 15 here, for the 16 Commodore 64 colors.

The chart in the previous article shows it all: the exterior (border) color; then four background colors (they may be selected as part of multicolor characters or bits); and finally, two colors reserved especially for sprites.

Sprites

Jim Butterfield

So far we have looked through the functions of the nonsprite
video control words at 53265 to 53286 (hex D011 to D026). Sprites
are completely separate from the conventional video circuitry.
You can lay a sprite on top of just about anything. But first, what's
a sprite and how do we define it?

MOBs

Sprites are sometimes called Movable Object Blocks (MOBs) —
and that's what they are, movable objects. The nice thing about
them is that they appear on the screen independently of the main
screen image, so that we can have a sprite airplane flying across
the screen, and, after it passes a background object, the object re-
appears. This can save a lot of programming.

   We noted earlier that the video chip can reach only 16K for its
information. This includes three things: the screen memory (or
video matrix), the Character Generator (or Character Base), and
the sprite information. It all has to come out of the same 16K section.

   When we learn how to draw sprites, we'll discover that each
sprite occupies 63 bytes and uses a 64-byte block. So within 16K,
we could draw up to 128 sprites. We can't use more than eight at a
time, but we can have up to 128 drawings waiting to be used. The
sprite positions number from 0 at address 0, through 1 at address
64, up to 127 at address 8128.

   We cannot use all of the 128 sprite positions, of course. For
one thing, the video matrix and the Character Base will use up a
total of 3K of memory, and this space won't be available for us to
use. That cuts us down to 80; and, depending on the 16K block
we have chosen, there may be other forbidden locations.

   The normal configuration is for the video chip to access 0 to
16383, and there's a lot of forbidden territory in there. Many of the
first 1024 bytes are busy as the BASIC work area; the screen is
normally 1024 to 2023 (more on that later); the Character Base appears in addresses 4096 to 8191, since there are two complete
character sets; and everything above 2048 that isn't used by the
Character Base is used to store your BASIC program. We haven't
started, but we seem to be out of sprite memory!

If we want to draw lots of sprite pictures, we would need to do one of two things: move BASIC RAM so that it starts at a much higher location, or move to another 16K block that is not so busy. For the moment, we can find room for a few sprites in the existing space. I find the following sprite areas available: sprite 11 at 704 to 766; sprite 13 at 832 to 894; sprite 14 at 896 to 958; and sprite 15 at 960 to 1022. These last three use the cassette tape buffer; if we use cassette tape during the program run, the sprites will become very strange.

The Hard Way

There are quite a few utility programs around that will help us draw sprites. You should use them; they will help make life easier. In the meantime, we can draw a sprite the hard way by using a sheet of squared paper. Let's draw a target reticule. First, we'll sketch it:

```
x x x x x x x x . . . . . . . . x x x x x x x x
x . . . . . . . . . . . . . . . . . . . . . . x
x . . . . . . . . . . . . . . . . . . . . . . x
_ _ _                                     _ _ _
. . . . . . . . . . . x . . . . . . . . . . . .
. . . . . . . . . . . x . . . . . . . . . . . .
. . . . . . . . . x x . x x . . . . . . . . . .
. . . . . . . . . . . x . . . . . . . . . . . .
. . . . . . . . . . . x . . . . . . . . . . . .
_ _ _                                     _ _ _
x . . . . . . . . . . . . . . . . . . . . . . x
x . . . . . . . . . . . . . . . . . . . . . . x
x x x x x x x x . . . . . . . . x x x x x x x x
```

There are 24 pixels across (that takes three bytes of eight bits each) and 21 down. We may analyze the pixel pattern eight at a time, using a binary system to describe each byte. We end up with a DATA statement something like:

```
10 DATA 255,0,255,128,0,1,128,0,1,128,0,
   1,128,0,1,128,0,1,128,0,1
20 DATA 0,8,0,0,8,0,0,8,0,0,52,0,0,8,0,0
   ,8,0,0,8,0
30 DATA 128,0,1,128,0,1,128,0,1,128,0,1,
   128,0,1,128,0,1,255,0,255
```

Now we place the sprite into slot 13 by:

```
40 FORJ=0TO62:READ X:POKEJ+832,X:NEXT J
```

81

Good. Running the program this far will place the sprite into slot 13, but it won't do anything. It's just a picture, and nobody is using it. That's OK. In fact, you'll often want to have dozens of pictures available, even though you might end up using only one or two at a time.

Let's tell a sprite to use this drawing. We do it in an odd way: we don't use the video chip control registers at all. Instead, we use the video matrix, or "screen memory." You may recall that 1024 addresses are set aside for the video memory, but the screen holds only 1000 characters. What about the extras? At least some of them are used to designate which sprite picture to use for a given sprite. The last "live" screen address is 2023. We could point sprite 0 to sprite drawing 13 (the one we have just done) by POKE 2040,13. Better yet, let's point all the sprites at this drawing:

```
50 FOR J=0 TO 7:POKE 2040+J,13:NEXT J
```

We're almost ready to energize the sprite. But, first, let's give it a position on the screen. For sprite 0, we set the position by POKEing to 53248 and 53249. Let's put a value of 99 in each, and then turn the sprite on. If you've run the above program, you may do this with a direct command, or give it a program line:

```
60 POKE53248,99:POKE53249,99:POKE53269,1
```

Either way, you should get your sprite on the screen. Now we can play with it and see how easy some things are to do. Notice how you can see right through the transparent portions of the sprite to the program listing behind. Now you can try changing the sprite color as desired by POKEing a value from 0 to 15 into location 53287. One color will be the same as the background, so that the sprite will be almost invisible, but not quite, since we can see when it covers part of the text.

You can move the sprite around at will by changing the values you have POKEd into 53248 and 53249. Try playing with the values; you may find that (vertically, at least) you can move the sprite partly or completely off the screen. If you like, try the following command:

```
FOR J= 99 TO 150:POKE 53248,J:NEXT J
```

and then substitute 53249 for 53248 and try it again. Neat? You bet. And there's more to come. But first, a small problem to be resolved.

Moving Left or Right

We can move the sprite vertically anywhere we like — including
partly or completely off the screen. But the screen is wider than it
is high; and we can't reach the whole screen with the range of
values (0 to 255) that we can POKE in 53248. We need a high bit to
cover the extra distance. You'll find this in 53264; POKEing 53264
with a value of one causes sprite zero to be moved to the right —
perhaps off screen.

Let's stop for a moment and look at video registers. When we
set the X and Y position for sprite zero by changing 53248 and
53249, we recognized that we would need a different set of locations for sprite one — 53250 and 53251, as it happens. And when
we set sprite zero's color to any one of the 16 combinations by
changing address 53287, we see that we'll need a new color
address for sprite one — 53288.

But the other sprite registers use a different system. One
register controls sprites: so that address 53269 allows us to turn
on one sprite, or all eight. We use a bitmap to arrange this; the
pattern is:

Sprite 0 — value 1
Sprite 1 — value 2
Sprite 2 — value 4
Sprite 3 — value 8
Sprite 4 — value 16
Sprite 5 — value 32
Sprite 6 — value 64
Sprite 7 — value 128

We use addition to signal a combination of sprites. If we
wished to turn on sprites zero and three, we would POKE 53269,9
(nine is the sum of eight and one). All other sprites would be
turned off.

That's how the X-position high bit works: we set sprite zero to
the right-hand sector of the screen by POKE 53264,1. All the other
registers we will discuss work the same way.

You may be pleased by the way that the sprite moves over the
top of the text on the screen — it would move over a background
picture just as easily, of course. But we have another option: you
can make the sprite move *behind* the main screen if you wish. Do
this with location 53275. For example, POKE 53275,1 will place the
sprite behind the screen text.

The sprite that we have drawn isn't very big. We can make it
larger in the X and Y directions with addresses 53277 and 53271

respectively. These addresses are often used together; when an object is drawn bigger it looks closer, and we often want this effect in games and animations. Try, separately or individually, POKE 53277,1 and POKE 53271,1.

Four-color Sprites

Our sprite is only one color, the color we selected in 53287. The other color is "transparent," so it isn't really a color at all. We may code our sprite in four colors (or three plus transparent, to be exact), but we would need to draw it slightly differently. Instead of one bit representing either "color" or "transparent," a grouping of two bits will be needed to describe four conditions: the sprite color (as before), special color #1, special color #2, and transparent. These extra special colors, by the way, are kept at 53285 and 53286: they are the same for all sprites; only the sprite color is individual.

Now we come to the last two registers, which tell you about collisions. PEEK(53279) will tell you if any sprites have collided with the background since you last checked. One certainly has, of course, if you've been messing around with the screen as suggested. PRINT PEEK(53279) will yield a value of one: checking the bit table above tells us that sprite zero has hit the background. Now, checking this location clears it; but if the sprite is still touching some of the screen text, it will flip right back on again. Move the sprite to a clear part of the screen. Print the PEEK again — it will likely still say one, since the sprite has hit characters since it was last checked. If the sprite is safely in a clear screen area, the next PEEK will yield a zero.

We've activated only one sprite, so that we won't see any collisions between sprites. You would see this in location 53278, but right now PEEK(53278) will yield zero; unless you have activated more sprites, there would not have been any collision. Again, when you get a signal here, you'll know which sprites have bumped; and testing the location clears it, so that only new "touches" will be shown on the next test.

A small comment here: these two PEEK locations are marked "Interrupt." Yet when such collisions occur, they are logged — they don't do anything. As we discussed earlier, the word *interrupt* has a special meaning to machine language programmers; and no interrupts seem to be happening. The machine language programmer who wants interrupt to happen must enable the interrupt by storing the appropriate value into address D01A hexadecimal, and then write the appropriate extra coding to make it all work.

This completes our roster of registers, but the plain mechanical facts don't convey the remarkable things that you can do with the Commodore 64. There's more to come.

Program Design

Jim Butterfield

We've examined all the bits in the video chip control registers. Now let's ease back and look at the 64's video structure. We'll talk a bit about program design considerations.

A Single 16K Slice

We have discussed how the video chip gets its screen information directly from memory. We indicated that the chip must dig out all of its information from a single 16K slice. We might draw this as a diagram (see the figure).

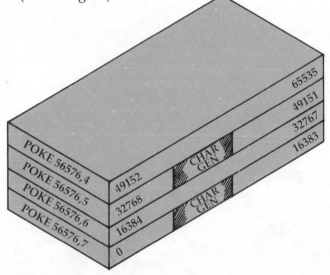

The video chip obtains its screen information from one of four 16K memory "slices." Two of the slices contain the ROM Character Generator.

We can control which slice we want by manipulating the two low bits in address 56576 (hex DD00). Normally, the processor picks the slice from 0 to 16383.

Once we've picked a 16K block, we must get all screen data from this block: the screen memory, the character set, and the sprites. We cannot get the screen data from one block, the Character Base from another, and sprites from still another. Because we are restricted, we must do a little planning and design our video information into our program.

After we have picked the 16K slice, we must set the video matrix (screen memory) to some point within it. We may pick any multiple of 1024 as a starting address. The normal 64 configuration is set to a value of one, meaning we take the screen information from memory starting at address 1024. The video matrix, you may remember, is stored in the high nybble (that means multiply it by 16) of 53272 (hex D018).

We must pick our Character Base next. If we're in normal resolution, we may pick any even multiple of 1024 as a starting address: i.e., 0, 2048, 4096, etc. If we're in high-resolution mode, we must pick only values of zero and eight, meaning that the hi-res starting address will be either 0 or 8192. The normal 64 configuration is set to four or six for either uppercase/graphics or upper-/lowercase mode, meaning we take our character set from 4096 to 6144. The Character Base is stored in the low nybble of 53272.

So we'd expect a normal 64 to place into address 53272: a video matrix of one, times 16, plus a Character Base of four or six, yielding a total of 20 or 22. You may in fact see 21 or 23 if you PEEK the location, but the extra bit doesn't matter — it's not used. And if we switch to high-resolution without changing anything else, our Character Base of four or six will be trimmed back to zero — explaining why we saw zero page when we tried POKE 53265,48 in the first article of this series.

Let's try a few specific design jobs.

Task 1: Simple Graphics

We're quite satisfied with the screen and character set, but we'd like to add a few sprites to liven things up. Fine, the normal 64 configuration leaves room for about four sprite drawings (numbers 11, 13, 14, and 15), provided we don't need to use cassette tape during the program run. This may be enough for a lot of animation; all eight sprites could use a single drawing, if that suited the task.

If we needed more than four drawings, we might be tempted to move the start-of-BASIC pointer to a higher location, making room for the extras. That can work quite well, but it will probably call for two programs: a configuring program and a final program. It's hard for a program to reconfigure itself and survive.

Task 2: New Character Sets

If we wish to use the regular character set as well as new characters that we might devise, we'll want to stay in the memory blocks
from 0 to 16383 or 32768 to 49151. These two blocks contain the
ROM Character Generator at offset 4096 to 8191. If we don't need
regular characters at all (if we intend to use our own), it may be
more convenient to switch to either of the other two blocks: 16384
to 32767 or 49152 to 65535. Since there's nothing but RAM in these
two, we may find more room.

Note that some of these RAM addresses are "hidden" beneath ROMs — BASIC from 40960 to 49151, and the Kernal from
57344 to 65535. The video chip sees only the RAM; but in a
normally configured 64 system, programs will see only the ROM.
You can POKE or store to the RAM beneath, but when you PEEK
or load from these addresses, you'll get the ROM. That's OK; the
video chip sees the RAM locations you have POKEd. Result:
something for nothing! You can build a Character Base into RAM,
and not lose any memory from your system.

Task 3: Emulating a PET

This is a clear-cut task. We want to move the screen to the same
place that the PET uses the screen. That's very straightforward
from a video chip standpoint. (Note: If you type the following
POKEs in one at a time, you may have to type blind for some of
them.) The PET screen belongs at 32768, so we must select that
slice with:

```
POKE 56576,5
```

so that we'll pick up RAM starting at 32768. The ROM Character
Generator is still in place.

Since we want the screen (video matrix) to be positioned
right at the start of the block, we must set it to a value of zero. The
Character Base can stay at its value of four (for graphics mode), so
we must set up address 53272 with zero times 16 plus four:

```
POKE 53272,4
```

That completes the video, but we have a few other things to do to
make BASIC work in a sound manner. We must tell BASIC where
the new screen is located:

```
POKE 648,128
```

And finally, we should set the start and end of BASIC to correspond with a 32K PET:

```
POKE 1024,0:POKE 44,4:POKE56,128:NEW
```

Clear the screen, and the job's done. Zero page usage is still different, so not all PEEKs and POKEs will automatically work on this reconfigured system; but BASIC and screen now match the PET.

Task 4: High-resolution Plotting

There are only eight places in memory that we can place a high-resolution screen: 0, 8192, 16384, 24576, 32768, 40960, 49152, and 57344. We tend to choose the two 16K blocks that don't have the Character Generator, 16384 to 32767 and 49152 to 65535. That way, we'll have more clear RAM to use; there will be more space left for our video matrix and any sprites we need.

If we want to write characters on the hi-res screen, we'll have to generate them ourselves or steal them from the Character Generator. Here's an odd thing — the video chip sees the character ROM at two different addresses, but the processor chip (and that includes your program) sees the same 4K ROM only at a third location, 53248 to 57343. Most of the time, the processor can't see the ROM anyway, since the addresses are overlaid with the I/O chips.

So if our program wants to see the character set, it must flip away the I/O chip with POKE 1,51 — stop, don't do it yet! There are two problems. First, once the I/O chips are moved out — sound, video, interface, everything — you won't be able to type on the keyboard; so you'll never be able to type the POKE to put everything back. Second, the interrupt program uses these I/O chips for quite a few things, and it will go berserk the moment you take them out of action. So we must use a program or a multiple direct command to do the job, and we must temporarily lock out the interrupt activity. Type the following statements as a single line:

POKE 56333,127:	(lock out the interrupt)
POKE 1,51:	(flip out I/O)
X =PEEK(53256):	(read part of character)
POKE 1,55:	(restore I/O)
POKE 56333,129	(restore interrupt)

X will contain the top row of pixels for the letter A. If you like, you can draw a character's shape with the following program:

```
100 INPUT "CHARACTER NUMBER";A
110 IF A<0 OR A>255 THEN STOP
120 B=53248+8*A
130 C=56333
140 FOR J=0 TO 7
150 POKE C,127:POKE 1,51:X=PEEK(B+J)/128
160 POKE 1,55:POKE C,129
170 FOR K=1 TO 8
180 X%=X:X=(X-X%)*2
190 PRINT CHR$(32+X%*3);
200 NEXT K:PRINT
210 NEXT J
220 GOTO 100
```

To terminate this program, enter a number over 255. You'll note that most of the characters are drawn with "double width" lines. A video technician would tell you that this reduces the video frequencies and is likely to cause less picture smear.

Arranging the video areas is almost an art. It takes a little practice, but you'll get the knack of it fairly quickly.

The Lunar Lander: The 64 in Action

Jim Butterfield

Now we'll write a small lunar lander program that demonstrates some of the features of the 64's video chip.

First, the Craft

First, let's draw the sprites for the rocket:

```
100 DATA 0,24,0,0,60,0,0,198,0,1,131,0,1
    ,131,0,3,1,128,3,1,128,3,1,128
110 DATA 3,1,128,3,1,128,3,1,128,3,1,128
    ,1,131,0,1,131,0,1,131,0
120 DATA 0,102,0,0,126,0,0,0,0,0,0,0,0,0
    ,0,0,0,0
```

A fairly crude craft — you can improve it if you like. We have drawn the sprite into 63 bytes of memory; one more and we can continue to the next sprite.

```
130 DATA 0:REM GAP BETWEEN SPRITES
```

Then the Flame

Now we're going to draw the rocket flame as a separate sprite. Why? Because later, when we look for collisions, we don't care what the flame hits, just what the rocket hits. There's another reason: when we're not thrusting, we can simply turn this sprite off, and the flame disappears.

```
140 DATA 0,0,0,0,0,0,0,0,0,0,0,0,0,0,0,0
    ,0,0,0,0,0,0,0,0,0,0,0,0,0,0,0,0
150 DATA 0,0,0,0,0,0,0,0,0,0,0,0,0,0,0,0
    ,0,0,0,66,0,0,36,0,0,24,0,0,24,0
```

Mostly zeros. The flame is only at the bottom of the sprite. OK, we're ready to go. Let's clear the screen and print instructions:

```
160 PRINT CHR$(147)
170 PRINT "LUNAR LANDER"
180 PRINT
190 PRINT "PRESS 'SPACE' FOR MAIN THRUST
    "
200 PRINT "PRESS 'F1'{4 SPACES}FOR LEFT
    THRUST"
210 PRINT "PRESS 'F7'{4 SPACES}FOR RIGHT
     THRUST"
220 PRINT
230 PRINT "WATCH OUT FOR THE MINES."
240 PRINT
250 PRINT "LAND GENTLY OR YOU'LL BOUNCE!
    "
```

While the user is reading the instructions, we can read in the sprites and put them into slots 13 and 14. We can also set our sprite "position" addresses as variables, and identify sprites 0 and 1 as using pictures 13 and 14.

```
260 REM SET UP
270 FOR J=0 TO 126:READ X:POKE 832+J,X:N
    EXT J
280 X0=53248:Y0=53249:C0=53279
290 X1=53250:Y1=53251:E=53269
300 POKE 2040,13:POKE 2041,14
```

We'll make the rocket exhaust go behind the main screen. This way, as we land, the exhaust will go behind the background. We'll also give it color to distinguish it from the rocket ship itself (you can pick your own).

```
310 POKE 53275,2
320 POKE 53288,3:REM THRUST COLOR
330 PRINT "READY TO START";
340 X$="Y":INPUT X$
```

Variable E is used to enable the sprites. When we're ready, we'll turn them on; for now they can stay off.

```
350 POKE E,0
360 IF X$<>"Y" AND X$<>"YES" THEN END
```

We're ready to fly. Let's put the sprite high on the left part of the screen. Then we'll draw a screen with mines for the player to avoid.

```
370 V=100:H=100:V0=0:H0=0
380 POKE 54296,15:POKE54278,240
390 REM DRAW SCREEN
400 PRINTCHR$(147)
410 FOR J=1 TO 18:PRINT:NEXT J
420 FOR J=1 TO 4:FOR K=1 TO 30
430 C$="":IF RND(1)<.1 AND (K<20 OR K>25
    ) THEN C$="#"
440 PRINT C$;:NEXT K:PRINT:NEXT J
450 FOR J=1 TO 30:PRINT"=";:NEXT J
```

Keyboard Checks

Let's place the sprite, and start the main play by checking the keyboard. We check for two different things: a new key (K$), or an old key still being held down (K):

```
460 POKE X0,H:POKE Y0,V:POKE X1,H:POKE Y
    1,V
470 K=PEEK(203):GET K$
480 REM MAIN FLIGHT LOOP-TEST KEYS
490 IF K$=""GOTO 550
500 K0=ASC(K$):V1=.1:H1=0
```

Let's check for the space bar. If it's on, we want to energize the rocket and the rocket flame. Our vertical thrust will be upwards (-.5), and we'll want to enable the flame video with a note that E0 =3. We'll spot lateral thrust as keys F1 and F7, and set value H1 accordingly.

```
510 E0=1:IF K0=32 THEN V1=-.5:E0=3
512 REM
520 IF K0=133 THEN H1=-.2
530 IF K0=136 THEN H1=.2
540 GOTO 560
550 IF K=64 THEN V1=.1:H1=0:E0=1
```

Here's where we turn on our sprites — either rocket only (E0 =1) or both rocket and flame (E0 =3). As long as we're turning rockets on and off, we might as well add sound effects, too:

```
560 IF PEEK(E)=E0 GOTO 600
570 REM THRUST SOUND
580 POKE E,E0:IF E0=1 THEN POKE 54276,0:
    GOTO 600
```

93

```
590 POKE 54273,8:POKE 54276,129
600 IF H1=H9 GOTO 630
610 H9=H1:K=SGN(ABS(H9))*129:POKE 54273,
    99:POKE 54276,K
```

Gravity, thrust, or lateral thrust — they all involve acceleration. We add acceleration to our speed to get new speed; then we add speed to position to get new position.

```
620 REM LET'S MOVE IT!
630 V0=V0+V1:H0=H0+H1
```

To prevent the player going off screen, we'll invent a force field around the screen boundary. If you hit it, you'll bounce; that is, your speed will flip to the opposite direction. We'll fudge a bit. The high bit of the X position is tricky to set in BASIC; there's often a flicker during the moment that we set the low and high values. So let's limit the player's travel to the left-hand three-quarters of the screen and avoid the problem.

```
640 REM FIELD FORCE BOUNDARIES
650 IF V<50 THEN V0=ABS(V0)
660 IF H<20 THEN H0=ABS(H0)
670 IF H>240 THEN H0=-ABS(H0)
680 V=V+V0:H=H+H0
```

We move the craft simply by changing its coordinates. Then we check the collision register to see if we've hit anything.

There's a problem here. It seems that collision is noted when the screen is drawn, not when you set the coordinates. BASIC isn't super fast, but it could be fast enough to miss that collision. If you watch the program closely, you will see that the rocket sometimes bounces after it goes below ground level.

There's an additional contributing factor. BASIC, being slow, may need to move the rocket several pixels in distance at a time. So, rather than just touching the ground and stopping, the rocket may leap from just above the ground to well into it, if it's going quite fast.

```
690 REM MOVE CRAFT, CHECK COLLISION
700 POKE X0,H:POKE Y0,V:POKE X1,H:POKE Y
    1,V
710 C=PEEK(C0):IF(C AND 1)=0 GOTO 470
```

Collision says we've hit something. We can look at our height (Y position) to see if it's the ground. If not, it must be a mine.

```
720 IF V>218 GOTO 780
730 IF V+V0<218 GOTO 470
```

We could do a sensational explosion here, but we'd need to define more sprites, or modify the ones we've got. Try your hand at it if you like. For the moment, hitting a mine will cause the rocket to disappear.

```
740 REM WE SEEM TO HAVE HIT A MINE
750 PRINT CHR$(19);"CRASHED!":POKE E,0
760 GOTO 820
```

Bounce and Overshoot

I arbitrarily decided to make the craft bounce if it hits too fast. If you'd rather crash, go ahead. See the previous note.

```
770 REM HIT THE DECK...TOO FAST?
780 IF V0>1 OR V0<0 THEN V0=-ABS(V0):GOT
    O 470
790 PRINT CHR$(19);"LANDED!":POKE E,1
```

Because we may overshoot the ground and dig a little hole, we'll reset the vertical position of a successfully landed rocket to look neat. Then we wind up the game or play another one.

```
800 POKE Y0,219
810 REM ALL DONE-SHUT DOWN
820 POKE 54276,0:POKE 54296,0
830 PRINT "WANT TO TRY AGAIN";
840 GOTO 340
```

There are many features you can add — such as a fuel supply.

We could have done a pretty background in high-resolution graphics, but this would make it difficult to add features (if you wish) like meter readouts. In fact, I've used very dull graphics, but you may consider that a challenge.

That's it. We've done a simple sprite exercise. It's really not hard, even in BASIC. In machine language, it's almost too easy; you'll find that you need to slow your program down, or everything will happen too fast.

The graphics capability is there, and it's not hard to use. A little experimentation and practice, and you too can animate a picture that's worth a thousand words.

Split Screens

Jim Butterfield

In this section we will deal with a fairly advanced technique: split screens. It's a new aspect of the computer, combining things we have already learned into a new set of capabilities. We'll demonstrate, via a machine language program, an amazing visual display.

We'll need to venture into more technical waters now, but with a little effort we can perform some minor miracles on the screen. All the limitations we have learned may be set aside with a little creative "cheating." We'll have a venture into machine language; but even if you're not an ML fanatic, it's worth knowing that the job can be done.

We have learned a number of limitations, largely based on the idea that the screen can do a lot of things, but only one at a time:

• We can have only one background color, unless we are in multicolor mode; and even in that case, we're restricted in our choice of colors.

• We can obtain information only from one 16K memory quadrant.

• We can use only one character set.

• We can be in character mode or bitmap (hi-res) mode, but not both.

• We may have only eight sprites on the screen at one time.

In fact, we have a more general set of rules. We may be in only one mode at a time — multicolor is either on or off; extended color is either on or off, and so on. It seems impossible to mix screen modes and have the best of both worlds, but we can do it.

Here's the trick: the Raster Register, address $D012 together with the high bit of $D011, can do more than tell us where the screen is being painted at this instant. We may store an interrupt value there and tell the computer: "Advise me when you get to this part of the screen." At this point, we can switch screen characteristics: color mode, high resolution, background color, character set, memory bank — whatever you want. Of course, we need to put it all back when we return to the top of the screen.

The Task

We're going to write a quick program to split the screen into two parts, each with a different characteristic. It won't be perfect; we're just trying to show the technique, not polish up all the loose ends. The fine points will come later. First, let's plan.

If we set a new interrupt into our machine, we'll need to make some careful distinctions. First, when an interrupt happens, we must establish: who caused this one? Was it the raster, or the traditional interrupt source of 1/60 second timing? Second, if it was a raster, which part of the screen is involved — the top or the "switch" point?

The Interrupt

Let's start to lay out the machine language program. All interrupts will come here, and we'll need to sort them out. We'll put the program into the cassette buffer.

033C	AD	19	D0	INT	LDA	$D019
033F	29	01			AND	#$01
0341	F0	19			BEQ	REGULR

The interrupt has happened and has come here. Check the Raster Interrupt Bit in $D019 — was this one caused by the raster? We'll need to mask out the bit we want with an AND. If we get nothing, it's a regular interrupt — go there.

0343	8D	19	D0		STA	$D019

It is indeed a raster interrupt, and we must shut off the alarm. We do this by storing the bit back where it came from (there's a 1 in the A register right now). Amazingly, this turns the bit off.

0346	A2	92		LDX	#$92
0348	A0	15		LDY	#$15

We'll prepare the registers, assuming we are doing the top-of-screen work. The hex 92 is decimal 146 — the scan line that hits about mid-screen; that's where we will want the next interrupt to take place. Note that hex 92 is considered a "negative" byte; we will use this fact in just a moment. Now, let's see if we are correct about being at mid-screen:

034A	AD	12	D0		LDA	#$D012
034D	10	04			BPL	MID

We look at the raster scan. If it's less than 127, we're near the top of the screen, and we don't see the negative byte. So we skip ahead. If, however, we are at the middle of the screen, we'll see a negative value. We won't branch; instead, we'll fix up the registers for mid-screen work:

| 034F | A2 | 01 | | LDX | #$01 |
| 0351 | A0 | 17 | | LDY | #$17 |

Both streams join again at this point. X contains the raster location where we will want the next interrupt: if we're at the top, we want to be interrupted at the middle (hex 92); if we're at the middle, we will want to be interrupted at the top (hex 01). Y contains information on the character set we want to choose: graphics or text. Let's proceed:

| 0353 | 8E | 12 | D0 | MID | STX | $D012 |

Place the next interrupt point into the raster register. The next interrupt will now hit at the right time.

| 0356 | 8C | 18 | D0 | | STY | $D018 |

Place the "character set" value — hex 15 for graphics, hex 17 for text — into the appropriate register.

| 0359 | 4C | BC | FE | | JMP | $FEBC |

We've done our job. We may now exit. Don't give an RTI; instead, go to a routine that cleans things up nicely, at $FEBC. And what of our regular interrupt?

| 035C | 4C | 31 | EA | REGULR | JMP | $EA31 |

It goes to the normal address ($EA31), to which regular interrupts go. We have more to do after we get this program into memory. We must also detour the interrupt vector to our new program and fire up the raster interrupt control.

Back to BASIC
Ready to put all this in BASIC? Here we go:

```
90  POKE 53265,27
100 FOR J=828 TO 862:READ X
110 T=T+X:POKE J,X
120 NEXT J
130 IF T<>3958 THEN STOP
200 DATA 173,25,208,41,1,240,25,141,25,2
    08,162,146,160,21,173,18
210 DATA 208,16,4,162,1,160,23,142,18,20
    8,140,24,208,76,188,254,76,49,234
300 POKE 56333,127
310 POKE 788,60:POKE 789,3
320 POKE 56333,129:POKE 53274,129
```

Let's look at the last three lines. Line 300 kills the interrupt for a
moment, so that we can mess with the interrupt vector without
running into disaster. Line 310 changes the interrupt vector to
point at our newly POKEd program. Line 320 restores the interrupt and adds an extra one: the raster interrupt.

An Amazing Split

When the program is run, an amazing thing happens: the screen
becomes graphic at the top and text at the bottom. Impossible,
you say? Not for us clever — and careful — people. The effect is
permanent: you may NEW the program and start something
else, and the split screen will still be there. You shouldn't use
cassette tape with program in place — it's there in the buffer.
And you may find that LOAD and SAVE don't work quite right.
RUN-STOP/RESTORE will put everything back to its former
state. (Please save this program for use in the next section.)

The Unsolved Problem

But it's not perfect (I warned you). Every once in a while, the bar-
rier seems to creep slightly, and then correct itself. Maybe it's
computer hiccups. It seems worse when you are using the keyboard. What's happening? And how can we fix it? Read "Son of
Split Screens."

Son of
Split Screens

Jim Butterfield

In the section called "Split Screens," we had a program similar
but not identical to the one below. Either type this in or load the
earlier version and make the necessary changes in lines 130, 200,
and 210.

```
90   POKE 53265,27
100  FOR J=828 TO 862:READ X
110  T=T+X:POKE J,X
120  NEXT J
130  IF T<>3929 THEN STOP
200  DATA 173,25,208,41,1,240,25,141,25,2
     08,162,146,160,6,173,18
210  DATA 208,16,4,162,1,160,0,142,18,208
     ,140,33,208,76,188,254,76,49,234
300  POKE 56333,127
310  POKE 788,60:POKE 789,3
320  POKE 56333,129:POKE 53274,129
```

Our previous example split the screen into two sections:
graphics and text. This one splits the screen into two background
color areas. It makes it easier for us to see the glitch — the hiccup
that occasionally disturbs our screen split. By the way, it's easier
to see the problem when you are using the keyboard.

Why the Problem?

Here's where the problem comes from: the timer interrupt strikes
about every 1/60 second. The screen display, too, runs at a
rate of about 60 times a second. But they are not synchronized.
The two processes run at similar, but not identical, speeds.

Every once in a while, the timer interrupt hits just before the
raster interrupt. The timer interrupt has quite a few jobs to do:
update the TI$ clock, check the cassette motor, flash the cursor,
and check the keyboard. It takes time to do these jobs, and extra
time is required if a key is being pressed.

Suppose we have just started on the timer interrupt, and the raster scan says, "I'm ready!" Sorry, raster, we're already into an interrupt routine, and other interrupts are locked out until we have finished. By that time, the screen scan might have moved along a few lines, and our split screen has crept from its normal position.

Some Possible Fixes

There are several possible approaches to fixing this jitter. The ones that come to mind first are complex; in a moment, we'll move on to an easy one.

When the timer interrupt strikes, we could ask it to look at the raster and see if the scan was close to the interrupt point. If so, we might wait things out or skip part of the timer interrupt jobs. Messy.

The timer interrupt could unlock the interrupt very quickly, using a CLI command. That way, we could interrupt the interrupt program itself to do the split screen job. Better — but some programmers feel it's dangerous to allow this kind of thing to happen.

A Better Way

There is an easier way: shut the timer interrupt off completely, and do its various jobs with our own programs. This *seems* complex, but it's not. We can call the timer interrupt routines ourselves, whenever it's time.

Let's look a little more closely into the timing of these interrupts. We expect to cause a raster scan interrupt about 120 times a second. That's twice as often as the timer interrupt needs to be handled. So our raster program could occasionally call in the timer interrupt program.

It seems that we could accomplish the task easily by calling the timer interrupt routines every second raster interrupt. That would certainly do the job, but there's a better way.

Even though we've shut off the timer interrupt, it's still signaling when the time is ready. Let's review: the timer leaves a signal in hex address $DC0D (56333) whenever it counts down to zero. Normally, this signal triggers the interrupt line (IRQ) and causes the processor to be interrupted. But we may "break" the connection between the timer signal and the interrupt line. In this case, the timer will not cause an interrupt, but the signal bit will still flash when the appropriate time has come.

We can see the plan in Figures 1 and 2. We will disconnect the timer from interrupt and service it ourselves when it flashes.

Easier done than said. Let's look at the machine language coding:

```
033C   A9   01          INTR    LDA    #$01
033E   8D   19   D0              STA    $D019
```

Raster interrupt is now the only game in town, so we don't need to test for it. We must, of course, turn off the raster interrupt flag.

```
0341   A2   92                  LDX    #$92
0343   A0   06                  LDY    #$06
```

Setup for top of screen. Next interrupt, line 92 hex; new color, number 6.

```
0345   AD   12   D0              LDA    $D012
0348   10   04                   BPL    MID
```

If it's really the top of screen, we can skip ahead. Otherwise, we change for mid-screen — line 1, new color, number 0:

```
034A   A2   01                  LDX    #$01
034C   A0   00                   LDY    #$00
```

Now we're ready to do the job, wherever the screen is:

```
034E   8E   12   D0   MID    STX    $D012
0351   8C   21   D0             STY    $D021
```

The job is done. Now let's see if the timer interrupt is calling for action:

```
0354   AD   0D   DC              LDA    $DC0D
0357   29   01                   AND    #$01
0359   F0   03                   BEQ    SKIP
```

If we didn't skip, the timer wants attention. Call it in:

```
035B   4C   31   EA              JMP    $EA31
```

If we did skip, the timer isn't needed. Quit with:

```
035E   4C   BC   FE   SKIP    JMP    $FEBC
```

We must remember, of course, to turn off the timer interrupt, set the IRQ vector to our new code, and turn on the raster interrupt. We'll do all that in BASIC.

BASIC-ally Yours

Here's the same program in BASIC.

```
90  POKE 53265,27
100 FOR J=828 TO 864:READ X
110 T=T+X:POKE J,X
120 NEXT J
130 IF T<>4077 THEN STOP
```

```
200 DATA 169,1,141,25,208,162,146,160,6,
    173,18,208,16,4,162,1
210 DATA 160,0,142,18,208,140,33,208,173
    ,13,220
220 DATA 41,1,240,3,76,49,234,76,188,254
300 POKE 56333,127
310 POKE 788,60:POKE 789,3
320 POKE 53274,129
```

Now we have a rock-solid color change at the appropriate screen point. No creeping, no jittering, no hiccups.

We've only touched upon the techniques of raster interrupt. A whole host of new possibilities open up with its use.

But we've shown it can be done — and some of the techniques that can be used to do it.

Figure 1. Conventional coding requires the program to distinguish between the two live timing sources. It may also cause timing jitter.

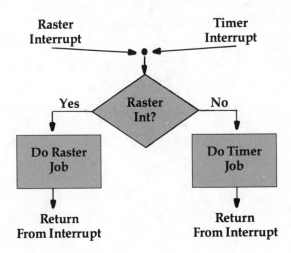

Figure 2. Single interrupt coding gives priority to the time-sensitive raster job.

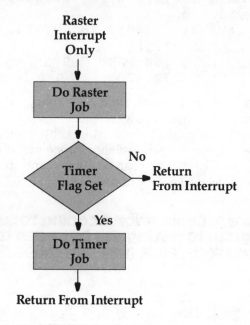

Chapter 4

Creating Games

Joysticks and Sprites

Sheldon Leemon

Fast movement of sprites can increase the appeal of any game. Try the demonstration programs here and learn how to add this technique to your games.

As the owner of an Atari 800 computer, I welcomed Commodore's announcement of the 64, because it closely parallels the Atari in its consumer orientation. One example is the inclusion of two ports for Atari-type joystick controllers. These controllers provide a simple way for the user to interact with any type of program, including, of course, arcade games.

A Fascinating Chip
When I bought the computer, however, I discovered, to my dismay, that the consumer-oriented design approach did not seem to carry through to the BASIC interpreter and *User's Guide.* Not only was there no BASIC command for reading the joystick controllers, but the BASIC manual also made no mention whatever of these ports! This meant that if I discovered how to use these sticks any time soon, I would have to play hardware detective.

Fortunately, the 64 is similar to the VIC-20 in a number of ways. Since the VIC reads the joystick through a VIA (Versatile Interface Adapter) chip, it stands to reason that the 64 would read its joystick through the analogous CIA (Complex Interface Adapter) chip. An early memory map from Commodore shows CIA #1 to be addressed at location $DC00, or 56320 decimal. The CIA is a fascinating I/O chip and could well serve as the basis for an article in itself, but here I'll focus attention on the registers that read the joysticks.

Like the VIC, the 64 uses Peripheral Data Registers A and B to read these sticks, and I/O (input/output) through these registers is controlled by Data Direction Registers A and B. These registers are

107

addressed at the chip's first four locations, so that on the 64 Data
Register A is addressed at 65320, Register B is addressed at 56321,
and Data Direction Registers A and B are addressed at 56322 and
56323, respectively.

Reading the Joysticks

Knowing this, with a bit of trial and error I was able to figure out
how to read the joysticks. A quick try seémed to indicate that it
was not necessary to write to the Data Direction Registers before
reading the sticks, as must be done on the VIC-20. Checking the
values of Registers A and B while moving joysticks connected to
Control Ports 1 and 2 revealed that the data from the stick connected to Control Port 1 appeared in Register B, and that the data
from the stick in Port 2 showed up in Register A.

The relationship of the data returned in the register to the
direction of stick movement is exactly the same as on the Atari.
Each of the low bits (0-3) corresponds to one of the switches that
is closed by moving the stick in one of the four primary directions.
These bits are normally set to 1, but are reset to 0 when the corresponding switch is closed. Bit 0 corresponds to the up switch, bit
1 corresponds to the down switch, bit 2 is left, and bit 3 right. Bit 4
is used to read the joystick trigger button. It is set to 1 normally
and reset to 0 if the button is pushed.

What this means to the hardware-weary reader who has
borne with me thus far, patiently waiting for an explanation in
plain English of how to use the Commodore 64 joysticks, is that it
takes only a couple of BASIC statements to do the job. Those
familiar with the Atari system of numbering the joystick positions
(as I am) may want to use the following statements:

```
S1=PEEK(56321) AND 15:REM READS STICK 1
S2=PEEK(56320) AND 15:REM READS STICK 2
```

Because these registers can contain irrelevant information in bits
4-7, the logical AND is used to mask (block out) those bits. The
figure on the next page shows the way in which the number
returned in variable S1 or S2 corresponds to the direction in
which the stick is pushed.

To read the trigger buttons, the following statements will return a 1 if a button is pressed, and a 0 if it is not:

```
T1=-((PEEK(56321) AND 16)=0)
T2=-((PEEK(56320) AND 16)=0)
```

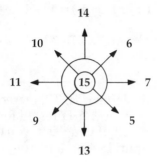

Of course, if you prefer a system where the variable will be 0 when the stick is not pressed, you can use the logical operator NOT to adjust the values accordingly.

```
S1=NOT PEEK(56321) AND 15
S2=NOT PEEK(56320) AND 15
```

This will produce the following pattern:

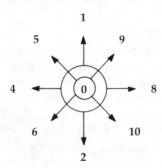

A Keyboard Bonus

The variations on these basic schemes are limited only by your applications. If you are using the joystick for an action game, for example, you may want to read the changes in horizontal position and vertical position separately. You can do this with the following formulas:

```
H1=((PEEK(56321) AND 4)=0)-((PEEK(56321)
    AND 8)=0)
H2=((PEEK(56320) AND 4)=0)-((PEEK(56320)
    AND 8)=0)
```

```
V1=((PEEK(56321) AND 1)=Ø)-((PEEK(56321)
   AND 2)=Ø)
V2=((PEEK(5632Ø) AND 1)=Ø)-((PEEK(5632Ø)
   AND 2)=Ø)
```

The value of H1 will be 1 if the stick is pressed to the right, -1 if the stick is pressed to the left, and 0 if centered. Likewise, the value of V1 will be -1 for an upward press, 1 for a downward press, and 0 if the stick is centered. If you wish, you can even read each switch separately. Program 1, short and not exciting, demonstrates the technique.

One interesting sidelight demonstrated with this program is the fact that some CIA registers that are used to read the joysticks are used also to read the keyboard. The four keys at the top left of the keyboard (Control, Left Arrow, 1, and 2) are read exactly the same as joystick switches 0-3. While you are running Program 1, try pressing these keys, and you will see what I mean.

Pressing the Control key has the same effect as moving the stick to the left, while the Left Arrow, 1, and 2 keys function like a joystick moved down, up, and to the right, respectively.

Sprite Movement
Program 2 sets up a sprite and moves it around based on the position of the joystick. The initialization routine, which I have put out of the way at the back of the program, starting with line 1000, sets up a flying saucer in double width, and then RETURNs to the movement loop at line 2. The ON-GOSUB routes the program to the proper line number without having to test each stick position, which would slow down the loop.

There are a couple of points to note. First, the registers that designate sprite horizontal and vertical positions are not write-only registers, as are the Atari horizontal position registers. This means that you can find out the current position of the sprite just by reading those registers, without having to set up separate RAM variables to keep track of them as must be done on the Atari. I set up variables X% and Y% in Program 2 only for purposes of readability.

To move a sprite one position to the right, we need only read the current horizontal position, add 1, and POKE that number back into the horizontal position register. Of course, you must keep in mind that you can't POKE in a value less than 0 or greater than 255. If you examine the move-down and move-up subroutines at lines 80 and 90, you will see that I have incorporated logical statements to move the sprite to the bottom of the screen if it hits the upper limit, and which will move it to the top if the value tries to get below 0. This wraparound feature guarantees that no errors will result from trying to POKE in an illegal quantity.

The Horizontal "Seam"

A more complicated situation arises when we deal with horizontal movement. Because there are 320 horizontal positions available, but only 256 combinations which can be accessed from the horizontal position register, we need to set the Most Significant Bit in the register located at 53264 whenever we wish to use a horizontal position between 256 and 320. Anytime the sprite moves into or out of this zone, therefore, special handling of this bit will be required.

Accordingly, the horizontal movement routines (lines 40-45 and 70-75) have to test to see if this "seam" is encountered before moving the sprite. If the horizontal position register reads 0, for example, we don't know whether the sprite is located at the left edge of the screen or at the "seam" (i.e., location 256) until we check the MSB register. This extra checking is time-consuming, and as a result the saucer moves noticeably faster up and down than it does right and left.

Because of the slowness of the motion in BASIC, I have multiplied all motion by the factor WUN, which is defined in line 1005, and which can be set from 1 to 3. When its value is 1, the motion is very smooth, but extremely slow. When it is 3, each push of the stick changes the position of the sprite by three places, speeding up the motion, but making it somewhat jerky.

Machine Language Motion

The best solution to the problem of achieving quick, smooth motion is the use of a machine language subroutine which will read a joystick and move the sprite accordingly. Program 3 uses just such a subroutine. Though I POKE it into memory starting at $C000 (49152 decimal), it is completely relocatable.

If it later proves that this large block of free RAM can be better used otherwise, you will be able to move the routine with no rewriting. You should be aware, however, that, as written, the routine checks only the joystick in Port 1, and moves only Sprite 0 in response to movement of that stick. Since some lines of Program

4 Creating Games

3 duplicate those of Program 2, you may want to edit the latter program rather than typing in Program 3 from scratch.

One difference that you will notice immediately is that this program asks you to select a speed (you should respond with a value from 1-5). The reason for this is that I wanted to demonstrate the degree to which even a machine language subroutine is slowed down by BASIC. At Speed 1, each time through the loop the program calls the subroutine once and returns to BASIC. Though this produces smooth motion, it is still somewhat slow. At Speed 2, the program calls the subroutine twice in a row before returning, and so on up to Speed 4, which produces rather quick motion. At Speed 5, the machine language subroutine goes into a continuous loop, without ever returning to BASIC. At this speed, if you push on the stick diagonally, it will appear as if there are dozens of saucers on the screen at once!

Though my examples may seem most applicable to game programs, do not overlook the joysticks as input devices for more mundane tasks. Because each stick has only four switches, it limits the number of choices available to the user. It therefore reduces the number of mistakes that can be made, as compared with a keyboard, which has over 60 keys, each key having both a shifted and nonshifted value.

Program 1. Joystick Demonstration

```
10 FOR I=1 TO 25:DOWN$=DOWN$+CHR$(17):NE
   XT:HOME$=CHR$(19):PRINTCHR$(147);CHR$
   (5)
15 PRINT" THIS PROGRAM READS STICK #1":P
   RINT" INSERT JOYSTICK, AND MOVE IT AR
   OUND!"
20 S=NOT PEEK(56321) AND 15
30 UP=S AND 1:IF UP THEN PRINT HOME$;LEF
   T$(DOWN$,10);TAB(15);"UP{3 SPACES}";:
   GOTO 50
40 DOWN=S AND 2:IF DOWN THEN PRINT HOME$
   ;LEFT$(DOWN$,10);TAB(15);"DOWN ";
50 LEFT=S AND 4:IF LEFT THEN PRINT HOME$
   ;LEFT$(DOWN$,10);TAB(25);"LEFT ";:GOT
   O70
60 RIGHT=S AND 8:IF RIGHT THEN PRINT HOM
   E$;LEFT$(DOWN$,10);TAB(25);"RIGHT";
70 IF S=0 THEN PRINT HOME$;LEFT$(DOWN$,1
   0);TAB(15);"{16 SPACES}"
80 GOTO 20
```

112

Program 2. Moving Sprites in BASIC

```
1 GOTO 1000
2 S=PEEK(S0)AND15:ONSGOSUB3,3,3,3,20,30,
  40,3,50,60,70,2,80,90,3:GOTO2
3 RETURN
20 GOSUB 40:GOSUB 80:RETURN
30 GOSUB 40:GOSUB 90:RETURN
40 X%=X%+WUN :IF X%>255 THEN X%=0:POKE S
  P+16,1
43 IF X%>65 AND PEEK(SP+16)=1 THEN POKE
  SP+16,0:X%=0
45 POKEHP,X%:RETURN
50 GOSUB 80:GOSUB 70:RETURN
60 GOSUB 90:GOSUB 70:RETURN
70 X%=X%-WUN:IF X%<1 AND PEEK(SP+16)=1 T
  HEN X%=255:POKE SP+16,0
73 IF X%< 1 AND PEEK(SP+16)=0 THEN X%=65
  :POKE SP+16,1
75 POKEHP,X%:RETURN
80 Y%=Y%+WUN+HI * (Y%>HI):POKEVP,Y%:RETU
  RN
90 Y%=Y%-WUN-HI * (Y%<WUN):POKEVP,Y%:RET
  URN
1000 FORI=871TO895:POKEI,0:NEXT:FOR I=83
     2TO870:READA:POKEI,A:NEXT:SP=53248
1005 HP=SP:VP=SP+1:X%=160:Y%=100:WUN=3:H
     I=252:S0=56321
1010 POKESP+21,1:POKE2040,13:POKESP+39,6
     :POKESP+29,1:POKEHP,X%:POKEVP,Y%
1020 POKESP+32,0:POKESP+33,0:PRINTCHR$(1
     47)
1030 FORI=1 TO 50:R=1024+INT(RND(0)*1000
     ):POKE R,46:POKE R+54272,1:NEXT
1040 DATA 0,56,0,0,124,0,0,254,0,0,170,0
     ,1,171,0,15,255,224,15,255,224,13,8
     5,96
1050 DATA 13,85,96,15,255,224,15,255,224
     ,0,254,0,0,124,0
1060 GOTO 2
```

Program 3. Moving Sprites in Machine Language

```
10 PRINTCHR$(147);CHR$(5): INPUT"SPEED "
   ;S:GOTO 1000
20 ON S GOTO 30,40,50,60,70
30 SYS(49409):GOTO 30
40 SYS(49406):GOTO 40
50 SYS(49403):GOTO 50
```

```
60 SYS(49400):GOTO 60
70 SYS(49413):GOTO 70
1000 FORI=871TO895:POKEI,0:NEXT:FOR I=83
     2TO870:READA:POKEI,A:NEXT:SP=53248
1010 POKESP+21,1:POKE2040,13:POKESP+39,6
     :POKESP+29,1:POKESP,160:POKESP+1,10
     0
1020 POKESP+32,0:POKESP+33,0:PRINT CHR$(
     147)
1030 FORI=1 TO 50:R=1024+INT(RND(0)*1000
     ):POKE R,46:POKE R+54272,1: NEXT
1040 DATA 0,56,0,0,124,0,0,254,0,0,170,0
     ,1,171,0,15,255,224,15,255,224,13,8
     5,96
1045 DATA 13,85,96,15,255,224,15,255,224
     ,0,254,0,0,124,0
1050 FOR I=1 TO 101:READ A:POKE 49151+I,
     A:NEXT
1055 FOR I=1 TO 19:READ A:POKE 49399+I,A
     :NEXT:GOTO 20
1060 DATA 173,1,220,74,176,3,206,1,208,7
     4,176,3,238,1,208,74,176,38,173
1070 DATA 0,208,208,15,173,16,208,41,1,2
     40,12,173,16,208,41,254,141,16
1080 DATA 208,206,0,208,96,173,16,208,9,
     1,162,63,141,16,208,142,0,208,96
1090 DATA 74,176,32,238,0,208,240,28,173
     ,16,208,41,1,240,20,169,64,205
1100 DATA 0,208,208,13,173,16,208,41,254
     ,162,0,141,16,208,142,0,208,96
1110 DATA 173,16,208,9,1,141,16,208,96
1200 DATA 32,0,192,32,0,192,32,0,192,32,
     0,192,96,32,0,192,76,5,193
```

Alfabug

Michael Wasilenko

Preschoolers will love this simple game. The child is required to press the correct letter in order to start the race.

"Alfabug" is for relatively young people, three to six years old. To a child learning the alphabet, the accomplishment of pressing the correct key to initiate a bug race is quite exhilarating.

The object of the game is to press the same letter of the alphabet on the keyboard that the computer displays on the screen. When the correct letter is pressed, a bug race starts: five bugs of different colors race across the screen. If the wrong letter is pressed, the computer responds with an unpleasant sound and then waits for the correct letter. The order in which the bugs finish is marked at the end of each lane, so the player(s) can also compete for points by guessing the winner. Upon completion of each race, the player is asked if another race is desired. At this point, a Y or N for *yes* or *no* is expected. Again, an unpleasant sound is heard when an invalid answer is given.

In the following program, the computer will select the letters alphabetically beginning with A (of course) and will reset to A after Z is reached. By simply deleting the remark statement (REM) from line 76, the program will select the letters randomly. You could also modify the program so it asks the player for the method of letter selection. But I have found that the fewer the prompts, the easier it is for the child. Remember, this is for young children who are just learning their alphabet or who are just learning to read. For instance, with the selection method fixed in the code, my five-year-old daughter can load and run the program without any assistance.

This simple program can provide hours of fun for young children while helping them practice the alphabet. But watch out! You may not get to use your computer again, unless they're all asleep.

Alfabug

```
0  PRINT"{CLR}INITIALIZING"
1  POKE52,48:POKE56,48:CLR:POKE56334,PEEK
   (56334)AND254:POKE1,PEEK(1)AND251
5  FORN=0TO1279:POKEN+12288,PEEK(N+53248)
   :NEXTN:POKE1,PEEK(1)OR4
6  POKE56334,PEEK(56334)OR1
10 PRINT"{BLK}{CLR}":POKE53281,1
20 DIMY(5),K(5),O(5),CO(5):AB=64
25 CO(0)=0:CO(1)=3:CO(2)=4:CO(3)=5:CO(4)
   =7
30 Z=05:A=45:CR=42:IN=-1:WX=54272
34 SS=12288+(41*8):FORI=0TO15:READQ:POKE
   SS+I,Q:NEXTI
36 DATA 36,72,123,254,254,123,72,36,144,
   72,123,254,254,123,72,144
40 FORN=0TO4:READY(N):NEXTN
50 DATA 1306,1386,1466,1546,1626
55 FORW=0TO4:K(W)=Y(W):NEXTW
57 PRINT"{WHT}{CLR}":FORP=0TO4:O(P)=48:N
   EXTP:X=1264:F=48
60 FORL=0TO5:FORI=0TO39:POKEX+I,A:POKEX+
   I+WX,0:{2 SPACES}NEXTI
70 POKEX+I-1,115:X=X+80:NEXTL
74 FORG=0TO4:POKEY(G)-1+WX,0:POKEY(G)+WX
   ,CR:NEXTG
75 FORG=0TO4:POKEY(G)-1,49+G:POKEY(G),CR
   :NEXTG
76 REM{3 SPACES}AB=INT(RND(1)*26)+64
77 AB=AB+1:IFAB>90THENAB=65
78 PRINT"{HOME}{BLK}{DOWN}PRESS ";CHR$(1
   8)CHR$(AB)CHR$(146);" TO START"
79 GETA$:IFA$=""THEN79
80 IFASC(A$)<>ABTHENGOSUB174:GOTO78
81 POKE53272,(PEEK(53272)AND240)+12: M=3
   5:FORC=0TO4:IFK(C)=Y(C)+35THEN105
85 POKEK(C),32
90 E=INT(RND(0)+.5)+1.5:K(C)=K(C)+E:IFK(
   C)=>Y(C)+M-1.5THENK(C)=Y(C)+M:F=F+1
100 POKEK(C),CR:POKEK(C)+WX,CO(C):FOR J=
    0TOZ:NEXTJ:IFK(C)=Y(C)+MTHEN105
102 GOTO110
105 IFO(C)<>1THENPOKEK(C)+1,F:POKEK(C)+1
    +WX,0:POKEK(C),42:O(C)=1:GOSUB200
110 NEXTC
115 CR=CR+IN:IN=IN*-1:IFF<53THEN81
118 POKE53272,21
```

```
120 PRINT"{HOME}{BLK}{19 DOWN}AGAIN? 'Y'
    OR 'N'"
130 GETY$:IFY$=""THEN130
140 IFY$="Y"THENCR=42:IN=-1:GOTO55
145 IFY$<>"N"THENGOSUB174:GOTO120
150 END
174 SO=54272:FORGH=SOTOSO+24:POKEGH,0:NE
    XT:POKESO+24,15:POKESO+1,34:POKESO,7
    5
175 POKESO+5,72:POKESO+6,72
176 POKESO+4,129:FORT=1TO500:NEXT
177 FORGH=10TO0STEP-1:POKESO+24,GH:NEXT
178 RETURN
200 SO=54272:FORGH=SOTOSO+24:POKEGH,0:NE
    XT:POKESO+24,15:POKESO+1,34:POKESO,7
    5
205 POKESO+5,72:POKESO+6,72
210 POKESO+4,17:FORT=1TO500:NEXT
215 FORGH=10TO0STEP-1:POKESO+24,GH:NEXT
220 RETURN
```

Chapter 5

Peripherals

The Confusing Catalog

Jim Butterfield

Have you ever wanted to have a program gain control of the disk catalog? There are a number of ways to use directory information, but getting hold of it is not as simple as it might seem at first glance.

On Commodore machines with 4.0 BASIC, you just type CATA-LOG or DIRECTORY to see a list of the programs on a disk. On other Commodore machines, you must LOAD "$",8 and then LIST. Either way, you get a directory with your disk header, information on the programs, and the number of blocks free. Very handy indeed.

Here's the problem: you would like your program to be able to read a directory. It seems simple: just OPEN it as a file and bring in the items. Unfortunately, it doesn't work that way.

Two Types
When you command LOAD "$",8 you are bringing in a directory with a LOAD command; it arrives in a certain format. If you OPEN 1,8,2,"$" within your program, you'll get an entirely different format. Why?

When you say LOAD, the disk manufactures a directory that imitates a BASIC program. After all, the next thing you'll say is LIST, and the only thing that can be listed is BASIC. If you say OPEN, however, the disk will give you its directory, in binary, just as it is stored on the disk surface. That seems to be a little better — until you realize that BASIC has a devil of a time understanding binary.

You can do an OPEN and get the imitation program. The trick is to use secondary address 0 — usually reserved for LOADing.

Another Problem
Either way, you get binary. You'll need to translate it and interpret it; and you'll need to cope with that annoying BASIC glitch, in-

putting a CHR$(0). Whenever BASIC GETs a CHR$(0), it changes it to a null string (" "), and you'll need to detect this and change it back.

The coding for this is fairly easy. After we get a character with GET A$, we may take its binary value with A =ASC(A$) — except that the null string won't work right. So,.we say, A =ASC(A$ + CHR$(0)) and everything works out.

Imitation BASIC

This is the easiest and most standard way of obtaining directory information; it works the same way with all Commodore disk drives. To understand it, we must see how a BASIC line is constructed:

First two bytes: forward chain or zero (dummy on directory)
Next two bytes: binary number
Then: text of line
Ending with: binary zero

Program 1 prints the directory. Big deal: you could do that anyway. But since it's a program, you can change it to do whatever functions you need. For example, you could dig into the text part in more detail, extracting the program name and type; that way, your program would know if a given data file were on the disk.

It's handy to be able to check how many blocks are free on the disk. Our program already does this: the last number that line 230 calculates will be the blocks-free value. You can abbreviate this procedure by making the program skip all the file names. Change the OPEN statement to read:

```
100 OPEN 1,8,0,"$0:S%Q"
```

Now, the program will catalog only those programs whose name happens to be exactly S%Q. Chances are you won't have many of these. Your directory is now shortened down to the header line and the BLOCKS FREE line. Let's telescope our program into a simple block-free checker. Try Program 2.

We've only scratched the surface. Try your hand at programming some directory search function of your choice.

Bit-image Directories

You can get more information from a bit-image directory than from a BASIC-imitator. For example, you can read the length parameter of relative files, see deleted files, and view file track and sector values.

But this comes with considerable difficulty. You might get any one of several different formats, depending on the disk. We won't do the whole job here: you can chase after some of the details for yourself. Look at Program 3.

Yes, you can go in there and drag out the BAM. Yes, you can dig useful data out of the stuff we skipped in lines 360-380. Check your disk manual for details.

It's not easy either way. The "imitation BASIC" is the shortest and works on all disks: use it when you can. But if you need the extra power of the bitmap, don't hesitate to go for it.

Program 1. Print Directory

```
95 REM GET THE DIRECTORY FOR DRIVE Ø
100 OPEN 1,8,0,"$Ø"
105 REM NULL STRING REPLACEMENT
110 N$=CHR$(Ø)
185 REM SKIP THE "LOAD ADDRESS" AT FILE S
    TART
190 GET#1,A$,A$
195 REM SKIP THE FORWARD CHAIN
200 GET#1,A$,A$
205 REM EXCEPT ZERO CHAIN MEANS END
210 IF A$=""GOTO 400
215 REM GET THE BINARY NUMBER
220 GET#1,A$,B$
225 REM PRINT "NUMBER OF BLOCKS"
230 PRINT ASC(A$+N$)+ASC(B$+N$)*256;
295 REM LET'S GET TEXT
300 GET#1,A$
305 REM END OF THIS LINE:GO BACK
310 IF A$="" THEN PRINT:GOTO 200
315 REM PRINT ONE CHARACTER
320 PRINT A$;
325 REM GET SOME MORE
330 GOTO 300
400 CLOSE1
```

Program 2. Block-free Checker

```
95 REM ANOTHER UNLIKELY NAME
100 OPEN 1,8,0,"$Ø:E7!N"
110 N$=CHR$(Ø)
195 REM THROW AWAY LOAD ADDRESS, LINK, N
    UMBER
200 GET#1,A$,A$,A$,A$,A$,A$
205 REM THROW AWAY THE HEADER LINE
```

```
210 GET#1,A$:IF A$<>""GOTO 210
215 REM THROW AWAY THE LINK,GET THE NUMB
    ER
220 GET#1,A$,A$,A$,B$
225 REM HERE'S OUR BLOCK-FREE COUNT
230 F=ASC(A$+N$)+ASC(B$+N$)*256
400 CLOSE1
410 PRINT F
```

Program 3. Bit-image Directory

```
95 REM WE MUST INITIALIZE FOR THIS ONE
100 OPEN 1,8,15,"I0":CLOSE1
105 REM HERE COMES THE BIT DIRECTORY
110 OPEN 1,8,2,"$0"
120 N$=CHR$(0)
125 REM DISK WILL IDENTIFY ITSELF
130 GET#1,A$
135 REM HERE'S THE IDENTITY
140 A=ASC(A$+N$)
145 REM JUST TO PROVE WE IDENTIFIED IT
146 REM 8250'S WILL GIVE TROUBLE HERE
150 IF A=67 THEN PRINT "8050"
160 IF A=65 THEN PRINT "1540/1541/4040"
170 IF A=1 THEN PRINT "2040"
195 REM SKIP THE(BIT) BAM
200 FOR J=1 TO 253
210 GET #1,A$
220 NEXT J
225 REM THE 8050 HAS A BIG BAM TO SKIP
230 IF A<>67 GOTO 300
240 FOR J=1 TO 254*2
250 GET#1,A$
260 NEXT J
295 REM EIGHT FILES PER BLOCK
300 FOR J=1 TO 8
305 REM FILE TYPE,TRACK,SECTOR
310 GET#1,F$,T$,S$
320 F=ASC(F$+N$)
325 REM GET 16-CHARACTER NAME
330 P$="":FOR K= 1 TO 16
340 GET#1,X$:P$=P$+X$
350 NEXT K
355 REM THERE'S USEFUL STUFF HERE, BUT WE
    'LL SKIP IT
360 FOR K= 1 TO 9
370 GET#1,X$
380 NEXT K
385 REM FILE LENGTH
```

```
390 GET#1,L1$,L2$
395 REM WEIRD; 254 BYTLES/8 LEAVES US TWO
    BYTES SHORT
400 IF J<8 THEN GET#1,X$,X$
405 REM TO ALLOW US TO TEST END-OF-DIRECT
    ORY
410 SW=ST
415 REM NOT A REAL FILE
420 IF F<129 OR F>132 GOTO 480
425 REM NAME AND LENGTH
430 PRINT P$;ASC(L1$+N$)+ASC(L2$+N$)*256
480 NEXT J
500 IF SW=0 GOTO 300
900 CLOSE1
```

Automatic Program Selector

Steven A. Smith

Here are several ways to make disks easier to use. A disk menu program that will run your programs automatically is included.

If you want to be able to choose from among a number of options within a program, one of the best methods available is a menu. The computer displays a list of items with numbers or letters assigned to each, and you press the number or letter corresponding to the option you want. This way, you don't have to worry about which responses are allowed or about how to spell a particular response, and it's much faster.

All this applies to disk drives, as well. Also, someone who is not familiar with the operating system of the computer can call up any of a number of programs without having to know about diskette directories or about LOADing or RUNning programs.

You can choose between two ways of automating program selection from a disk. The first one we'll describe uses specific, predefined menus for each diskette or function. The second can be used with any diskettes, determining at runtime which programs are available on the disk.

Predefined Menus

A predefined menu is written right into the BASIC menu program. Because of this, a new program must be written for each diskette for which you want a menu. However, there are several advantages to using a predefined menu. First, it's fast. As soon as you RUN it, the menu program knows what programs should be on the diskette and can go about the business of displaying the menu. Also, you can add program descriptions to the menu screens to show more information about the programs than just their names.

Another, less obvious advantage to predefined menus is that you can set up a menu for just a few of the programs on a diskette, have another menu for some others, and have other programs that are not accessed by any menus. This way, you can let someone have access to only the programs that a particular application requires.

Program 1 is a sample of a predefined menu for an inventory file maintenance system. Although it is short, it is surprising how impressive it can be in operation, especially to someone who is used to having to load and run individual programs via the traditional directory method.

Lines 120-130 set up an array of program names, one per array element.

Lines 140-230 display the actual menu. The numbers 1 through 8 are displayed in reverse, with a description of the associated programs next to them. The number of items on the menu is not significant — eight just happened to fit well on this menu.

In this menu, the programs are grouped by type of operation to make things clearer for the user. Inventory file operations, transaction file operations, and setup operations are each grouped together and separated from the others by a line. Of course, you can display and group items on your menus any way you wish, remembering to have your item numbers and array elements correspond properly.

Lines 240-260 accept your menu item choice, making sure it is between one and the maximum item number on the menu. On this menu, choice number 8 simply ends the program.

Lines 270-300 are the heart of the menu program. Using the dynamic keyboard technique (where the computer *enters its own instructions*), the computer types the LOAD and RUN instructions on the screen, and then forces RETURNs into the keyboard buffer to make it execute them. To accomplish this dynamic effect, you need to POKE a value of 13 into the first two keyboard buffer bytes, and a value of two into the byte which contains the number of characters in keyboard buffer (line 300).

This sample menu program will expect to find a "Library Inventory System" diskette in drive 0 containing programs with the filenames stored in the array C$ (lines 120-130). To use Program 1 with your own disks, substitute the names of your own programs in lines 120-130 and short descriptions in lines 140-230. You may need to change the DIM statement in line 110 and the entry number checking in lines 250-260 if you have more or fewer than eight menu items.

Increasing Menu Items

Nine items can be placed on this menu before the screen begins to look crowded. There are two ways to improve on this number: the first is simply to use several menus and let each menu chain (call in) the next. You can let one menu item be the next menu program, or add a line:

```
245 IF A$=CHR$(13) THEN C$(0)="MENU2":A$=
    "1":GOTO 270
```

This line will call the next menu program (here named MENU2) if RETURN, rather than one of the options shown, is pressed.

While this works quite well, you do have to wait for the new menu to be loaded each time you chain from one to the next. A faster way is shown in Program 2. Several menus can be stored in the same program. By pressing RETURN, you can go from one menu to the next without waiting to load a new menu program. A message is added to the bottom of the screen indicating that you can press RETURN to go on to the next menu. After the last menu is shown, pressing RETURN again will bring you back to the first menu. Of course, going to the next menu could itself be made a menu option, instead of being automatic.

To make menus especially useful to people unfamiliar with computers, you can make the programs called by the menu call the menu back when they finish. To do this, find where your program ends, whether by an END statement or by reaching the last of the line numbers. Change your END statements to GOTO 62000 and add the following lines:

```
62000 PRINT "{CLR}{4 DOWN}"
62010 PRINT"LOAD"CHR$(34)"0:MENU"CHR$(34
      )",8{4 DOWN}"
62020 PRINT"RUN":PRINT"{9 UP}"
62030 POKE 631,13:POKE 632,13:POKE 198,2
      :END
```

This assumes that your menu program is named "MENU".

Once you load the menu program, you don't need to worry about loading any more programs. Each time you finish one program, the machine will take you back to your menu. This is why menus are especially helpful for inexperienced operators. A menu also works well at parties — you set it up with games which call back the menu, and you don't have to worry about being around to show people how to LOAD and RUN their choices.

Fully Automatic Menus

Program 3 is a different method of generating menus, a fully automatic diskette menu. When you run this program, you can put any disk in the drive and it will find out what programs are on the disk and build a menu around them. Although you can't add descriptions to the program names, with disk files you do have 16-character names to work with, and you can make them quite descriptive.

This method is slower than using predefined menus because, before the program can generate the menus, it must read the diskette directory and fill its own array of program names. However, you don't have to write a new menu program for each diskette or change a menu program when you change the contents of a diskette.

The following is a description of the variables used in Program 3:

AE$: Filename Array
AN : Array Entry Number
A0 : Files From Drive 0
C$: Character Read In
DE : Directory Entry
DR$: Drive Number
ER : Disk Error Number
F$: Filename Found
FL : Filename Length
I : Iteration Variable
J : Iteration Maximum
MM : Maximum #On Menu
MN : Menu Number

Lines 190-210 set up the variables and the program name array used by the program. Line 220 initializes the diskette in the drive currently being checked. This sets things up for line 230, which checks to see if a diskette was found in the drive. If not, the program prints an error message.

Lines 240-250 are in the program mostly to let you know something is happening. While the program is reading the disk directory, it lets you know how many programs it has found on that drive.

In lines 260-390, the diskette directory is opened and read as a sequential file. After skipping over the directory header, each directory block of eight file entries is checked for programs until the last entry is reached.

Line 310 skips entries which have their first byte equal to anything other than 130. That would indicate that the file was not a program file. You could use this line to create menus which displayed only USR or SEQ files if you wished. Line 330 puts the program name into string F$. Line 340 keeps the DOS support program from showing up on the menus. Line 340 also shows how a program can be excluded from the menu if you don't want it displayed. Line 350 updates your screen to tell you how many program entries have been found, and line 360 puts this program name and drive number into the array of filenames found. Lines 370-380 then read past the proper number of bytes to be ready to read in the next file entry.

Line 410 finishes up the work. If no programs were found, the program ends with line 430. Otherwise, the first menu is ready to be displayed.

Entering Your Choices

Line 440 prints the menu heading. The heading will include a menu number starting with 1 and going as high as necessary to show all of the program names found, in groups of nine. Line 450 checks to see if there are enough program names left in the array to display nine menu items. If not, the menu is shortened. Line 460 displays the menu item itself, and lines 470-480 display the message at the bottom of the screen.

Lines 490-530 check for your choice of menu item. It must be between 1 and the maximum number on the menu, or it can be RETURN, in which case the program will display the next menu. If there are no more items in the program name array, the first menu is redisplayed.

If the key you pressed was one of the menu items shown, the program continues to line 540. Variable AE$ is now the drive number, a colon, and the 16-character name of the program you have chosen. Any blanks in the name are stored in the directory as *shifted* spaces, with an ASCII value of 160.

Lines 560-580 check to see how long the program name is by looking backwards from the end for the first character that is not a shifted space. When one is found, variable FL contains the length of the name plus the drive number. Then, the LOAD and RUN instructions are displayed, and the keyboard buffer is POKEd with RETURNs to load the chosen program, just as in the predefined menu programs.

Program 1. Predefined Disk Menu

```
100 REM ** LIBRARY INVENTORY SYSTEM DRIVE
    R MENU **
110 DIMC$(6):PRINT CHR$(14)
120 C$(0)="SLIB":C$(1)="SLIBPRINT":C$(2)=
    "SLIBINQ":C$(3)="STRANPRINT"
130 C$(4)="STRANPURGE":C$(5)="SLIBSETUP":
    C$(6)="FORMAT"
140 PRINT"{CLR}{2 DOWN}{10 SPACES}{RVS} P
    ROGRAM CHOICE MENU {OFF}{2 DOWN}"
150 PRINT"{7 SPACES}{RVS}1{OFF} INVENTORY
     FILE MAINTENANCE{DOWN}"
160 PRINT"{7 SPACES}{RVS}2{OFF} INVENTORY
     FILE LISTING{DOWN}"
170 PRINT"{7 SPACES}{RVS}3{OFF} INVENTORY
     FILE INQUIRY{2 DOWN}"
180 PRINT"{7 SPACES}{RVS}4{OFF} TRANSACTI
    ON FILE LISTING{DOWN}"
190 PRINT"{7 SPACES}{RVS}5{OFF} TRANSACTI
    ON FILE PURGE{2 DOWN}"
200 PRINT"{7 SPACES}{RVS}6{OFF} FIRST-TIM
    E FILE SETUP{DOWN}"
210 PRINT"{7 SPACES}{RVS}7{OFF} FORMAT A
    DISKETTE{2 DOWN}"
220 PRINT"{7 SPACES}{RVS}8{OFF} END OF LI
    BRARY WORK{DOWN}"
230 PRINT"{8 SPACES}{RVS} CHOOSE ONE OF T
    HE ABOVE {OFF}";
240 GETA$:IFA$=""THEN240
250 IFA$<"1"ORA$>"8"THEN240
260 IFA$="8"THENEND
270 PRINT"{CLR}{6 DOWN}"
280 PRINT"LOAD"CHR$(34)"0:"C$(VAL(A$)-1)C
    HR$(34)",8"
290 PRINT"{4 DOWN}RUN":PRINT"{9 UP}"
300 POKE631,13:POKE632,13:POKE198,2:END
```

Program 2. Multiple Predefined Menus

```
100 REM ** INVENTORY SYSTEM DISK MENU #1
    **
110 DIMC$(9):PRINT CHR$(14)
120 C$(1)="SLIB":C$(2)="SLIBPRINT":C$(3)=
    "SLIBINQ":C$(4)="STRANPRINT"
```

```
130 C$(5)="STRANPURGE":C$(6)="SLIBSETUP":
    C$(7)="FORMAT":C$(8)="DIRECT"
140 PRINT"{CLR}{DOWN}{7 SPACES}{RVS} LIBR
    ARY INVENTORY MENU 1 {OFF}{2 DOWN}"
150 PRINT"{7 SPACES}{RVS}1{OFF} LIBRARY F
    ILE MAINTENANCE{DOWN}"
160 PRINT"{7 SPACES}{RVS}2{OFF} LIBRARY F
    ILE LISTING{DOWN}"
170 PRINT"{7 SPACES}{RVS}3{OFF} LIBRARY F
    ILE INQUIRY{2 DOWN}"
180 PRINT"{7 SPACES}{RVS}4{OFF} TRANSACTI
    ON FILE LISTING{DOWN}"
190 PRINT"{7 SPACES}{RVS}5{OFF} TRANSACTI
    ON FILE PURGE{2 DOWN}"
200 PRINT"{7 SPACES}{RVS}6{OFF} SETUP INV
    ENTORY FILES{DOWN}"
210 PRINT"{7 SPACES}{RVS}7{OFF} FORMAT A
    DISKETTE{DOWN}"
220 PRINT"{7 SPACES}{RVS}8{OFF} PRINT A D
    ISKETTE DIRECTORY{2 DOWN}"
230 PRINT"{5 SPACES}{RVS}{4 SPACES}CHOOSE
    ONE OF THE ABOVE{4 SPACES}{OFF}"
240 PRINT"{5 SPACES}{RVS} OR PRESS RETURN
    FOR NEXT MENU {OFF}";
250 GETA$:IFA$=""THEN250
260 IFA$=CHR$(13)THEN290
270 IFA$<"1"ORA$>"8"THEN250
280 GOTO450
290 C$(1)="SLIBPRT1":C$(2)="SLIBPRT2":C$(
    3)="SLIBPRT3":C$(4)="SLIBPRT4"
300 C$(5)="SLIBPRT5":C$(6)="SLIBPRT6":C$(
    7)="SLIBPRT7":C$(8)="SLIBPRT8"
310 PRINT"{CLR}{DOWN}{7 SPACES}{RVS} LIBR
    ARY INVENTORY MENU 2 {OFF}{2 DOWN}"
320 PRINT"{7 SPACES}{RVS}1{OFF} PRINT SAL
    ES REPORT{DOWN}"
330 PRINT"{7 SPACES}{RVS}2{OFF} PRINT BAC
    KORDER REPORT{DOWN}"
340 PRINT"{7 SPACES}{RVS}3{OFF} PRINT DEL
    INQUENT ACCOUNTS{DOWN}"
350 PRINT"{7 SPACES}{RVS}4{OFF} PRINT HIS
    TORICAL REPORT{DOWN}"
360 PRINT"{7 SPACES}{RVS}5{OFF} PRINT HIS
    TORICAL SUMMARY{DOWN}"
370 PRINT"{7 SPACES}{RVS}6{OFF} PRINT SAL
    ES TAX REPORT{DOWN}"
380 PRINT"{7 SPACES}{RVS}7{OFF} PRINT MON
    THLY REPORTS{DOWN}"
```

```
390 PRINT"{7 SPACES}{RVS}8{OFF} PRINT YEA
    RLY REPORTS{DOWN}"
400 PRINT"{5 SPACES}{RVS}{4 SPACES}CHOOSE
    ONE OF THE ABOVE{4 SPACES}{OFF}"
410 PRINT"{5 SPACES}{RVS} OR PRESS RETURN
    FOR NEXT MENU {OFF}";
420 GETA$:IFA$=""THEN420
430 IFA$=CHR$(13)THEN120
440 IFA$<"1"ORA$>"9"THEN420
450 PRINT"{CLR}{6 DOWN}"
460 PRINT"LOAD"CHR$(34)"0:"C$(VAL(A$))CHR
    $(34)",8"
470 PRINT"{4 DOWN}RUN":PRINT"{9 UP}"
480 POKE631,13:POKE632,13:POKE198,2:END
```

Program 3. Automatic Disk Menus

```
100 REM * AUTOMATIC DISKETTE MENU *
190 AE$="":AN=0:A0=0:C$="":DE=0:DR$="0"
200 ER=0:F$="":FL=0:I=0:J=0:MM=0:MN=0
210 DIM AE$(150)
220 OPEN15,8,15:PRINT#15,"I"+DR$
230 INPUT#15,ER:IFER=21THEN400
240 PRINT"{CLR}{DOWN}READING DIRECTORY OF
    DRIVE ";DR$
250 PRINT"{DOWN}PROGRAMS FOUND: 0"
260 OPEN8,8,8,"$"+DR$+",SEQ"
270 FORI=1TO254:GET#8,C$:NEXT
280 FORDE=1TO8:F$="":GET#8,C$
290 IFC$=CHR$(199)THEN410
300 IFC$=""THENJ=29:GOTO370
310 IFASC(C$)<>130THENJ=29:GOTO370
320 AN=AN+1:J=11:GET#8,C$:GET#8,C$
330 FORI=1TO16:GET#8,C$:F$=F$+C$:NEXT
340 IFLEFT$(F$,3)="DOS"THEN AN=AN-1:GOTO3
    70
350 PRINT"{UP}"TAB(15)AN-A0
360 AE$(AN)=DR$+":"+F$
370 FORI=1TOJ:GET#8,C$:NEXT
380 IFDE<>8THENGET#8,C$:GET#8,C$
390 NEXT:GOTO280
400 PRINT"{DOWN}NO DISKETTE FOUND IN DRIV
    E "DR$"{DOWN}"
410 CLOSE8:CLOSE15
430 IFAN=0THENPRINT"{2 DOWN}{RVS} NO PROG
    RAMS FOUND {OFF}{2 DOWN}":END
440 MM=9:PRINT"{CLR}{DOWN}"TAB(12)"{RVS}P
    ROGRAM MENU #"STR$(MN+1)"{OFF}{DOWN}"
450 FORI=1TO9:IFAE$(MN*9+I)=""THENMM=I-1:
    I=9:GOTO470
```

```
460 PRINTTAB(12)"{RVS}"RIGHT$(STR$(I),1)"
    {OFF} "MID$(AE$(MN*9+I),3,16)"{DOWN}"
470 NEXT:PRINT"{4 SPACES}{RVS}{4 SPACES}C
    HOOSE ONE OF THE ABOVE OR{3 SPACES}
    {OFF}"
480 PRINT"{4 SPACES}{RVS} PRESS RETURN TO
     GO TO NEXT MENU {OFF}"
490 GETC$:IFC$=""THEN490
500 IFC$<>CHR$(13)THEN530
510 MN=MN+1:IFMN*9+1>ANTHENMN=0
520 GOTO440
530 IFVAL(C$)<1 OR VAL(C$)>MM THEN490
540 AE$=AE$(MN*9+VAL(C$))
550 PRINT:PRINT"{CLR}{4 DOWN}MENU ITEM CH
    OSEN: #"C$" - "MID$(AE$,3,16)
560 FORI=18TO1STEP-1:FL=I
570 IFASC(MID$(AE$,I,1))<>160THENI=1
580 NEXT:PRINT"{4 DOWN}LOAD"CHR$(34)LEFT$
    (AE$,FL)CHR$(34)",8{4 DOWN}"
590 PRINT"RUN":PRINT"{9 UP}"
600 POKE631,13:POKE632,13:POKE198,2:END
```

64 DOSmaker

Charley Kozarski

Changing disks to load DOS 5.1 can at times be inconvenient. You can use these short programs to save time — by putting the Wedge on your own disks.

If you've bought a 1541 disk drive for your Commodore 64, you've probably noticed that the Test/Demo disk which comes with it contains several useful programs. In particular, there is a program called "DOS 5.1" which simplifies many disk-handling operations for you. For example, you can just use the symbol for division (/) followed by the name of a file, and the file will be LOADed in for you.

Despite the misleading name, DOS 5.1 is *not* a Disk Operating System (DOS) for the 1541. Like all Commodore disk drives, the 1541 is "intelligent," which means that its DOS is contained in ROM inside the drive itself. DOS 5.1 is actually a *DOS support program* which makes the built-in DOS easier to use.

All of the helpful functions of the DOS support program, however, are available only on that disk. If, for some reason, you need to turn off power, you've got to reload DOS 5.1 from the demo disk. Wouldn't it be nice to be able to put this useful program on any of your disks?

Program 1 must be saved onto each disk on which you want to put DOS 5.1. It is the "wedge," which ties DOS 5.1 into BASIC. Type Program 1 in and SAVE it on a disk. Then type NEW and type in Program 2 which is the DOS 5.1 Creator. SAVE Program 2 to the same disk. It is necessary to SAVE Program 2 to only one of your disks because after it creates DOS 5.1, it serves no further purpose. You'll only need Program 1 and DOS 5.1 on each disk.

Now replace your disk with the Test/Demo disk. (Program 2 will get DOS 5.1 from the demo disk.) RUN Program 2 and, after a few seconds, it will ask if you have replaced the demo disk with your own. Make that replacement and you're halfway through creating a new DOS 5.1. When your disk is in the drive, type Y for *yes* and hit RETURN. The Creator program will now SAVE DOS 5.1 onto your disk and then erase itself from memory. If you forgot to remove the demo disk, there will be no problem because the tab on the disk prevents anything from being SAVEd onto it. Program 2, however, will have erased itself and you'll need to start over.

After you've got a copy of DOS 5.1 on one of your disks, you're all set to use it anytime you use that disk. Simply load in the Wedge (Program 1) from that disk and RUN it.

Program 1. DOS Wedge

```
10 REM DOS WEDGE FOR C-64
20 PRINT "{CLR}"
30 IF IM=YOU THEN YOUR=1:LOAD"DOS 5.1",8
   ,1
40 IF YOUR=1 THEN SYS 52224
50 NEW
```

Program 2. DOS Creator

```
10 REM DOS WITHOUT LOADING DEMO DISK
20 IF IM=YOU THEN YOUR=1:LOAD"DOS 5.1",8
   ,1
30 IF YOUR=1 THEN SYS 52224
40 INPUT "{CLR}DEMO DISK REPLACED YET? (
   Y OR N )";I$:IF I$<>"Y" THEN 40
50 POKE 43,255:POKE 44,203:POKE 45,90:PO
   KE 46,207
60 SAVE"DOS 5.1",8,1
70 POKE 43,1:POKE 44,8:POKE 46,8:NEW
```

Backup 1540/1541 Disks

Harvey B. Herman

LOAD, switch disks, SAVE, LOAD, switch, SAVE — it can be cumbersome and tedious to make backups of disks when you don't have a dual disk drive. What's worse, you need to go through special extra steps to transfer machine language programs. This utility makes creating safe backups on single disk drives nearly automatic.

I recently purchased a 1541 disk drive. The diskette that came with it included a few sample programs. Conspicuous by its absence, however, was a program to make duplicate copies of diskettes for *backup* purposes. I have learned the hard way that diskettes do not last forever, and it is foolish to have only one copy of important programs.

What to do? Well, I was lucky to have acquired an excellent backup program for the Commodore 2031 single disk drive (written by Jim Law and Keith Hope and distributed by the Toronto PET Users Group). I adapted this program to work on the Commodore 64. The modifications in the original program were quite modest — a few PEEKs and POKEs were changed, and the machine language portion was relocated to the cassette buffer and POKEd in from DATA statements.

Using the Program

The program is quite easy to use; no knowledge of machine language is necessary. First, the destination diskette is formatted, a good idea if you will be using it later on the same drive. Please be careful to format only blank diskettes, or ones that are no longer needed. Next, the diskettes are swapped and the source diskette is read to determine how much to copy. Successive blocks are then read from the source into the available computer memory. (I can read 124 blocks on the Commodore 64.) The diskettes are swapped again, and identical blocks on the destination disk are written from data saved in memory. The swapping of source and destination diskette continues until the entire diskette has been copied.

Of course, it would be easier (but not much faster) if a second drive were available. However, this program is the next best thing. It surely beats loading and saving BASIC programs, one at a time, or finding the loading address of machine language files. Try *that* sometime if you doubt it.

Disk Backup

```
1 FORI=828TO883:READA:POKEI,A:NEXTI
10 REM"D=DSAVE"@BACK2",DØ:?DS$:CATALOGDØ
20 BB=PEEK(44)+27:POKE995,BB
30 POKE998,PEEK(55):POKE999,PEEK(56):POKE
   55,Ø:POKE56,BB:CLR
40 BB=PEEK(995)
50 N=PEEK(999)-BB-1:BA=BB*256:MA=828
60 DIMBM%(35,24)
70 FORJ=ØTO7:TA(J)=2↑J:NEXT
80 PRINT"{CLR}{3 RIGHT}{RVS}BACKUP 1541
   {OFF}"
90 PRINT"{DOWN}'GOTO10ØØØ' IF PROGRAM QUI
   TS ABNORMALLY"
100 PRINT"{DOWN}"N"BUFFERS AVAILABLE"
110 OPEN1,8,15
200 REM *** MAIN FUNCTIONS ****
210 GOSUB1000
220 D$="S":GOSUB3200:I2$=IR$
230 IFDR$<>"2A"THENPRINT"{RVS}ILLEGAL DOS
    1.Ø DISK{OFF}":GOTO10ØØØ
240 IFI2$=I1$THENPRINT"{RVS}SOURCE AND DE
    STINATION HAVE SAME ID CODE{OFF}":GOT
    O10ØØØ
250 GOSUB2500
260 T=TS:S=Ø:NU=1:T1=T:S1=S
270 PRINT#1,"IØ":OPEN3,8,3,"#"
280 PRINT"READING BLOCK #";
290 IFBM%(T1,S1)=ØTHENGOSUB2000:NU=NU+1:I
    FNU>NTHEN320
300 S1=S1+1:IFS1>20THENS1=Ø:T1=T1+1
310 IFT1<TF+1THEN290
320 PRINT"{DOWN}"
330 CLOSE3
340 D$="D":GOSUB3200:IFIR$<>I1$THENGOTO34
    Ø
350 PRINT#1,"IØ":OPEN3,8,3,"#"
360 PRINT"WRITING BUFFER #";
370 NU=1:T1=T:S1=S
380 IFBM%(T1,S1)=ØTHENGOSUB2200:NU=NU+1:I
    FNU>NTHEN410
390 S1=S1+1:IFS1>20THENS1=Ø:T1=T1+1
```

```
400 IFT1<TF+1THEN380
410 PRINT"{DOWN}"
420 CLOSE3
430 S=S1+1:IFS>20THENS=0:T1=T1+1
440 T=T1:IFT>TFTHEN500
450 D$="S":GOSUB3200:IFIR$<>I2$THEN450
460 NU=1:T1=T:S1=S:GOTO270
500 REM FINISHED XFERS
510 CLOSE1
520 POKE55,PEEK(998):POKE56,PEEK(999):CLR
530 PRINT"{2 DOWN}BACKUP COMPLETE"
540 OPEN1,8,0,"$0"
550 GET#1,A$:IFA$<>"{RVS}"THEN550
560 PRINTA$;:GOTO610
570 GET#1,A$:SS=ST:A=LEN(A$):IFATHENA=ASC
    (A$)
580 GET#1,B$:SS=ST:B=LEN(B$):IFBTHENA=ASC
    (B$)
590 IFSSTHEN660
600 IFA=1ANDB=1THENGOSUB630
610 GET#1,A$:IFA$=""THENPRINT:GOTO570
620 PRINTA$;:GOTO610
630 GET#1,A$:SS=ST:A=LEN(A$):IFATHENA=ASC
    (A$)
640 GET#1,B$:SS=ST:B=LEN(B$):IFBTHENB=ASC
    (B$)
650 N=B*256+A:PRINTN;:RETURN
660 CLOSE1
670 END
1000 REM HEADER DEST DISK
1010 PRINT"{DOWN}INSERT DESTINATION DISK
     TO BE FORMATTED"
1020 INPUT"{2 DOWN}DISK NAME{3 RIGHT}
     {SHIFT-SPACE}{16 SPACES}{19 LEFT}";D
     N$
1030 IFDN$="{SHIFT-SPACE}"THENPRINT"
     {3 UP}";:GOTO1020
1040 IFLEN(DN$)>16THENCLR:GOTO40
1050 F=0:FORJ=1TOLEN(DN$):S1$=MID$(DN$,J,
     1)
1060 IFS1$="{SHIFT-SPACE}"ORS1$=CHR$(34)T
     HENF=1
1070 NEXTJ:IFFTHENPRINT"{3 UP}";:GOTO1020
1080 INPUT"{DOWN}UNIQUE DISK ID{3 RIGHT}
     {SHIFT-SPACE}{20 SPACES}{23 LEFT}";I
     1$
1090 IFI1$="{SHIFT-SPACE}"THENPRINT"
     {2 UP}";:GOTO1080
1100 IFLEN(I1$)<>2THENPRINT"{2 UP}";:GOTO
     1080
```

```
1110 PRINT#1,"NØ:"+DN$+","+I1$
1120 GOSUB3000
1130 IFERTHENPRINTER$:GOTO10000
1140 RETURN
2000 REM READ BLOCK T1,S1 TO BUFFER # NU
2010 C=.
2020 PRINT#1,"U1";3;Ø;T1;S1
2030 GOSUB3000:IFNOTERTHEN2060
2040 C=C+1:IFC<3GOTO2020
2050 PRINTER$:FORJ=(BB+NU)*256TO(BB+NU)*2
     56+255:POKEJ,.:NEXTJ:GOTO2100
2060 PRINT#1,"B-P";3;Ø
2070 IFNU<>ØTHENPRINT"{3 SPACES}{3 LEFT}"
     ;RIGHT$("{2 SPACES}"+STR$(NU),3);"
     {3 LEFT}";
2080 POKE996,PEEK(3):POKE997,PEEK(4):POKE
     4,BB+NU:SYSMA
2085 POKE3,PEEK(996):POKE4,PEEK(997)
2090 IFST<>.ANDST<>64THENGOSUB3000:GOTO20
     50
2100 RETURN
2200 REM WRITE BLOCK T1,S1 FROM BUFFER #
     NU
2210 C=.
2220 PRINT#1,"B-A";Ø;T1;S1:PRINT#1,"B-P";
     3;Ø
2230 PRINT"{3 SPACES}{3 LEFT}";RIGHT$("
     {2 SPACES}"+STR$(NU),3);"{3 LEFT}";
2240 POKE996,PEEK(3):POKE997,PEEK(4):POKE
     4,BB+NU:SYSMA+3
2245 POKE3,PEEK(996):POKE4,PEEK(997)
2250 IFST<>.ANDST<>64THENPRINT"{RVS}IEEE
     WRITE ERROR"ST"{OFF}":GOTO10000
2260 PRINT#1,"U2";3;Ø;T1;S1
2270 GOSUB3000:IFNOTERTHEN2300
2280 C=C+1:IFC<3THEN2260
2290 PRINT"{RVS}UNRECOVERABLE WRITE ERROR
     "ER$:GOTO10000
2300 RETURN
2500 REM GET BAM TO BM%(T,S)
2510 TS=1:TF=.
2520 PRINT#1,"IØ":OPEN3,8,3,"#"
2530 S9=Ø
2540 PRINT"{DOWN}TRACK #{3 SPACES}BLOCKS
     TO XFER"
2550 PRINT"{24 T}"
2560 NU=0:T1=18:S1=Ø:CØ$=CHR$(.):GOSUB200
     Ø
2570 BY=4
```

```
2580 T%=(BY-4)/4+1
2590 PRINT"{2 SPACES}";T%;
2600 IFPEEK(BA+BY)=.THENFORJ=.TO20:BM%(T%
     ,J)=.:NEXT:BY=BY+4:GOTO2650
2610 S=0
2620 BY=BY+1:A0=PEEK(BA+BY):FORJ=.TO7:BM%
     (T%,S)=A0ANDTA(J):S=S+1:NEXT
2630 IFS<22THEN2620
2640 BY=BY+1
2650 ES=21:IFT%>17THENES=19
2660 IFT%>24THENES=18
2670 IFT%>30THENES=17
2680 FORJ=ESTO24:BM%(T%,J)=-1:NEXT
2690 SM=.:FORJ=.TO20:IFBM%(T%,J)=.THENSM=
     SM+1
2700 NEXT:PRINTTAB(12);SM:S9=S9+SM
2710 IFSM=.ANDTS=T%THENTS=TS+1:GOTO2730
2720 IFSM<>.THENTF=T%
2730 IFBY<143THEN2580
2740 CLOSE3
2750 PRINT"START =";TS;" FINISH =";TF
2760 PRINT"{DOWN}A TOTAL OF";S9;"BLOCKS T
     O XFER"
2770 S8=90+25+(.650+.980)*S9
2780 S7=INT(S8/60):PRINT"APPROX";S7":"INT
     (S8-S7*60);"FOR COPY"
2790 RETURN
3000 REM READ ERR CH TO ER,ER$
3010 INPUT#1,E0$,E1$,E2$,E3$:ER$=E0$+","+
     E1$+","+E2$+","+E3$
3020 ER=LEN(E0$):IFERTHENER=VAL(E0$)
3030 RETURN
3200 REM INSTRUCT TO SWAP TO DISK GIVEN I
     N D$
3210 IFD$="D"THENS1$="DESTINATION":GOTO32
     30
3220 S1$="SOURCE"
3230 PRINT"{DOWN}INSERT ";S1$;" DISK, PRE
     SS {RVS}SPACE{OFF}"
3240 GETA$:IFA$<>" "THEN3240
3250 OPEN2,8,0,"$0"
3260 GOSUB3000:IFER>0THEN10000
3270 FORJ=1TO26:GET#2,A$:NEXTJ
3280 GET#2,A$:GET#2,B$:IR$=A$+B$
3290 GET#2,A$:GET#2,A$:GET#2,B$:DR$=A$+B$
3300 CLOSE2:RETURN
10000 REM DROP OUT
10010 POKE55,PEEK(998):POKE56,PEEK(999):C
      LR:STOP
```

```
15000 DATA 76,66,3,76,91,3,162,3,32,198,2
      55,160,0,132,3,32,207,255,145
15010 DATA 3,165,144,208,3,200,208,244,32
      ,204,255,96,162,3,32,201,255,160
15020 DATA 0,132,3,177,3,32,210,255,165,1
      44,208,3,200,208,244,32,204,255,96
```

Using the User Port

John Heilborn

The User Port on the 64 gives you direct access to your computer. This article explains exactly how to program for and connect to this port.

Located on the back and side of the 64 are several different connectors (see Figure 1). Each of them (except one) has a specific purpose. For example, the video port connects to a television or monitor; the game ports on the side of the computer connect to various kinds of game controllers such as paddles or joysticks; the serial plug on the back of the computer connects to a Commodore printer or disk drive; and the expander slot accepts program cartridges.

Figure 1. 64 Ports

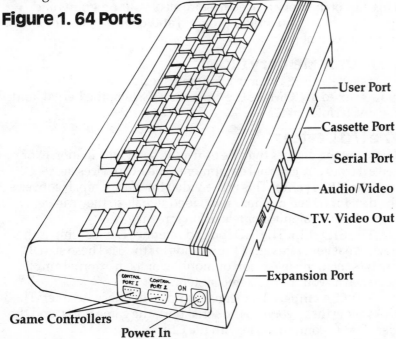

User Port

Cassette Port

Serial Port

Audio/Video

T.V. Video Out

Expansion Port

Game Controllers

Power In

143

There is one connector, however, that was designed to be used by you, the user, and is called (appropriately enough) the User Port.

What Is the User Port?

To get an idea of what the User Port is, let's take a look at the 64 system as a whole. Figure 2 is a block diagram of the major components of the 64. As you can see, the 64 consists of a Central Processing Unit (CPU), some memory (lots of memory), and some I/O (Input/Output) devices. The television (or monitor), the printer, disk drive, and even the keyboard are connected to the 64 through the I/O devices.

The following is a brief description of each of the major components of the 64.

The Central Processing Unit (CPU)

This is the device that performs all of the logical and numerical functions for the 64. The central processor in the 64 is a microprocessor called a 6510.

Random Access Memory (RAM)

This part of memory is used to store all of your programs and data. Whenever you write a program and/or enter data, the computer stores it here.

Read Only Memory (ROM)

This is where the 64's control programs reside. Some of the programs stored in ROM are the Operating System, the Kernal, and the BASIC interpreter.

The I/O Devices

These are the devices that the 64 uses to send information to or receive it from any external equipment. The I/O devices are:

The VIC-II chip. This is the Video Interface Chip. It converts the data for screen memory into video signals so they can be viewed on the monitor or television screen.

The SID chip. The SID (Sound Interface Device) chip is the device that generates all of the sounds for the 64. These signals can be sent to the television or monitor, or to an external amplifier, such as your home stereo system.

The CIA chips. CIA means Complex Interface Adapter. The CIAs allow the keyboard, the serial port, the game ports, and the User Port to communicate with the CPU.

Figure 2. 64 Computer System

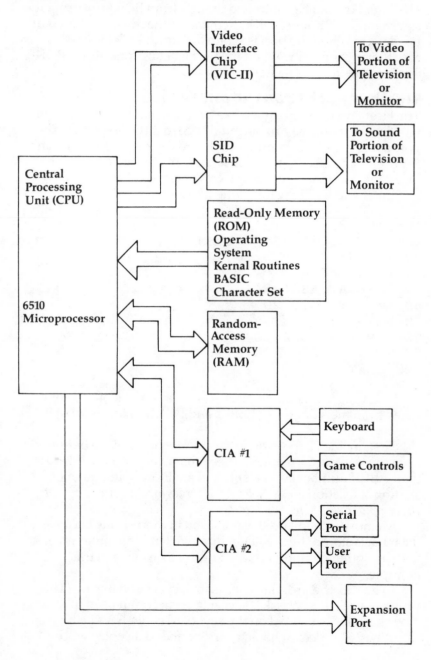

How the User Port Works

The User Port can be controlled directly from BASIC by using the
commands PEEK and POKE. Remember that the User Port is an
I/O device. When the port is set up for input, PEEK is used to *read*
data that is coming in. When the port is set up for output, POKE
is used to *write* the data going out.

The User Port as an Output Device

The User Port operates much like a typical memory location, and
while we're using it as an output device, data can be sent to the
port using the POKE command. Before we examine the specific
features of the User Port, however, let's review the process of
POKEing using some ordinary RAM locations.

Enter and RUN the following routine:

```
10 A=6000
20 GET A$: IF A$="" THEN 20
30 IF A$="*" THEN 70
40 PRINT A$;
50 POKE A, ASC(A$)
60 A=A+1: GOTO 20
70 PRINT
80 FOR R = 6000 TO A
90 PRINT CHR$(PEEK(R));
100 NEXT
```

This program demonstrates how data can be stored and re-
called from memory using PEEKs and POKEs. Here is what it
does:

First, in line 20 the program waits for characters to be entered
from the keyboard. In line 50, these characters are converted into
their ASCII number equivalents and are POKEd into memory
starting at location 6000. *Note: ASCII codes are numeric values that
the computer uses to represent text.*

Memory location 6000 was chosen in this routine because
data that is stored there will not interfere with this program or
with any other computer operations we'll be using in this
example.

In line 30, the program checks for a special character. (This
program uses the asterisk [*] because it isn't often used in text.
Any character or symbol on the keyboard could have been used.)

When the special character is detected, data entry will end. At that point the program will skip to line 70, which starts PEEKing memory locations beginning with location 6000. The characters stored there will be displayed, one character at a time, up to the last character we stored.

When Memory Is Not Memory

Not every memory location in the 64 is used to store information. Some memory locations are actually *control registers* for the I/O chips which perform special functions. For example, location 53280 is one of the VIC-II chip control registers. POKEing different numbers into that location will change the color of the screen border. To look at this, enter and RUN the following program:

```
10 FOR R=0 TO 15
20 POKE 53280, R
30 FOR G=0 TO 500: NEXT
40 NEXT
50 GOTO 10
```

This routine displays all of the 16 possible screen border colors. It does this by POKEing numbers between 0 and 15 into the control register (at memory location 53280) which controls this function.

A Closer Look at the Control Numbers

Normally, when the 64 displays the contents of PEEKed memory locations, it displays them as decimal numbers. This is because BASIC converts the numbers it finds in memory into their decimal equivalents before displaying them. The values are actually stored in memory as binary numbers.

Binary numbers are made up of only 1's and 0's instead of the decimal numbers 0-9 that we are used to. The reason they are stored that way is because digital circuits (like the ones in the 64) are actually tiny electronic switches. Each switch (like a light switch) can be either *on* or *off*. Numerically, these conditions correspond to the numbers 1 and 0. By using these 1's and 0's, we can represent any character we want.

Every memory location in the 64 contains eight of these tiny switches. In computer jargon, the switches are called *bits*.

"Bit Display," the program at the end of this article, looks at the number stored in a memory location (we can use 6000 again) and displays the bits in that memory location as black and white squares. We'll use a light square to represent a binary 1 and a black square to represent a binary 0.

The keys numbered 1-8 will be used as toggle switches for each of the eight bits. Pressing a number once will turn the switch on and pressing it again will turn it off.

In lines 10-240, the program sets up the variables and bit displays. Program control is then transferred to the subroutine in lines 330-380 which reads the number stored in our memory location and displays its binary value as black and white squares.

The program jumps to line 260 and GETs a keyboard entry. Line 270 checks it to make sure it is a number between 1 and 8, and if it is, its value is assigned to the variable B and lines 290-300 POKE the new value into memory location 6000.

With the new data in variable B, the program jumps to the subroutine at location 330 again, which converts the number to its binary value and displays them on the screen. After that, the program returns to line 260, awaiting another keystroke.

The number in the upper left-hand corner of the screen is the decimal value of the binary number being displayed.

It should be noted that the numbers 1 to 8 do not represent the number of the bit, but rather the keys to be pressed in order to turn the bits on and off. Bit patterns are usually numbered from the right starting with zero. Thus, the bit toggled by pressing the 8 key would normally be called bit 0, while the bit toggled by pressing the 1 key would be called bit 7.

Rerouting the Data

The program ("Bit Display") will display and toggle the contents of any memory location except one that contains ROM. ROM means Read Only Memory, and by definition, cannot be changed. If we had used a location that was a control register instead of a RAM location, however, the numbers being stored and displayed would have also affected the device controlled by the register, just as it did in the program that changed the screen border colors.

To see how this works, replace all references to memory location 6000 in the program with 53280 (the screen border color control register we used in the earlier example). These references occur in lines 290, 300, 330, and 350.

```
290 IF(PEEK(53280)ANDA(B))=0THENPOKE53280
    ,PEEK(53280)+A(B):GOTO310
300 POKE53280,PEEK(53280)-A(B)
330 PRINT"{HOME}{2 DOWN}{4 SPACES}{HOME}
    {2 DOWN}";PEEK(53280)
```

```
350 IF((2↑J)AND(PEEK(53280)))=0THENPRINTB
    $(7-J):GOTO370
```

When you run the program now, it will behave quite differently. To begin with, the four left-hand bits (numbered 1-4) are all *on*, and cannot be changed by pressing the corresponding keys.

Look at what happens when you toggle the four right-hand bits. Each time a bit is changed, the screen border changes to another color. Notice that the control register limits us to only 16 different number combinations — one for each color that can be generated for the screen border. You will find that many of the control registers have rules such as this governing their use.

Sending Data to the User Port

In the previous example, we sent data to the control register at memory location 53280 which controls the color of the screen border. This is not the only control register for the VIC-II chip, however. In order to control the screen display, the VIC-II chip has several control registers at various memory locations. Another memory location that controls the functions of the VIC-II chip is 53281. It controls the screen background color. If you replace the number 53280 with 53281 in the previous example, you will be able to manipulate the screen color instead of the border color.

The User Port is also controlled by several memory locations. One of the memory locations is 56577. Numbers that you POKE into that location will appear as data on pins of the User Port connector.

Figure 3. User Port Edge Connector

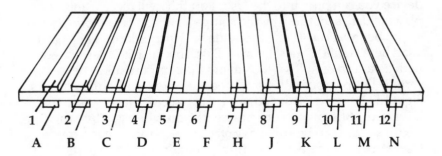

Figure 3. User Port Edge Connector

TOP SIDE		BOTTOM SIDE		
Pin	Function	Pin	Function	
1	Ground	A	Ground	
2	+ 5 volts DC	B	FLAG2 *	
3	RESET	C	User Port bit 0	
4	CNT1 *	D	User Port bit 1	
5	SP1 *	E	User Port bit 2	
6	CNT2 *	F	User Port bit 3	
7	SP2 *	H	User Port bit 4	
8	PC2 *	J	User Port bit 5	
9	Serial ATN *	K	User Port bit 6	
10	9 volts AC	L	User Port bit 7	
11	9 volts AC	M	PA2 *	
12	Ground	N	Ground	

*Assorted serial input/output and "handshaking" functions. See Chapter 6 of the *Programmer's Reference Guide* for further details.

A Simple Peripheral Device

For those of you who are inclined to build circuits, here is a simple device you can plug into the User Port that will receive and display the data sent there by the computer. It can be built on a small circuit board about 1½ inches wide by 3 inches long. The board used here is called "perf board." That's because it is perforated with a pattern of holes which allow the components to be inserted. The components you'll need are eight 3.3K ohm resistors, eight LEDs, and a 24-pin edge-card connector that fits onto the User Port. (Bring your computer with you when you buy the connector so you can be sure its contacts match the contacts on the User Port.) Most electronic supply stores carry these parts.

Figure 4 is a picture of the top of the circuit board, showing where all of the components go.

Figure 4. Top of Circuit Board

NOTE: Position Flat Surface on Flange of LED Toward Connector

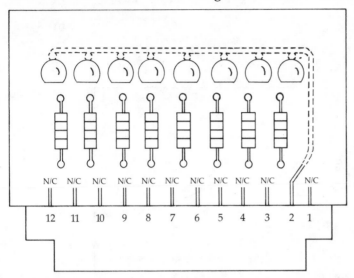

Figure 5 is a picture of the bottom of the board, showing the connections that need to be made there.

Figure 5. Bottom of Circuit Board

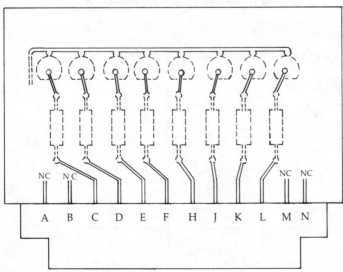

Figure 6 is a schematic diagram of the circuit.

Figure 6. Circuit Board

**24-Pin
Edge Connector**

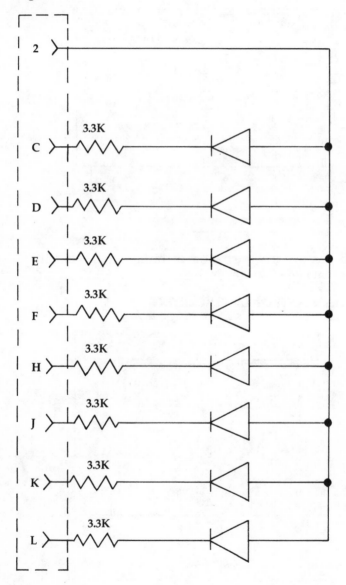

When you install this device, be sure you turn off power to the 64 first, and push the connector all the way onto the User Port, making sure it fits securely.

Running the Port

The purpose of building the device above is to demonstrate how an external device can be connected to and controlled by the 64. If you choose not to build the device, leave the bit display program in the computer and make the following changes to it:

1) Delete lines 250-320 and line 380,
2) And change these lines:

```
10 POKE 53280,0:POKE 53281,0:POKE 56579,2
   55
330 PRINT"{HOME}{2 DOWN}{4 SPACES}{HOME}
    {2 DOWN}";PEEK(56577)
350 IF((2↑J)AND(PEEK(56577)))=0THENPRINTB
    $(7-J):GOTO370
```

With these changes to the program, the video display will show the output just like the external device.

Programming the User Port

As was mentioned earlier, the User Port can be either an input device or an output device. In this article we'll be using it as an output device, so we'll need to program it to receive data from the computer and send it out. Memory location 56579 is called the data direction register for the User Port. By changing the number in this register, you can control each bit on the port, making it either an input or an output bit. To make a bit on the User Port an output, the corresponding bit in the data direction register must contain a 1. To make all of the bits equal to 1 in the data direction register, we'll need to POKE memory location 56579 (the data direction register) with the binary number 11111111. This is equal to the decimal number 255.

```
5 POKE 56579,255
```

Experimenting with the User Port

The examples that follow show various method of controlling the LEDs (or lighted squares on the video screen). More practical applications would suggest connecting the User Port to real appliances such as the lights in your home, a radio, or perhaps your coffee maker. However, interfacing with such appliances presents a risk of serious electric shock or damage to the computer, and should not be attempted by the inexperienced.

Keeping this philosophy in mind, enter the examples and think of how you might apply them to your needs.

Binary Counter

Video Version. Remember to make the changes to Program 1 as outlined above before adding the following routine:

```
500 IF A=255 THEN A=0
510 POKE 56577, A
520 A=A+1
530 GOTO 330
```

External Board Version. This routine has exactly the same function as the one above, but because the 64 can send data directly to the port much faster than it can change the screen display, a delay loop was added at line 520 to allow you to see the counter. Additionally, the LEDs are the reverse of the screen; that is, a one is represented by a dark LED and a zero by a lit LED. To compensate for this, line 510 inverts the number.

```
500 IF A=255 THEN A=0
510 POKE 56577, 255-A
520 FOR G=0 TO 100: NEXT
530 A=A+1
540 GOTO 500
```

Sequential Lights

This program is similar to the previous program, but instead of performing a full count, it lights the lamps individually.

Video Version.

```
500 A(0)=128: A(1)=64: A(2)=32:A(3)=16: A
    (4)=8: A(5)=4: A(6)=2: A(7)=1
510 IF B>7 THEN B=0
520 POKE 56577, A(B)
530 B=B+1
540 GOTO 330
```

External Board Version.

```
500 A(0)=128: A(1)=64: A(2)=32:A(3)=16: A
    (4)=8: A(5)=4: A(6)=2: A(7)=1
510 IF B>7 THEN B=0
```

```
520 POKE 56577, 255-A(B)
530 B=B+1
540 GOTO 500
```

Incidentally, to make the lights flash in the other direction, all you need to do is change line 520 to:

```
520 POKE 56577, A(7-B)
```

for the video version, or:

```
520 POKE 56577, 255-A(7-B)
```

if you are using the external board.

Random Lights

This program lights the LEDs (or screen lights) randomly.
Video Version.

```
500 A(0)=128: A(1)=64: A(2)=32:A(3)=16: A
    (4)=8: A(5)=4: A(6)=2: A(7)=1
510 B = INT(RND(0)*8)
520 POKE 56577, A(B)
530 GOTO 330
```

External Board Version.

```
500 A(0)=128: A(1)=64: A(2)=32:A(3)=16: A
    (4)=8: A(5)=4: A(6)=2: A(7)=1
510 B = INT(RND(0)*8)
520 POKE 56577, 255-A(B)
530 GOTO 510
```

Bit Display

```
10 POKE 53280,0: POKE53281,0
20 A(1)=128:A(2)=64:A(3)=32:A(4)=16:A(5)=
   8:A(6)=4:A(7)=2:A(8)=1
21 A$="{HOME}{12 DOWN}"
22 B$="{G} {M}{DOWN}{3 LEFT}{G} {M}"
23 C$="{RVS}{G}{2 SPACES}{DOWN}{3 LEFT}
   {G}{2 SPACES}"
24 D$="{M}{G} {M}{G} {M}{G} {M}{G} {M}{G}
   {M}{G} {M}{G} {M}{G} {M}{G}"
30 B$(0)=A$+"{7 RIGHT}"+B$
40 C$(0)=A$+"{7 RIGHT}"+C$
50 B$(1)=A$+"{10 RIGHT}"+B$
60 C$(1)=A$+"{10 RIGHT}"+C$
70 B$(2)=A$+"{13 RIGHT}"+B$
```

```
80 C$(2)=A$+"{13 RIGHT}"+C$
90 B$(3)=A$+"{16 RIGHT}"+B$
100 C$(3)=A$+"{16 RIGHT}"+C$
110 B$(4)=A$+"{19 RIGHT}"+B$
120 C$(4)=A$+"{19 RIGHT}"+C$
130 B$(5)=A$+"{22 RIGHT}"+B$
140 C$(5)=A$+"{22 RIGHT}"+C$
150 B$(6)=A$+"{25 RIGHT}"+B$
160 C$(6)=A$+"{25 RIGHT}"+C$
170 B$(7)=A$+"{28 RIGHT}"+B$
180 C$(7)=A$+"{28 RIGHT}"+C$
190 PRINT"{WHT}{CLR}{10 DOWN}{8 RIGHT}1
    {2 SPACES}2{2 SPACES}3{2 SPACES}4
    {2 SPACES}5{2 SPACES}6{2 SPACES}7
    {2 SPACES}8{DOWN}";
200 PRINT"{23 LEFT}";
210 PRINT"{24 @}{DOWN}{25 LEFT}";
220 PRINT D$;"{DOWN}{26 LEFT}";
230 PRINT D$;"{DOWN}{29 LEFT}";
240 PRINT"{DOWN}{36 LEFT}{24 T}"
250 GOSUB330
260 GETK$:IFK$=""THEN260
270 IFASC(K$)>57ORASC(K$)<49THEN260
280 B=VAL(K$)
290 IF(PEEK(6000)ANDA(B))=0THENPOKE6000,P
    EEK(6000)+A(B):GOTO310
300 POKE6000,PEEK(6000)-A(B)
310 GOSUB330
320 GOTO260
330 PRINT"{HOME}{2 DOWN}{4 SPACES}{HOME}
    {2 DOWN}";PEEK(6000)
340 FORJ=0TO7
350 IF((2↑J)AND(PEEK(6000)))=0THENPRINTB$
    (7-J):GOTO370
360 PRINTC$(7-J)
370 NEXT
380 RETURN
```

Chapter 6

Utilities

Data Searcher

Jerry Sturdivant

Programmers are always looking for ways to make their programs more "friendly," easier to use.
  This special search routine will accept all kinds of wrong input and still come up with the right match.

Have you ever searched through a file for something but just couldn't find it? You know it's in there, but your spelling may be off by one letter and the strings just won't match?
  Or you know the city of Albuquerque is in the program, but you can't spell it? Or you don't know if you're supposed to add the state? And if you *do* need to type the state, should you use the two-letter abbreviation? Is New Mexico supposed to be NE or NM?
  In short, if a program has to search for a string match, you can solve all these problems by adding a Truncating Search Routine.
  Let's look at the example program. Here a user enters the name of a city, and the program gives the elevation. If no match is found for the user's request, rather than having line 120 report "CITY NOT FOUND": GOTO 70, the program performs a *truncating search* (lines 160 to 210).
  The routine searches only that first part of each City string equal to the length of the Request string. If there is no match, it shortens the end of the Request string by one letter and searches the shorter portion of each City string. It will continue to shorten and search until it finds a match or runs down to two letters. It will print all matches found for that length Request string.
  Suppose the user gets the two-letter abbreviation of Maine wrong. If the user requests PORTLAND MA rather than ME or types out the complete word "MAINE", it will still find PORTLAND ME. If the user requests just PORTLAND, the search will print both PORTLANDs. As for our Albuquerque problem, the word can be badly misspelled and still be found. A user who understands the Truncating Search would just enter ALBU. It's a very handy and user-friendly routine, especially for poor spellers.

Data Search Demonstration

```
10 REM PICK CITY - PRINT CITY AND ELEVAT
   ION
20 NUMBER OF CITIES=5
30 DIM CITY$(NUMBER OF CITIES),ELEV$(NUM
   BER OF CITIES)
40 FOR I=1 TO NUMBER OF CITIES
50 READ CITY$(I),ELEV$(I)
60 NEXT
70 T=0:PRINT"ENTER CITY NAME"
80 INPUT REQUEST$
90 FOR I=1 TO NUMBER OF CITIES
100 IF REQUEST$=CITY$(I) THEN PRINT CITY
    $(I),ELEV$(I):GOTO 70
110 NEXT
120 REM{7 SPACES}NOTHING FOUND
130 REM{2 SPACES}SEARCH SIMILAR SPELLING
140 REM ==========================
150 PRINT"SEARCHING FOR SOMETHING SIMILA
    R"
160 FOR Z=LEN(REQUEST$) TO 2 STEP -1
170 FOR I=1 TO NUMBER OF CITIES
180 IF LEFT$(REQUESTS$,Z)=LEFT$(CITY$(I)
    ,Z) THEN PRINT CITY$(I),ELEV$(I):T=1
190 NEXT I
200 IF T THEN 70
210 NEXT Z
220 PRINT"CITY NOT FOUND":GOTO 70
250 DATA ALBUQUERQUE NM,4500
260 DATA BISHOP CA,4100
270 DATA PORTLAND MA,45
280 DATA PORTLAND OR,37
290 DATA THE DALLES OR,85
```

Music Keyboard

Bryan Kattwinkle

The 64 has amazing sound capabilities. This program will allow you to experiment with sound by creating a music synthesizer with your 64.

"Music Keyboard" allows convenient experimentation with the 64's built-in synthesizer, the SID chip. With this program, the 64's synthesizer becomes almost as easy to adjust as a professional synthesizer with knobs to control and buttons to push.

Using the computer's keyboard as your control panel, the top two rows become the piano keys, while the function keys control the octave and waveform. The attack, decay, sustain, release, length, filter, band pass, resonance, and pulse functions are controlled by pressing the appropriate key as shown on the screen. The program will inform you of the present value of any of the functions you may wish to change.

The Functions

The filter and pulse rates can vary from 1 to 4095. The band pass can be varied between 1 and 7 and will interact with the filter. All the other functions will have a value from 1 to 15.

A quick review of each function:

• Attack is the rate at which a note rises to its maximum volume.

• Decay is the rate at which a note falls to the sustain level.

• Sustain allows you to extend a note.

• Release allows you to free a note once it is sustained.

• Length is the number of seconds before a note is released (use .5 for ½ second).

• Pulse affects only the pulse waveform (F6) by changing its tone quality.

• Filter will cut off the highs *or* lows of a wave.

• Band pass cuts off both the highs *and* lows of a wave.

• Resonance has little audible effect.

161

Waveform refers to the shape of the sound wave: triangle (F2), sawtooth (F4), pulse (F6), or noise (F8).

Try experimenting with the different functions to see what kinds of sound you can create with your 64. Try changing the functions to simulate different instruments such as a piano, flute, or drum. When you really feel you've got the hang of it, try composing a tune.

Music Keyboard

```
90 REM ----- MUSIC KEYBOARD -----
100 GOSUB 1000{4 SPACES}:REM SET UP DISP
    LAY
102 PRINT TAB(12); "...THINKING..."
110 S=13*4096+1024 :REM BASE FOR POKES
120 FOR I=0 TO 28 :POKE S+I,0 :NEXT
130 DIM F(26) :REM FREQUENCY TABLE
140 F1=7040 :TW=2↑(1/12) :REM CONSTANTS
150 FOR I=1 TO 26 :F(27-I)=F1*5.8+30 :F1
    =F1/TW :NEXT
160 DIM K(255) :REM KEY TABLE
170 K$="Q2W3ER5T6Y7UI9O0P@-*ᖯ↑"
180 FOR I=1 TO LEN(K$) :K(ASC(MID$(K$,I)
    ))=I :NEXT I
200 GOSUB 1200{4 SPACES}:REM SET UP ADSR
210 FOR I=0 TO 14 STEP 7 :POKE S+I+5,0 :
    POKE S+I+6,0{2 SPACES}:REM TONES OFF
220 WV=32:W=1:M=2:OC=3:HB=256:Z=0:PY=1
225 PRINT "{UP}"; TAB(12); "{14 SPACES}"
235 REM ENTER HERE AFTER PARAM CHANGE
240 FOR I=0 TO 2{4 SPACES}:REM PULSE PAR
    AMS
245 POKE S+2+I*7,P(8) AND 255
250 POKE S+3+I*7,P(8)/256
255 NEXT I
260 POKE S+24,P(7)*16 + 15 :REM BP,VOL
270 POKE S+23,P(9)*16 + 7 :REM RES,FV
275 POKE S+22,P(6)/16 :REM FILTER HI
276 POKE S+21,P(6) AND 15 :REM LO
280 AV = P(1) * 16 + P(2) :REM ATT/DEC
285 SV = P(3) * 16 + P(4) :REM SUS/REL
300 GET A$ :IF A$="" THEN 300
310 FR=F(K(ASC(A$)))/M :T=V*7+S
    {9 SPACES}:IF FR=Z THEN 500
315 IF PY=1 THEN V=V+1 :IF V=3 THEN V=0
320 POKE T+6,Z :REM CLEAR SUSTAIN/REL
325 POKE T+5,Z :REM CLEAR ATTACK/DECAY
330 POKE T+4,0 :REM TURN OFF SOUND
```

```
340 POKE T,FR-HB*INT(FR/HB) :REM LOW FR
350 POKE T+1,FR/HB :REM SET HI FREQ
360 POKE T+6,SV{4 SPACES}:REM SET SUS/RE
    L
365 POKE T+5,AV{4 SPACES}:REM SET ATT/DE
    C
370 POKE T+4,WV+1 :FOR I=1 TO 160*P(5)
375 GET A$ :IF A$="" THEN NEXT I
380 POKE T+4,WV :IF A$<>"" THEN 310
385 FOR I=1 TO 1+(P(4)/2.2)↑4
390 GET A$ :IF A$<>"" THEN 310
395 NEXT I :POKE S+4,Z :POKE S+11,Z :POK
    E S+18,Z
400 GOTO 300
500 IF A$="{F1}" THEN M=1 :OC=4 :GOTO 30
    0
510 IF A$="{F3}" THEN M=2 :OC=3 :GOTO 30
    0
520 IF A$="{F5}" THEN M=4 :OC=2 :GOTO 30
    0
530 IF A$="{F7}" THEN M=8 :OC=1 :GOTO 30
    0
540 IF A$="{F2}" THEN W=0 :WV=16 :GOTO 3
    00
550 IF A$="{F4}" THEN W=1 :WV=32 :GOTO 3
    00
560 IF A$="{F6}" THEN W=2 :WV=64 :GOTO 3
    00
570 IF A$="{F8}" THEN W=3 :WV=128 :GOTO
    300
580 IF A$<>" " THEN 600
585 PY=1-PY :IF PY<>0 THEN 300
590 POKE S+11,0 :POKE S+18,0 :V=0
595 GOTO 300
600 N=0
610 IF A$="A" THEN N=1 :MX=15
620 IF A$="D" THEN N=2 :MX=15
630 IF A$="S" THEN N=3 :MX=15
640 IF A$="Z" THEN N=4 :MX=15
650 IF A$="L" THEN N=5 :MX=15
660 IF A$="F" THEN N=6 :MX=4095
670 IF A$="B" THEN N=7 :MX=7
680 IF A$="K" THEN N=8 :MX=4095
690 IF A$="N" THEN N=9 :MX=15
700 IF N=0 THEN 300
750 PRINT "{UP} "; P$(N); " ="; P(N);
755 PRINT "{2 SPACES}NEW VALUE ";
760 GET A$ :I=P(N) :INPUT I
770 PRINT "{UP}{38 SPACES}"
```

163

```
780 IF (I<0) OR (I>MX) THEN PRINT "{UP}
    MAXIMUM =";MX; :GOTO 755
785 P(N) = I
790 GOTO 240 :REM RE-CALCULATE PARAMS
1000 REM ---DISPLAY SETUP SUBROUTINE---
1002 C=29{2 SPACES}:REM COLUMN
1003 POKE 53280,PEEK(53281) :REM BORDER
1005 PRINT"{CLR} " : PRINT " "
1007 PRINT "{2 SPACES}2 3{3 SPACES}5 6 7
     {3 SPACES}9 0{3 SPACES}- £"; TAB(C
     ); "{4 SPACES}F1C£S£"
1010 PRINT " {RVS} {RIGHT} {RIGHT} B
     {RIGHT} {RIGHT} {RIGHT} B {RIGHT}
     {RIGHT} B {RIGHT} {RIGHT} "; TAB(C)
     ; "{OFF}£A£CF2{3 SPACES}B"
1015 PRINT " {RVS} {RIGHT} {RIGHT} B
     {RIGHT} {RIGHT} {RIGHT} B {RIGHT}
     {RIGHT} B {RIGHT} {RIGHT} "; TAB(C)
     ; "{OFF}B{3 SPACES}F3C£W£"
1020 PRINT " {RVS} {RIGHT} {RIGHT} B
     {RIGHT} {RIGHT} {RIGHT} B {RIGHT}
     {RIGHT} B {RIGHT} {RIGHT} "; TAB(C)
     ; "{OFF}£Q£CF4{3 SPACES}B"
1030 PRINT " {RVS} B B B B B B B B B B
      B "; TAB(C); "{OFF}B{3 SPACES}F5C
     £W£"
1040 PRINT " {RVS}QBWBEBRBTBYBUBIBOBPB@B
     *B↑"; TAB(C); "{OFF}£Q£CF6
     {3 SPACES}B"
1050 PRINT TAB(C); "B{3 SPACES}F7C£W£"
1060 PRINT "{4 SPACES}{RVS} SOLO / POLYP
     HONIC {OFF}"; TAB(C); "£Q£CF8
     {3 SPACES}B"
1065 PRINT TAB(C); "B{3 SPACES}OCTAVE"
1070 PRINT "{RVS}A{OFF} ATTACK{5 SPACES}
     {RVS}S{OFF} SUSTAIN"; TAB(C-4); "WA
     VEFORM"
1075 PRINT " {RVS}D{OFF} DECAY{6 SPACES}
     {RVS}L{OFF} LENGTH"
1080 PRINT "{2 SPACES}{RVS}Z{OFF} RELEAS
     E{4 SPACES}{RVS}N{OFF} RESONANCE"
1082 PRINT "{3 SPACES}{RVS}F{OFF} FILTER
     {5 SPACES}{RVS}K{OFF} PULSE RATE"
1084 PRINT "{4 SPACES}{RVS}B{OFF} BAND P
     ASS"
1085 PRINT "{3 DOWN}"
1090 RETURN
1200 REM -- SETUP A-D-S-R SUBROUTINE --
1210 DIM P(9) :DIM P$(9)
```

```
1212 P$(1)="ATTACK" :P(1)=2
1214 P$(2)="DECAY" :P(2)=4
1216 P$(3)="SUSTAIN" :P(3)=4
1218 P$(4)="RELEASE" :P(4)=1Ø
122Ø P$(5)="LENGTH" :P(5)=1
1222 P$(6)="FILTER" :P(6)=5ØØ
1224 P$(7)="BAND PASS" :P(7)=7
1226 P$(8)="PULSE RATE" :P(8)=4ØØ
1228 P$(9)="RESONANCE" :P(9)=1
123Ø RETURN
```

Programmer's Alarm Clock

Bruce Jaeger

Translated for the 64 by Gregg Peele

You'll never work too long on your 64 if you use "Programmer's Alarm Clock."

Have you ever sat down at your computer after dinner to "touch up that program a bit," only to find again that you've lost all notion of time and you've just missed the first half of that movie you've waited for all week? Or you're supposed to pick someone up at 6:00, and by the time you look up from the screen it's 7:30? Me too!

That's why "Programmer's Alarm Clock" came about. When you first sit down at your computer, LOAD and RUN the program. It will ask you for the alarm time and current time of day. You must enter the time based on a 24-hour clock. The following chart will help you in entering the times.

HHMMSS

000500	12:05AM (and no seconds)
010030	1:00AM (and 30 seconds)
103045	10:30AM (and 45 seconds)
120000	12 noon (and no seconds)
133030	1:30PM (and 30 seconds)
180000	6:00PM (and no seconds)
233000	11:30PM (and no seconds)

As soon as you set the time of day, the clock begins counting toward the alarm time. When the time of day equals the alarm time you selected, a beep will sound and the word "QUIT" will be printed on the screen.

Since the internal clock is affected by using the cassette, the program will give unpredictable results if you use the cassette unit. Disk operation and TOOLKIT do not seem to affect the clock.

This program is a good one to study if you are interested in learning about simple machine language and interrupt-driven routines. Since the program is so short, it is fairly simple to understand and adapt for use in other programs.

Programmer's Alarm Clock

```
80 S=54272:FORR=STOS+24:POKER,0:NEXT
95 GOSUB195
100 PRINT"{CLR}SET ALARM TIME"
110 PRINT"{DOWN}( HHMMSS )"
120 INPUT"{DOWN}{2 SPACES}000000{8 LEFT}
    ";TI$
130 POKE956,PEEK(160)
140 POKE957,PEEK(161)
150 PRINT"{DOWN}INPUT TIME OF DAY"
160 PRINT"{DOWN}( HHMMSS )"
170 INPUT"{DOWN}{2 SPACES}000000{8 LEFT}
    ";TI$
180 PRINT"{CLR}":SYS49152:END
195 FORG=49152TO49284:READE:POKEG,E:NEXT
    :RETURN
200 DATA 120, 173, 20, 3, 141, 186, 3, 1
    73, 21, 3, 141
210 DATA 187, 3, 169, 25, 141, 20, 3, 16
    9, 192, 141
220 DATA 21, 3, 88, 96, 173, 160, 0, 205
    , 188, 3
230 DATA 208, 92, 173, 161, 0, 205, 189,
    3, 208, 84
240 DATA 169, 145, 141, 17, 4, 169, 149,
    141, 18, 4
250 DATA 169, 137, 141, 19, 4, 169, 148,
    141, 20, 4
260 DATA 169, 161, 141, 21, 4, 169, 15,
    141, 24, 212
270 DATA 169, 9, 141, 5, 212, 169, 6, 14
    1, 6, 212
280 DATA 169, 34, 141, 1, 212, 169, 70,
    141, 0, 212
290 DATA 169, 33, 141, 4, 212, 169, 255,
    160, 255, 136
300 DATA 208, 253, 202, 208, 248, 169, 0
    , 141, 24, 212
310 DATA 120, 173, 186, 3, 141, 20, 3, 1
    73, 187, 3
320 DATA 141, 21, 3, 88, 76, 49, 234, 13
    4, 223, 32
330 DATA 223, 0, 223, 32, 223, 32, 223,
    32, 223, 0
```

Chapter 7

Memory

A Window on Memory

Gregg Peele

Ready to actually look at the 64 memory? This article will take you on a visual tour of your computer's memory.

Our brain's memory is where we store information for future use. Like the human brain, a computer has memory also. And like the human brain, a computer stores information for future use. But unlike our memory, a computer does not forget what it has in its ROM memory. The computer *will* forget what it has in its RAM memory when you turn it off.

Computers' memories allow them to store data and programs. Computers are designed so we can manipulate and change much of the data. One of the most significant features of the Commodore 64 is its large memory capacity. On power-up, the 64 allows the user 38,000 bytes to use with BASIC and over 40,000 bytes for use with machine language. It is this memory that we will be actually looking at in this article.

The Nature of Memory

Nybbles, Bits, and Bytes

Memory is organized into several structural levels, each based on the binary (base two) number system. At the lowest level, a computer's memory consists of units called *bits* (from binary digits). Bits can be in only one of two states — on or off. One bit can thus define only two possible conditions. This seems extremely limited until you consider that two bits can define four different conditions (two to the second power), three bits can define eight different combinations (two to the third power), and four bits can describe 16 different combinations.

Four bits seen as a unit are called a *nybble*. If you want to change the color of the screen border or background on the 64, you can choose from among 16 different colors. The POKE com-

171

mand in BASIC allows you to alter a nybble in location 53281 for screen and a nybble in location 53280 for background. Altering these two nybbles provides the necessary color combinations for all 16 colors.

If you utilize eight bits as a unit — called a *byte* — you can describe a total of 256 unique numbers. The byte is the most useful unit within the Commodore 64. Each letter, number, or graphics symbol has its own pattern of eight bits. This pattern provides the unit for most functions which occur within the 64. For instance, the keyboard initiates the pattern 00000001 when you press the letter A. This pattern of bits travels through the computer and is stored in a byte of screen memory. This byte is then decoded into the familiar symbol A which appears on the screen.

A single byte can hold any number from zero to 255. A unique character can be made with each of these values; thus it is possible to represent a value within a byte by using a single character. This ability will come in handy as we try to decipher the contents of memory in our memory view program.

Pages and Kilobytes

The next structural level within memory consists of collections of bytes. One such level is the *page,* consisting of 256 bytes. There are 256 pages of memory within the Commodore 64 (256*256 =65536 bytes). Four pages (256*4 =1024) make up one K or kilobyte. The word *kilobyte* refers to 1024 rather than 1000 bytes since 1024 is two to the tenth power. A 64K computer has 64*1024 bytes or 65536 bytes.

Kinds of Memory

Memory may have many different functions. From a practical point of view, these functions can be separated into three different categories: memory available for user program space, memory used exclusively by the operating system (unavailable to the user), and memory which provides a connection between the computer's operating system and the user or his or her programs. The 64 has the unique ability to "shift" function of its memory space from one of these functions to the other. (See Jim Butterfield's "Commodore 64 Architecture," the next article in this book.) This chapter will be concerned with the memory functions of the computer in its normal configuration.

A Picture in Memory

Before embarking on our tour of the Commodore 64's memory, type in, SAVE, and RUN the program at the end of this section. The screen should be blank except for the words "LOADING MAZE." While the maze is loading, get a pencil or pen and prepare to take a few notes. In about one minute you will see a screen full of what may appear to be random characters.

These characters represent bytes in memory. In the upper-left corner of the screen is the decimal number of the first location shown; this number should be flashing. For example, if the flashing number is 100, then the first character shown is the character equivalent to what is stored in byte 100. Notice that the first few characters in the upper-left corner share the same space with the decimal number.

If you press the F1 or F3 keys, you can scroll backward and forward through memory. Use the screen display codes on pages 132-34 in your user's manual to decipher the numbers which represent the characters on the screen.

The Journey

Our journey begins at page zero. Move the display up or down until the number at the upper-left corner of the screen is at or near zero. Page zero takes up about one-fourth of the screen. Locations 161 and 162 are the most active locations visible in this area. These locations provide the internal clock for the system. Location 162 cycles through 256 times for each time that 161 changes.

Just below locations 161 and 162 on the screen are the locations which hold the value for the last key pressed: locations 197 and 203. These locations will change if you press a key. Press a few keys and watch the values change. The characters produced do not match the characters on the keys, but they do produce unique values for each key pressed.

Location 198 contains the number of keystrokes in the keyboard buffer. If you press many keys at one time, then this number increments to hold the keystroke values until they can be processed. Then, as the keystrokes are processed, the buffer gradually empties, and the value in location 198 returns to zero.

Page zero contains many locations specifically used by the operating system. Caution should be the rule when changing locations in this area.

The Stack

As you move forward within memory, the next activity that you see occurs in an area known as the stack. This area holds important information for both BASIC and machine language programs. The BASIC command GOSUB sends a program to the line indicated. The stack is where the computer stores the necessary information it needs to RETURN to the proper part in the program. Since this program contains subroutines which are repeatedly executing, the contents of the stack also display a pattern of repeated values.

Continue forward until the screen contains no activity. When the value in the upper-left corner is around 820, you are looking at the cassette buffer. The cassette buffer provides a good place for machine language programs. Since it is unused by the operating system except for tape input and output, values can be safely stored in and retrieved from this section of memory. If you scroll past the cassette buffer, you will find screen memory. Screen memory provides an interesting phenomenon: like a mirror, screen memory is now looking at itself. This phenomenon produces a delayed reaction time while the program copies the new contents of screen memory to itself.

Past screen memory, the contents of the BASIC program are visible. If you look closely in this area, you can see bits and pieces of the BASIC program. The BASIC commands are unrecognizable in their normal form but are "tokenized" into unique numbers.

At the end of our relatively small BASIC program, a pattern of characters continues until it ceases around 32768. Here, I have placed a simple interface between the user and memory. Hit the CLR key. The screen should freeze for a few moments. Continue forward in memory until you find a clear screen. Now type a few words and watch them appear on the screen. If you wish to delete, merely use the delete key. The cursor control keys work, but no visible cursor can be found. This display of typed characters demonstrates how memory is used to store data. Word processors utilize memory in just this fashion.

The Journey Continues

Continue forward in memory until the pattern of memory changes to random characters. This is the end of free memory for user BASIC programs. The next area in memory contains the BASIC ROM. This area begins at 40960 and contains the machine language program which runs the BASIC language. If you hit

SHIFT and the COMMODORE key simultaneously to put the machine into lowercase mode, then you may even see some of the error messages that BASIC utilizes.

Continue even further to around 49152, and you will see the maze that was generated while you were waiting for the program to begin. Use the lower two function keys to center the maze and then scroll through it. After 49152 ($C000) there are four kilobytes of user area available to the programmer. The first part of this area is where the machine language for this program resides. The rest of it is used for the maze. Since the 64 contains large quantities of RAM available for programs or other data, you can place any sort of design or playfield into memory and scroll through it. Think of the fantastic adventure games you could create.

Nearing the End of the Journey

Continue past 50000 and we enter the area of input/output devices. First, the 6566 chip with its periodic raster scans which constantly change. Further within the code, the next obvious area of change is the color RAM. The first nybble of each byte in this area contains the color for the screen, while the other nybble contains random values. This produces an almost hypnotic effect on the screen as the values change continuously. (Due to a change in operating systems, some 64s may not contain random values in the upper nybble of color memory.) The last area of memory is the Kernal ROM (57344-). Change to lowercase and you can see the Commodore logo which is on the screen upon power-up. I/O (Input/Output) messages are also found in this area.

If you continue further than 65536, then your trip begins again back at zero page.

We have made the journey through over 65,000 bytes of memory and have seen how the operating system interacts with the user and how the user can use the memory as a palette for his or her own designs. I hope our trip has provided you with new ideas for better use of the vast quantities of memory on the Commodore 64.

A Look at Memory

```
1 POKE53281,1:GOSUB190:GOSUB300
2 X=0:POKE191,0:POKE55,0:POKE56,128:R=33
  024
3 IFPEEK(191)=255ORPEEK(191)=0THENPOKE19
  1,PEEK(191)
```

```
5 GOSUB1000
10 A=PEEK(197):IFA=4THENX=X+40:IFX+40>25
   5THENX=X+40-256:Fl=1:GOTO20
11 A=PEEK(197):IFA=3THENX=X+1:IFX+1>255T
   HENX=X+1-256:Fl=1:GOTO20
12 A=PEEK(197):IFA=6THENX=X-1:IFX+1<0THE
   NX=X+1+256:Fl=1:GOTO20
13 A=PEEK(197):IFA=5THENX=X-40:IFX-40<0T
   HENX=256+X-40:Bl=1:GOTO25
20 IFPEEK(191)<>255THENIFA=4ANDFl=1THENZ
   =1:POKE191,PEEK(191)+Z:Fl=0:GOTO28
21 IFPEEK(191)=255THENIFA=4ANDFl=1THENZ=
   1:POKE191,PEEK(191)-256+Z:Fl=0:GOTO28
22 IFPEEK(191)=0THENIFA=5ANDBl=1THENZ=-1
   :POKE191,PEEK(191)+256+Z:Bl=0:GOTO28
25 IFPEEK(191)<>0THENIFA=5ANDBl=1THENZ=-
   1:POKE191,PEEK(191)+Z:Bl=0
28 IFPEEK(191)=255ANDPEEK(2)=255THENPOKE
   191,0:POKE2,0
35 IFX>255THENX=255
36 IFX<0THENX=0
39 POKE2,X:SYS49152
40 PRINT"{HOME}";PEEK(191)*256+PEEK(2);:
   GOTO3
190 FORR=49152TO49152+65:READJ:POKER,J:N
    EXT:RETURN
200 DATA 165, 2, 133, 251, 165, 191, 133
    , 252, 169, 0, 133
210 DATA 253, 169, 4, 133, 254, 162, 4,
    177, 251, 145
220 DATA 253, 200, 208, 249, 230, 252, 2
    30, 254, 202, 208
230 DATA 242, 169, 0, 133, 251, 169, 216
    , 133, 252, 162
240 DATA 4, 169, 0, 145, 251, 200, 208,
    251, 230, 252
250 DATA 202, 208, 246, 96, 0, 255, 255,
    0, 0, 255
260 DATA 255, 40, 10, 255, 255
300 DIMA(3)
310 A(0)=2:A(1)=-80:A(2)=-2:A(3)=80
320 WL=160:HL=32:SC=49658:A=SC+81
330 PRINT"{CLR}{BLK}LOADING MAZE (C. BON
    D)"
340 FORZ=SCTOSC+40:POKEZ,160:NEXT
350 FORM=SCTOSC+3072:POKEM,160:NEXT
360 FORM=SCTOSC+3072STEP40:POKEM,32:NEXT
370 FORM=SC+39TOSC+3072STEP40:POKEM,32:N
    EXT
```

```
410 POKEA,4
420 J=INT(RND(1)*4):X=J
430 B=A+A(J):IFPEEK(B)=WLTHENPOKEB,J:POK
    EA+A(J)/2,HL:A=B:GOTO420
440 J=(J+1)*-(J<3):IFJ<>XTHEN430
450 J=PEEK(A):POKEA,HL:IFJ<4THENA=A-A(J)
    :GOTO420
500 J=2
510 RETURN
1000 REM
1010 GETD$:IFD$=""THEN1040
1011 IFD$=CHR$(20)THENPOKER,32:POKER+1,3
     2:R=R-1:GOTO1040
1012 IF D$=CHR$(157)THEN:R=R-1:GOTO1040
1013 IF D$=CHR$(29)THENR=R+1:GOTO1040
1014 IF D$=CHR$(145)THENR=R-41:GOTO1040
1015 IF D$=CHR$(17)THENR=R+39:GOTO1040
1016 IF D$=CHR$(133)ORD$=CHR$(134)THEN10
     40
1017 IF D$="{CLR}"THENFORT=RTOR+1024:POK
     ET,32:NEXT:GOTO1040
1020 E=ASC(D$):IFE>64THENE=E-64
1030 R=R+1:IFR<40959ANDR>32768THENPOKER,
     E
1040 RETURN
```

Commodore 64 Architecture

Jim Butterfield

This article allows you a peek inside the structure of the Commodore 64 and demonstrates some of its extraordinary features.

Let's build a Commodore 64 — at least in principle. We'll put the memory elements together and see how they all fit.

RAM — 64K

We start with a full 64K of RAM. That's the maximum amount of memory that the 6510 microprocessor chip can address.

If we stopped at this point, we'd have problems. First of all, the screen is fed from memory, but it would contain nonsense. We'll need to put in two extra things: a video chip, and a character generator for the video chip to use. Then again, we have no programs of any sort, and no way to get them into RAM.

Building It Out

Here's what we will do: we'll add the extra features we need by piling them on top of RAM. That way, RAM will be "hidden" — if we look at that part of memory, we will see the new elements. But we'll include a set of switches which will allow us to "flip away" the overlaying material and expose the RAM beneath any time we choose. More about these later.

Keep in mind: the RAM is still there, but it's hidden behind the new chips.

Input/Output

We'll take the block of memory at hexadecimal D000 to DFFF and reserve it for our interface chips. These include two CIAs for timing and input/output, a SID chip for sound, and a video chip to deliver a screen to the television set.

About the 6566 video chip: its "registers" are located at hex D000 to D02E; these locations control how the chip works. But when the video chip needs information to put on the screen, it gets it directly from RAM memory. For example, the usual place for the screen characters is hex 0400 to 07E7. There's a distinction here: we control or check the chip by using its register addresses, but the chip gets display information from almost anywhere it likes.

The video chip needs to look at RAM to get characters for the screen. It also needs to look somewhere else to get a "picture" of each character; this allows it to light up the individual dots, or "pixels," that make up a character. There needs to be a table which gives details of each character: what it looks like, and how to draw it. This table is called the Character Base Table; hardware types may just call it the character generator.

We could put this Character Base Table in RAM and point the video chip to it. In fact, we are likely to do this if we want to define our own graphics. But on a standard 64, we'd just as soon have these characters built-in, in other words, we'll put the Character Base Table into ROM memory.

Now comes the tricky bit. We will put our ROM character base (it's 4K long when we allow for both graphics and text) into locations hex D000 to DFFF. Wait a minute! We just put our interface chips there!

No problem. We just pile the memory elements higher. The ROM character base sits above the RAM, and then we put the I/O on top. Any time we PEEK these locations, we'll see the I/O. The video chip, by the way, has a special circuit allowing it to go directly to the ROM character base, so there's no confusion there.

If you wanted to look at the character ROM, you'd have to flip it to the top somehow. It turns out you are allowed to do this: clearing bit two of address one will do the trick. But be sure you disable the interrupt first, or you're in serious trouble. After all, the interrupt routines expect the I/O to be in place. Bit 2 of address 0 is called the CHAREN control line.

Let's look at a small part of the character base — in BASIC! Be sure to do this on a single line, or as part of a program. First, to turn the interrupt off and back on again:

```
POKE 56333,127:... ...:POKE 56333,129
```

Now, while the interrupt is disabled, flip in the character base:

```
POKE 56333,127:POKE 1,51:...:POKE 1,55:POK
E 56333,129
```

Finally, let's PEEK at part of a character:

```
POKE 56333,127:POKE1,51:X=PEEK(53248):POK
E 1,55:POKE 56333,129:PRINT X
```

You should see a value of 60; this is the top of the @ character. To see its pixels, we would write it in binary as 00111100 and to see the next line of pixels we would repeat the above code with X =PEEK(53249).

Remember that this is ROM; we can PEEK but can't POKE. If we wanted a new character set, we would point the video chip to some new location.

Kernal ROM

To allow the computer to work at all, we must have an operating system in place. The 64's system is called the Kernal: it's in ROM, and placed above RAM at addresses $E000 to $FFFF.

We can flip the Kernal away and expose the RAM beneath by clearing bit one of address one. Be very careful! The computer can't exist for long without an operating system. Either put one into the RAM or be prepared for a crash.

Even if you flip out the Kernal for a moment, you must be sure to disable the interrupt. The interrupt vectors themselves are in the Kernal; if the interrupt strikes while the Kernal is flipped away, we'll have utter confusion.

Flipping out the Kernal automatically flips out BASIC as well. So bit one of address one, called the HIRAM control bit, switches out both ROMs. We can switch BASIC alone, however, by using bit zero — the LORAM control bit.

BASIC ROM

To run BASIC, we have another ROM which is placed above RAM at addresses $A000 to $BFFF. We may flip it out by clearing bit zero (mask one) of address one.

This is a very useful thing to do. When a word processor, spreadsheet calculator, or other program is in the computer, we may not need BASIC at all. Flip it away, and we have extra memory for our program.

Do Your Own BASIC

We can do even more. If we copy BASIC — carefully! — from its ROM into the RAM behind it, we can get BASIC-in-RAM — a BASIC we can change to meet our own needs.

Let's do this, just to show how. Type the following program into your Commodore 64:

```
100 FOR J=40960 TO 49151
110 POKE J, PEEK(J)
120 NEXT J
```

Run the program. It will take a minute or so. While it's running, let's talk about that curious line 110. What's the point in POKEing a value into memory identical to what's already there? Here's the secret: when we PEEK, we see the BASIC ROM; but when we POKE, we store information into the RAM beneath.

The program should say READY; now we have made a copy of BASIC in the corresponding RAM. Flip the ROM away with POKE 1,54. If the cursor is still flashing, we're there. BASIC is now in RAM. How can we prove this?

Let's try to fix one of my pet peeves (PET peeves?). Whenever I try to take the ASC value of a null string, BASIC refuses. Try it:

PRINT ASC(" ")
.. will yield an ?ILLEGAL QUANTITY ERROR.

Now, it's my fixation that you should be able to take the ASCII value of a null string, and have BASIC give you a value of zero. (Don't ask why; that would take a couple more pages.) By peering inside BASIC, I have established that the situation can be changed by modifying the contents of address 46991. There is usually a value of eight there. Normally, we couldn't change it: it's in ROM. But now BASIC is in RAM, and we'll change the ASC function slightly by:

```
POKE 46991,5
```

Now try PRINT ASC(" "); it will print a value of zero. In every other way, BASIC is exactly the same.

Just for fun: you can change some of BASIC's keywords or error messages to create your own style of machine. For example, POKE 41122,69 changes the FOR keyword ; you must type the new keyword to get the FOR action. Say LIST and see how line 100 has changed. Alternatively, POKE 41230,85; now you must say LUST instead of LIST.

You may go back to ROM BASIC at any time with a POKE 1,55.

Combination Switch

When we use the HIRAM control to flip out the Kernal, BASIC ROM is also removed. Is there any point in flipping both HIRAM and LORAM? If you do, the I/O and Character Generator also disappear, giving you a solid 64K of RAM. You can't talk to anybody, since you have no I/O, but you can do it.

We have named three control lines: CHAREN, which flips I/O with the Character Base; HIRAM, which flips out Kernal and BASIC ROMs; and LORAM, which controls BASIC. In my memory maps I've called them D-ROM switch, EF-RAM switch, and AB-RAM switch in an attempt to make them more descriptive.

But there are two other control lines, and your program cannot get to them. They are called EXROM and GAME and may be changed only by plugging a cartridge into the expansion slot. When these lines are switched by appropriate wiring inside the cartridge, the memory map changes once again.

But that's another story.

For the first time, the machine's architecture is at your disposal. If you don't like BASIC, throw it out and replace it with your own. The same is true of the Kernal operating system; it's accessible or replaceable.

New horizons are opening. We'll need to do a lot of traveling to reach them.

Commodore 64 Memory

Addresses shown in hexadecimal.

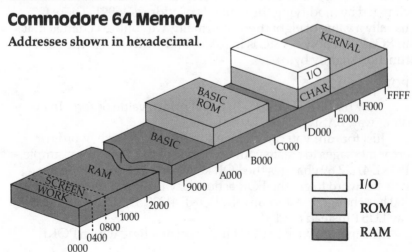

Commodore 64 Memory Map

Compiled by Jim Butterfield

Hex	Decimal	Description
0000	0	Chip data direction register
0001	1	Chip I/O; memory and tape control
0003-0004	3-4	Float-Fixed vector
0005-0006	5-6	Fixed-Float vector
0007	7	Search character
0008	8	Scan-quotes flag
0009	9	TAB column save
000A	10	0 =LOAD, 1 =VERIFY
000B	11	Input buffer pointer/ # subscript
000C	12	Default DIM flag
000D	13	Type: FF =string, 00 =numeric
000E	14	Type: 80 =integer, 00 =floating point
000F	15	DATA scan/LIST quote/memory flag
0010	16	Subscript/FNx flag
0011	17	0 =INPUT; $40 =GET; $98 =READ
0012	18	ATN sign/Comparison eval flag
0013	19	Current I/O prompt flag
0014-0015	20-21	Integer value
0016	22	Pointer: temporary string stack
0017-0018	23-24	Last temporary string vector
0019-0021	25-33	Stack for temporary strings
0022-0025	34-37	Utility pointer area
0026-002A	38-42	Product area for multiplication
002B-002C	43-44	Pointer: Start-of-BASIC
002D-002E	45-46	Pointer: Start-of-Variables
002F-0030	47-48	Pointer: Start-of-Arrays
0031-0032	49-50	Pointer: End-of-Arrays
0033-0034	51-52	Pointer: String-storage (moving down)
0035-0036	53-54	Utility string pointer
0037-0038	55-56	Pointer: Limit-of-memory
0039-003A	57-58	Current BASIC line number
003B-003C	59-60	Previous BASIC line number
003D-003E	61-62	Pointer: BASIC statement for CONT
003F-0040	63-64	Current DATA line number

0041-0042	65-66	Current DATA address
0043-0044	67-68	INPUT vector
0045-0046	69-70	Current variable name
0047-0048	71-72	Current variable address
0049-004A	73-74	Variable pointer for FOR/NEXT
004B-004C	75-76	Y-save; op-save; BASIC pointer save
004D	77	Comparison symbol accumulator
004E-0053	78-83	Miscellaneous work area, pointers, etc.
0054-0056	84-86	Jump vector for functions
0057-0060	87-96	Miscellaneous numeric work area
0061	97	Accum #1: Exponent
0062-0065	98-101	Accum #1: Mantissa
0066	102	Accum #1: Sign
0067	103	Series evaluation constant pointer
0068	104	Accum #1 hi-order (overflow)
0069-006E	105-110	Accum #2: Exponent, Mantissa, sign
006F	111	Sign comparison, Acc #1 vs #2
0070	112	Accum #1 lo-order (rounding)
0071-0072	113-114	Cassette buffer length/Series pointer
0073-008A	115-138	CHRGET subroutine; get BASIC character
007A-007B	122-123	BASIC pointer (within subroutine)
008B-008F	139-143	RND seed value
0090	144	Status word ST
0091	145	Keyswitch PIA: STOP and RVS flags
0092	146	Timing constant for tape
0093	147	LOAD =0, VERIFY =1
0094	148	Serial output: deferred character flag
0095	149	Serial deferred character
0096	150	Tape EOT received
0097	151	Register save
0098	152	Number of open files
0099	153	Input device, normally 0
009A	154	Output CMD device, normally 3
009B	155	Tape character parity
009C	156	Byte-received flag
009D	157	Run = 0, Direct mode = $80
009E	158	Tape Pass 1 error log/character buffer
009F	159	Tape Pass 2 error log corrected
00A0-00A2	160-162	Jiffy clock HML
00A3	163	Serial bit count/EOI flag
00A4	164	Cycle count
00A5	165	Countdown, tape write/bit count
00A6	166	Tape buffer pointer
00A7	167	Tp Wrt ldr count/Rd pass/inbit
00A8	168	Tp Wrt new byte/Rd error/inbit count
00A9	169	Wrt start bit/Rd bit err/stbit

00AA	170	Tp Scan; Count; Ld; End/byte assembly
00AB	171	Wr lead length/Rd checksum/parity
00AC-00AD	172-173	Pointer: tape buffer, scrolling
00AE-00AF	174-175	Tape end address/End of program
00B0-00B1	176-177	Tape timing constants
00B2-00B3	178-179	Pointer: start of tape buffer
00B4	180	1 =Tape timer enabled; bit count
00B5	181	Tape EOT/RS-232 next bit to send
00B6	182	Read character error/outbyte buffer
00B7	183	Number of characters in filename
00B8	184	Current logical file
00B9	185	Current secondary address
00BA	186	Current device
00BB-00BC	187-188	Pointer to filename
00BD	189	Wr shift word/Rd input character
00BE	190	# blocks remaining to Wr/Rd
00BF	191	Serial word buffer
00C0	192	Tape motor interlock
00C1-00C2	193-194	I/O start address
00C3-00C4	195-196	Kernal setup pointer
00C5	197	Last key pressed
00C6	198	Number of characters in keyboard buffer
00C7	199	Screen reverse flag
00C8	200	Pointer: end of line for INPUT
00C9-00CA	201-202	Input cursor log (row, column)
00CB	203	Which key: 64 if no key
00CC	204	0 =flash cursor
00CD	205	Cursor timing countdown
00CE	206	Character under cursor
00CF	207	Cursor in blink phase
00D0	208	Input from screen/from keyboard
00D1-00D2	209-210	Pointer to screen line
00D3	211	Position of cursor on above line
00D4	212	Quote mode flag, 0 = off
00D5	213	Current screen line length
00D6	214	Row where cursor lives
00D7	215	Last inkey/checksum/buffer
00D8	216	Number of INSERTs outstanding
00D9-00F2	217-242	Screen line link table
00F3-00F4	243-244	Screen color pointer
00F5-00F6	245-246	Keyboard pointer
00F7-00F8	247-248	Pointer: RS-232 input buffer
00F9-00FA	249-250	Pointer: RS-232 output buffer
0100-010A	256-266	Floating point to ASCII work area
0100-013E	256-318	Tape error log
0100-01FF	256-511	Processor stack area

0200-0258	512-600	BASIC input buffer
0259-0262	601-610	Logical file table
0263-026C	611-620	Device # table
026D-0276	621-630	Secondary address table
0277-0280	631-640	Keyboard buffer
0281-0282	641-642	Start of BASIC Memory
0283-0284	643-644	Top of BASIC Memory
0285	645	Serial bus time-out flag
0286	646	Current color code
0287	647	Color under cursor
0288	648	Screen memory page
0289	649	Maximum size of keyboard buffer
028A	650	Repeat all keys
028B	651	Repeat speed counter
028C	652	Repeat delay counter
028D	653	Keyboard Shift/Control flag
028E	654	Last shift pattern
028F-0290	655-656	Pointer: keyboard table setup
0291	657	Keyboard shift mode
0292	658	0 =scroll enable
0293	659	RS-232 control register
0294	660	RS-232 command register
0295-0296	661-662	Bit timing
0297	663	RS-232 status register
0298	664	Number of bits to send
0299-029A	665-666	RS-232 speed/code
029B	667	RS-232 end of input buffer index
029C	668	RS-232 start of input buffer
029D	669	RS-232 start of output buffer
029E	670	RS-232 end of output buffer index
029F-02A0	671-672	IRQ save during tape I/O
02A1	673	CIA2 (NMI) Interrupt Control
02A2	674	CIA1 Timer A control log
02A3	675	CIA1 Interrupt Log
02A4	676	CIA1 Timer A enabled flag
02A5	677	Screen row marker
02C0-02FE	704-766	(Sprite 11)
0300-0301	768-769	Error message link
0302-0303	770-771	BASIC warm start link
0304-0305	772-773	Crunch BASIC tokens link
0306-0307	774-775	Print tokens link
0308-0309	776-777	Start new BASIC code link
030A-030B	778-779	Get arithmetic element link
030C	780	6510 accumulator store
030D	781	6510 X-register store
030E	782	6510 Y-register store

030F	783	6510 status register store	
0310	784	USR function jump instruction	(4C)
0311-0312	785-786	USR function jump address	(B248)
0313	787	Unused	
0314-0315	788-789	Hardware interrupt vector	(EA31)
0316-0317	790-791	Break interrupt vector	(FE66)
0318-0319	792-793	NMI interrupt vector	(FE47)
031A-031B	794-795	OPEN vector	(F34A)
031C-031D	796-797	CLOSE vector	(F291)
031E-031F	798-799	Set-input vector	(F20E)
0320-0321	800-801	Set-output vector	(F250)
0322-0323	802-803	Restore I/O vector	(F333)
0324-0325	804-805	INPUT vector	(F157)
0326-0327	806-807	Output vector	(F1CA)
0328-0329	808-809	Test-STOP vector	(F6ED)
032A-032B	810-811	GET vector	(F13E)
032C-032D	812-813	Abort I/O vector	(F32F)
032E-032F	814-815	Warm start vector	(FE66)
0330-0331	816-817	LOAD vector	(F4A5)
0332-0333	818-819	SAVE vector	(F5ED)
0334-033B	820-827	Unused	
033C-03FB	828-1019	Cassette buffer	
0340-037E	832-894	(Sprite 13)	
0380-03BE	896-958	(Sprite 14)	
03C0-03FE	960-1022	(Sprite 15)	
0400-07FF	1024-2047	Screen memory	
0800-9FFF	2048-40959	BASIC RAM memory	
8000-9FFF	32768-40959	Alternate: ROM plug-in area	
A000-BFFF	40960-49151	ROM: BASIC	
A000-BFFF	49060-49151	Alternate: RAM	
C000-CFFF	49152-53247	RAM memory, including alternate	
D000-D02E	53248-53294	Video Chip (6566)	
D400-D41C	54272-54300	Sound Chip (6581 SID)	
D800-DBFF	55296-56319	Color nybble memory	
DC00-DC0F	56320-56335	Interface chip 1, IRQ (6526 CIA)	
DD00-DD0F	56576-56591	Interface chip 2, NMI (6526 CIA)	
D000-DFFF	53248-57294	Alternate: Character set	
E000-FFFF	57344-65535	ROM: Operating System	
E000-FFFF	57344-65535	Alternate: RAM	
FF81-FFF5	65409-65525	Jump Table, Including:	

    FFC6 - Set Input channel
    FFC9 - Set Output channel
    FFCC - Restore default I/O channels
    FFCF - INPUT
    FFD2 - PRINT
    FFE1 - Test Stop key
    FFE4 - GET

Figure 1. 6510 Processor I/O Port

	IN	IN	Out	IN	Out	Out	Out	Out		
$0000									DDR	0
$0001			Tape Motor	Tape Sense	Tape Write	D-Rom Switch	EF-RAM Switch	AB-RAM Switch	PR	1

Figure 2. 6566 SID Chip

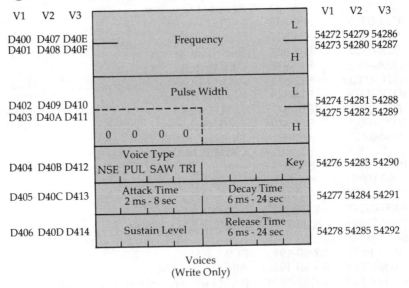

	V1	V2	V3			V1	V2	V3
	D400	D407	D40E	Frequency	L	54272	54279	54286
	D401	D408	D40F		H	54273	54280	54287
	D402	D409	D410	Pulse Width	L	54274	54281	54288
	D403	D40A	D411	0 0 0 0	H	54275	54282	54289
	D404	D40B	D412	Voice Type NSE PUL SAW TRI	Key	54276	54283	54290
	D405	D40C	D413	Attack Time 2 ms - 8 sec	Decay Time 6 ms - 24 sec	54277	54284	54291
	D406	D40D	D414	Sustain Level	Release Time 6 ms - 24 sec	54278	54285	54292

Voices
(Write Only)

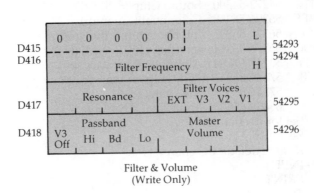

D415	0	0	0	0	0		L	54293
D416			Filter Frequency				H	54294
D417	Resonance			Filter Voices EXT V3 V2 V1				54295
D418	V3 Off	Passband Hi Bd Lo			Master Volume			54296

Filter & Volume
(Write Only)

188

D419	Paddle X	54297
D41A	Paddle Y	54298
D41B	Noise 3 (Random)	54299
D41C	Envelope 3	54300

(Read Only)   Sense

Special voice features (TEST, RING MOD, SYNC) are omitted from the above diagram.

Figure 3. 6526 CIA1 Chip

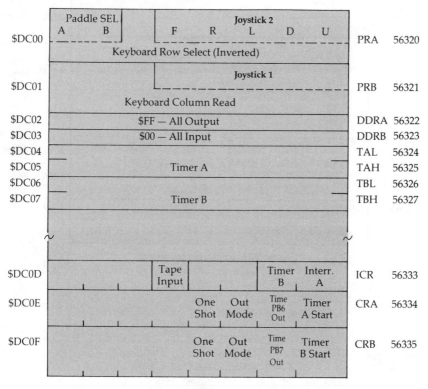

$DC00	Paddle SEL A B		Joystick 2 F R L D U					PRA	56320
	Keyboard Row Select (Inverted)								
$DC01			Joystick 1					PRB	56321
	Keyboard Column Read								
$DC02	$FF — All Output							DDRA	56322
$DC03	$00 — All Input							DDRB	56323
$DC04								TAL	56324
$DC05	Timer A							TAH	56325
$DC06								TBL	56326
$DC07	Timer B							TBH	56327
$DC0D			Tape Input		Timer B	Interr. A		ICR	56333
$DC0E			One Shot	Out Mode	Time PB6 Out	Timer A Start		CRA	56334
$DC0F			One Shot	Out Mode	Time PB7 Out	Timer B Start		CRB	56335

189

Figure 4. 6526 CIA2 Chip

$DD00	Serial In	Clock In	Serial Out	Clock Out	ATN Out	RS-232 Out			PRA	56576
$DD01	DSR In	CTS In		DCD* In	RI* In	DTR Out	RTS* Out	RS-232 In	PRB	56577
			Parallel User Port							
$DD02	IN	IN	Out	Out	Out $3F	Out	Out	Out	DDRA	56578
$DD03	$06 For RS-232								DDRB	56579
$DD04 $DD05	Timer A							—	TAL TAH	56580 56581
$DD06 $DD07	Timer B							—	TBL TBH	56582 56583
~								~		
$DD0D			RS-232 In			Timer B	Timer A		ICR	56589
$DD0E							Timer A Start		CRA	56590
$DD0F							Timer B Start		CRB	56591

*Connected but not used by system.

Soft-16

Douglas D. Nicoll

This program, "USR(PEEK)", demonstrates several interesting concepts about managing the memory of the 64. BASIC programs can be run essentially without BASIC, and you can switch between ROM and RAM during a program RUN to access an additional 16K of RAM for data storage. You'll also see how to use the USR( ) statement.

An inexpensive 16K RAM expansion for the Commodore 64? Run BASIC programs without BASIC or the Kernal? Well, almost. The 6510 microprocessor has the three ROM banks (BASIC [AB] $A000-$BFFF; characters [D] $D000-$DFFF; and Kernal [EF] $E000-$F000) with blocks of RAM. It switches between ROM and RAM with the control port located at $0001. Bit zero in $0001 controls AB, bit one controls EF, and bit two controls D. Setting the bit to one switches in ROM (the normal state), and zero switches in RAM memory.

   In normal BASIC operation, it is possible to POKE values to the RAM at the AB and EF locations, but PEEKing these locations will show *only* the ROM data. POKEs and PEEKs to the RAM at D work fine, but you can't PEEK the character ROM without setting a number of switches so the system won't crash. Thus, without the ability to PEEK the hidden RAM memory, AB and EF locations are effectively eliminated from use in BASIC programs.

   "USR(PEEK)" is a valuable machine language utility program that opens up the hidden RAM for use in BASIC programs, giving the user 16K of additional memory for data storage. The program is loaded into $C001-$C0E4 and uses $C000 as a temporary storage cell. The vector for the USR( ) function is set (POKE 785,1:POKE 786,192). BASIC programs are loaded normally, and any RAM location can be PEEKed by using X =USR(N), where X is any variable and N is any number from 1 to 65535. Any number less than 0.5 will set X to -1, 0.5 to 1.9 evaluate as 1, and all other decimal numbers are truncated to the integer. If a negative number is given for N, the value returned is for ABS(N). If a number is greater than 65535, then X is -1. If N is between 53248 and 57343, X is the value of data stored in character ROM (D).

Automatic Switching

How does USR(PEEK) work? The statement X =USR(N) in a
BASIC program loads N into the floating point accumulator and
sends the computer to the machine language program pointed to
by the USR vector. The machine language program evaluates the
number in the FP accumulator, switches out BASIC and Kernal
ROM, loads the desired RAM data into the FP accumulator,
switches BASIC and Kernal ROM back in, and finally sets up the
FP accumulator so that X contains the values on return to the
BASIC program. When character ROM is desired, it is switched in
for the manipulation.

The techniques used to dynamically switch between RAM
and ROM have many other uses for programmers who use both
BASIC and machine language. For example, machine language
programs can be LOADed under BASIC or Kernal ROM and run
with BASIC programs — this leaves more space for BASIC programs and variable storage. It is possible to envision LOADing a
BASIC program editor under BASIC ROM and calling it for re-
numbering, searching, etc.

Type in the program and, after saving a copy, RUN it to see a
demonstration of how easy it is to use. Then eliminate lines 10-540
and SAVE it with the name USR(PEEK). To use with your programs, LOAD and RUN USR(PEEK) and then LOAD and RUN
your own BASIC programs that can be constructed to utilize the
additional 16K of RAM data storage.

USR (PEEK)

```
1 GOSUB1000:REM SET UP USR(PEEK)
5 REM**{9 SPACES}USR(PEEK){12 SPACES}**
10 PRINT"{CLR}USR(PEEK) AT CHARACTER ROM
   "
20 V$="{HOME}{24 DOWN}"
30 H$=""+"{39 RIGHT}"
40 UC=53248:LC=55296:GC=53760
50 H=0:V=10:L=83*8+UC:GOSUB500
60 H=8:V=10:L=3*8+UC:GOSUB500
70 H=14:V=5:L=85*8+UC:GOSUB500:H=14:V=14
   :L=74*8+UC:GOSUB500
80 H=22:V=10:L=54*8+UC:GOSUB500
90 H=30:V=10:L=52*8+UC:GOSUB500
100 PRINTLEFT$(V$,5);LEFT$(H$,18);"SC
    {UP}U{2 DOWN}{LEFT}J{UP}64";LEFT$(V$
    ,22)
110 PRINT"PRESS ANY KEY TO CONTINUE";
```

```
120 GETA$:IFA$=""THEN120
130 PRINT"{CLR}USR(PEEK) INTO BASIC HIDD
    EN RAM"
140 PRINTLEFT$(V$,5);"INPUT 10 NUMERS(0-
    255) TO STORE IN $A000TO $A00A :"
150 FORI=1TO10
160 PRINT"NUMBER ";I;": ";:INPUT"";X
170 IFINT(X)<>XORX<0ORX>255THENPRINT"INV
    ALID ENTRY...":GOTO160
180 POKE40959+I,X:NEXT
190 PRINT"{CLR}USR(PEEK) INTO HIDDEN BAS
    IC RAM"
200 PRINT:PRINT:PRINT"LOCATION{3 SPACES}
    PEEK{3 SPACES}USR(PEEK)"
205 PRINT"-------------------------"
210 FORI=1TO10:PRINTI+40959,PEEK(I+40959
    ),USR(I+40959):NEXT
220 PRINTLEFT$(V$,22);"PRESS ANY KEY TO
    CONTINUE ";
230 GETA$:IFA$=""THEN230
240 PRINT"{CLR}USR(PEEK) INTO KERNAL HID
    DEN RAM"
250 PRINTLEFT$(V$,5);"INPUT 10 NUMERS(0-
    255) TO STORE IN $F000TO $F00A :"
260 FORI=1TO10
270 PRINT"NUMBER ";I;": ";:INPUT"";X
280 IFINT(X)<>XORX<0ORX>255THENPRINT"INV
    ALID ENTRY...":GOTO160
290 POKE61439+I,X:NEXT
300 PRINT"{CLR}USR(PEEK) INTO HIDDEN KER
    NAL RAM"
310 PRINT:PRINT:PRINT"LOCATION{3 SPACES}
    PEEK{3 SPACES}USR(PEEK)"
320 PRINT"-------------------------"
330 FORI=1TO10:PRINTI+61439,PEEK(I+61439
    ),USR(I+61439):NEXT
340 END
500 FORJ=LTOL+7:X$="":X=USR(J)
510 FORI=7TO0STEP-1:IFX=>2↑ITHENX=X-2↑I:
    X$=X$+"{WHT}{RVS} {OFF}":GOTO530
520 X$=X$+"{RIGHT}"
530 NEXTI:IFJ=LTHENPRINTLEFT$(V$,V);
540 PRINTLEFT$(H$,H);X$:NEXT:RETURN
1000 POKE785,1:POKE786,192:REM USR VECTO
     R
1010 FORI=49153TO49380:READX:POKEI,X:NEX
     T
1015 RETURN
```

```
1020 DATA173,97,0,201,144,208,3,76,188,1
     92,56,201,128,176,3,76,163,192,201,
     145
1030 DATA144,3,76,163,192,73,128,141,97,
     0,56,169,16,237,97,0,240,13,170,24
1040 DATA78,98,0,110,99,0,202,224,0,208,
     244,173,98,0,141,78,192,173,99,0
1050 DATA141,77,192,173,1,0,141,0,192,12
     0,73,7,141,1,0,173,255,255,141,98,0
1060 DATA173,0,192,141,1,0,88,173,98,0,2
     01,0,208,3,76,140,192,162,8,173,98,
     0
1070 DATA24,42,176,5,202,224,0,208,247,1
     06,141,98,0,73,128,141,102,0,138
1080 DATA9,128,141,97,0,169,0,141,99,0,1
     41,100,0,141,101,0,96,169,0,141,97,
     0
1090 DATA141,99,0,141,100,0,141,101,0,14
     1,102,0,169,128,141,98,0,96,169,129
1100 DATA141,97,0,169,128,141,98,0,141,1
     02,0,169,0,141,99,0,141,100,0,141,1
     01,0
1110 DATA96,56,173,98,0,201,224,144,3,76
     ,223,192,201,208,176,3,76,223,192,1
     69,4
1120 DATA141,72,192,173,97,0,32,26,192,1
     69,7,141,72,192,96,173,97,0,76,11,1
     92
```

Chapter 8

Advanced Memory

Assembler in BASIC

Ronald Thibault

Here is a symbolic Assembler in BASIC for the Commodore 64. The original version of this was written by Eric Brandon for the PET. I modified this Assembler because there were none available for the 64 and no symbolic assemblers that use only a cassette (I have no disk). [Disk users need only make the changes shown in lines 12025 and 13025 — Editor.] In addition, being cheap, this Assembler is good for those who are just starting out in machine language programming.

A symbolic assembler is one that allows the use of variable names in the label and operand fields. This Assembler could also be used on many other machines using the 6502 with slight modifications, most notably the LOAD and SAVE commands.

Since the Assembler is in BASIC, it does have a couple of disadvantages. The first is that it is slow. The other is that, because it resides in memory and needs the BASIC Interpreter, the amount of memory available for machine language programs is reduced.

The major additions to the Assembler from the original are:

1. Bounds checking on the commands that affect the line numbers.
2. The LOAD and SAVE commands modified for cassette.
3. Compact Command eliminates blank lines between code.
4. 40-column screen printout.
5. Instructions internal to the program.

The Assembly Listing
The assembled listing is broken into two segments: the first segment is the memory locations of the variables and labels; the second is the actual code. The format is as follows:

Column	Value
0-5	Line #
6-10	Start of Instruction Address
11-13	Opcode Value

14-16 & 17-19	Other Bytes of Instruction
20-26	Label Field
27-30	Opcode Field
31-40	Operand Field

A note about this program specifically and all Commodore 64 programs in general. This listing (except where all code would not fit on the line) has spaces between code elements to make it more readable. Now that we have more memory available there is no longer a need to compact the code just to fit it in memory. The spaces and REM statements (remember them?) can be taken out later for speed. It is much easier to type in and correct/modify readable code instead of 80-character strings. So start putting in spaces and REM statements.

Also, you will notice that in the instructions portion of the program there is code that stops the printing of the instructions after the screen is full, until any key is hit. This is of great help to those of us without printers who cannot read 800 characters per minute.

Typing in the Assembler in BASIC

I have left spaces between the code elements to make the code more readable. I have omitted the spaces when the line would not fit otherwise. If you wish to save typing and memory space, the spaces and REM statements can be removed. The instructions come at the end of the listing. With the proper adjustments to the code, the instructions can also be removed.

Well, there it is. You are now ready to begin writing your machine language routines using this BASIC Assembler.

BASIC Assembler / Editor

```
1 REM ASSEMBLER/EDITOR 2.0 -MODIFIED FOR
  {SPACE}C-64
2 MEM=50:M2=20
5 PRINT"{CLR}{WHT}":POKE 53281,0:POKE 532
  80,11
6 PRINT"INTRUCTIONS ? (Y/N)";
8 GET Z$:IF Z$="" OR (Z$<>"Y" AND Z$<>"N"
  ) THEN 8
9 IF Z$="Y" THEN GOSUB 11000
10 PRINT"{CLR}"
11 DIM A$(MEM),S$(M2),V(M2),LI(3)
15 H$="0123456789ABCDEF"
100 LN=1
110 PRINT LN;:TB=5:LT=6:GOSUB 4000:IF IN$
   ="EXIT" THEN 300
```

```
120 IF IN$="FIX" THEN LN=LN-1:PRINT CHR$(
    -13*(ASC(GT$)<>13));:GOTO 110
125 IF GT$=CHR$(13) THEN PRINT"{UP}";
126 IF LN>MEM THEN PRINT"{DOWN}{RIGHT}
    {RVS}LINE LIMIT EXCEEDED":GOTO 300
130 A$(LN)=IN$+" ":TB=13:LT=3:GOSUB 4000:
    A$(LN)=A$(LN)+IN$+" "
160 IF GT$=CHR$(13) THEN 200
170 TB=18:LT=10:GOSUB 4000:A$(LN)=A$(LN)+
    IN$
190 IF GT$<>CHR$(13) THEN PRINT
200 LN=LN+1:GOTO 110
300 PRINT"{DOWN}{RVS}C{OFF}OMPACT {RVS}I
    {OFF}NPUT {RVS}D{OFF}ELETE I{RVS}N
    {OFF}SERT"
305 PRINT"{RVS}L{OFF}IST {RVS}S{OFF}AVE L
    {RVS}O{OFF}AD {RVS}A{OFF}SSEMBLE
    {RVS}Q{OFF}UIT"
310 PRINT"COMMAND ?";
320 GET CM$:IF CM$="" THEN 320
325 PRINT CM$:IF CM$<>"I" THEN 360
340 INPUT"LINE ";LN:IF LN>MEM THEN PRINT"
    {RVS}LINE NUMBER TO LARGE":GOTO 300
345 IF LN<=0 THEN PRINT"{RVS}LINE NUMBER
    {SPACE}TO SMALL":GOTO 300
350 GOTO 110
360 IF CM$="O" THEN 12000
370 IF CM$="S" THEN 13000
410 IF CM$<>"D" THEN 460
420 INPUT"{DOWN}LINES - FROM,TO ";FL,LL
421 IF FL>LL THEN PRINT"{RVS}INCORRECT LI
    NE NUMBERS":GOTO 300
423 IF FL>MEM OR LL>MEM THEN PRINT"{RVS}L
    INE NUMBER TO LARGE":GOTO 300
424 IF FL<=0 OR LL<=0 THEN PRINT"{RVS}LIN
    E NUMBER TO SMALL":GOTO 300
425 IF FL<>LL THEN 430
427 FOR T=FL TO MEM-1:A$(T)=A$(T+1):NEXT
    {SPACE}T:GOTO 300
430 FOR T=LL TO MEM:A$(T-LL+FL)=A$(T):A$(
    T)="":NEXT T:GOTO 300
460 IF CM$<>"N" THEN 500
470 INPUT"FIRST LINE,NUMBER";FL,LL
474 IF FL>MEM THEN PRINT"{RVS}LINE NUMBER
    TO LARGE":GOTO 300
475 IF FL<=0 OR LL<=0 THEN PRINT"{RVS}INC
    ORRECT DATA":GOTO 300
476 MARK=0:FOR T=1 TO MEM:IF LEN(A$(T))>2
    THEN MARK= T
```

```
477 NEXT T
478 IF LL+MARK>MEM THEN PRINT"{RVS}NUMBER
    OF INSERTIONS TO LARGE":GOTO 300
480 FOR T=MEM-LL TO FL STEP-1:A$(T+LL)=A$
    (T):NEXT T
490 FOR T=FL TO FL+LL-1:A$(T)="":NEXT T:G
    OTO 300
500 IF CM$<>"L" THEN 580
510 INPUT"LINES FIRST,LAST";FL,LL
512 IF FL>LL THEN PRINT"{RVS}INCORRECT LI
    NE NUMBERS":GOTO 300
515 IF FL>MEM OR LL>MEM THEN PRINT"{RVS}L
    INE NUMBER TO LARGE":GOTO 300
517 IF FL<=0 OR LL<=0 TH?EN PRINT"{RVS}LIN
    E NUMBER TO SMALL":GOTO 300
521 FOR T=FL TO LL:IF LEN(A$(T))=0 THEN P
    RINT T:GOTO 565
525 LI(1)=0:LI(2)=0:LI(3)=0:LI=0:FOR Q=1
    {SPACE}TO LEN(A$(T))
540 IF MID$(A$(T),Q,1)=" " THEN LI=LI+1:L
    I(LI)=Q
545 NEXT Q:IF LI(3)=0 THEN LI(3)=Q-1
550 PRINT T TAB(5) LEFT$(A$(T),LI(1)) TAB
    (13) MID$(A$(T),LI(1)+1,LI(2)-LI(1));
560 PRINT TAB(18) RIGHT$(A$(T),LI(3)-LI(2
    )+1)
565 NEXT T:GOTO 300
580 IF CM$<>"Q" THEN 600
590 PRINT"{DOWN}GET BACK IN WITH {RVS}GOT
    O 300{OFF}":END
600 IF CM$<>"A" THEN 1300
605 PRINT"{CLR}{RVS}S{OFF}CREEN OR {RVS}P
    {OFF}RINTER ?";
610 GET DV$:IF DV$="" THEN 610
620 PRINT DV$:IF DV$="S" THEN DV=3:GOTO 6
    50
640 DV=4
650 CLOSE 1:OPEN 1,DV:SB=1
660 FOR T=1 TO MEM:GOSUB 10000:IF LB$=""
    {SPACE}THEN 710
670 IF OC$<>"=" THEN 700
680 GOSUB 6000:IF LB$="*" THEN PC=NU:OG=N
    U:GOTO 770
690 S$(SB)=LB$:V(SB)=NU:SB=SB+1
692 N=V(SB-1):GOSUB 9000
695 PRINT# 1,S$(SB-1)" =" LEFT$("
    {8 SPACES}",8-LEN(S$(SB-1)))"$"R$:GOT
    O 770
700 S$(SB)=LB$:V(SB)=PC:SB=SB+1
```

```
702 N=V(SB-1):GOSUB 9000
705 PRINT# 1,S$(SB-1)" =" LEFT$("
    {8 SPACES}",8-LEN(S$(SB-1)))"$"R$
710 IF OC$="" THEN 770
715 IF OP$="" THEN PC=PC+1:GOTO 770
717 IF OP$="A" THEN PC=PC+1:GOTO 770
720 IF LEFT$(OC$,1)<>"B" OR OC$="BIT" OR
    {SPACE}OC$="BRK" THEN 740
730 PC=PC+2:GOTO 770
740 IF LEFT$(OC$,1)="J" THEN PC=PC+3:GOTO
    770
750 GOSUB 6000:IF NU<256 THEN PC=PC+2:GOT
    O 770
760 PC=PC+3
770 NEXT T
790 PC=OG:ER=0
800 FOR T=1 TO MEM:GOSUB 10000:IF OC$=""
    {SPACE}THEN 1220
805 IF OC$="=" THEN O1$=OP$:MV$="
    {2 SPACES}":PC$="{4 SPACES}":IL=0:GOT
    O 1160
810 IF OP$="" THEN AM$="G":IL=1:GOTO 1060
820 IF OP$="A" THEN AM$="H":IL=1:GOTO 106
    0
825 X=0:Y=0:I=0:M=0:Z=0
830 FOR Q=1 TO LEN(OP$):Q$=MID$(OP$,Q,1):
    IF Q$=")" THEN I=1:GOTO 865
840 IF Q$="#" THEN M=1:GOTO 865
865 NEXT Q
866 FOR Q=1 TO LEN(OP$)-1:Q$=MID$(OP$,Q,2
    )
867 IF Q$=",Y" THEN Y=1:GOTO 870
868 IF Q$=",X" THEN X=1
870 NEXT Q
875 O1$=OP$:GOSUB 6000
876 IF NU<256 THEN Z=1
880 IF LEFT$(OC$,1)="B" AND OC$<>"BRK" AN
    D OC$<>"BIT" THEN 1000
890 IF Z THEN 940
900 IF X THEN AM$="K":GOTO 1030
910 IF Y THEN AM$="L":GOTO 1030
920 IF I THEN AM$="M":GOTO 1030
930 AM$="N":GOTO 1030
940 IF M THEN AM$="I":GOTO 1030
950 IF I AND Y THEN AM$="O":GOTO 1030
960 IF I AND X THEN AM$="P":GOTO 1030
970 IF X THEN AM$="Q":GOTO 1030
980 IF Y THEN AM$="R":GOTO 1030
990 AM$="S":GOTO 1030
```

```
1000 AM$="J":IF NU>PC+1 THEN OS=NU-PC-2:I
     F OS>127 THEN ER=1
1010 IF NUMBER<PC+1 THEN OS=254+NU-PC:IF
     {SPACE}OS<128 THEN ER=1
1020 IF ER=1 THEN PRINT"{RVS}TOO LONG CON
     DITIONAL BRANCH":GOTO 300
1025 FO=OS:IL=2:GOTO 1060
1030 IF Z=0 THEN 1050
1040 FO=NU:IL=2:GOTO 1060
1050 SO=INT(NU/256):FO=(NU/256-SO)*256:IL
     =3
1060 RESTORE:FOR W9=1 TO 56:READ I$:IF LE
     FT$(I$,3)=OC$ THEN CD$=I$:W9=100
1070 NEXT W9:IF W9=57 THEN PRINT"{RVS}ILL
     EGAL MNEMONIC":GOTO 300
1080 FOR W9=4 TO LEN(CD$) STEP 3:IF MID$(
     CD$,W9,1)=AM$ THEN LW=W9:W9=100
1090 NEXT W9:IF W9<100 THEN PRINT"{RVS}IL
     LEGAL ADDRESSING MODE":GOTO 300
1100 MV$=MID$(CD$,LW+1,2):N$=MV$:GOSUB 70
     00
1110 POKE PC,V:IF IL=1 THEN 1140
1120 POKE PC+1,FO:IF IL=2 THEN 1140
1130 POKE PC+2,SO
1140 N=PC:GOSUB 9000:PC$=R$:PC=PC+IL
1150 N=FO:GOSUB 9000:FO$=R$:N=SO:GOSUB 90
     00:SO$=R$
1160 IF IL<3 THEN SO$="{2 SPACES}"
1170 IF IL<2 THEN FO$="{2 SPACES}"
1175 IF AM$="H" THEN O1$="A"
1180 PRINT# 1,T LEFT$("{4 SPACES}",4-LEN(
     STR$(T))) PC$ " ";
1190 PRINT# 1,MV$ " " RIGHT$(FO$,2) " " R
     IGHT$(SO$,2) " ";
1200 PRINT# 1,LB$ LEFT$("{7 SPACES}",7-LE
     N(LB$)) OC$ LEFT$("{4 SPACES}",4-LEN
     (OC$));
1210 PRINT# 1,O1$:O1$=""
1220 NEXT T:CLOSE 1:GOTO 300
1300 IF CM$<>"C" THEN 320
1310 FOR T=1 TO MEM:IF LEN(A$(T))>2 THEN
     {SPACE}1340
1320 FOR TT=MEM TO T+1 STEP -1:IF LEN(A$(
     TT))>2 THEN A$(T)=A$(TT):MARK=TT
1330 NEXT TT:A$(MARK)=""
1340 NEXT T
1350 GOTO 300
3999 END
4000 IN$="":NL=0:PRINT TAB(TB);
```

```
4020 PRINT"{RVS} {OFF}{LEFT}";
4030 GET GT$:IF GT$="" THEN 4030
4031 IF GT$>"Z" OR GT$<" " AND GT$<> CHR$
     (13) AND GT$<>CHR$(20) THEN 4030
4035 NL=NL+1
4040 IF GT$=CHR$(20) OR GT$=CHR$(13) THEN
      4100
4045 IF GT$=" " THEN PRINT" ";:RETURN
4050 PRINT GT$;:IN$=IN$+GT$
4060 IF NL=LT THEN 4100
4070 GOTO 4020
4100 IF GT$<>CHR$(20) THEN 4150
4105 IF LEN(IN$)<2 THEN 4120
4110 PRINT" {2 LEFT}";:NL=NL-2:IN$=LEFT$(
     IN$,LEN(IN$)-1):GOTO 4020
4120 IF LEN(IN$)=0 THEN NL=NL-1:GOTO 4020
4130 PRINT" {2 LEFT}";:NL=NL-2:IN$="":GOT
     O 4020
4150 IF GT$=CHR$(13) THEN PRINT" "
4160 RETURN
5000 DATA ADCN6DS65I69K7DL79P61O71Q75
5010 DATA ANDN2DS25I29K3DL39P21O31Q35
5020 DATA ASLH0AN0ES06K1EQ16
5030 DATA BCCJ90,BCSJB0,BEQJF0
5060 DATA BITN2CS24
5070 DATA BMIJ30,BNEJD0,BPLJ10,BRKG00
5110 DATA BVCJ50,BVSJ70,CLCG18,CLDGD8
5150 DATA CLIG58,CLVGB8
5170 DATA CMPNCDSC5IC9KDDLD9PC1OD1QD5
5180 DATA CPXNECSE4IE0
5190 DATA CPYNCCSC4IC0
5200 DATA DECNCESC6KDEQD6
5210 DATA DEXGCA,DEYG88
5230 DATA EORN4DS45I49K5DL59P41O51Q55
5240 DATA INCNEEESE6KFEQF6
5250 DATA INXGE8,INYGC8
5270 DATA JMPN4CM6C
5280 DATA JSRN20
5290 DATA LDANADSA5IA9KBDLB9PA1OB1QB5
5300 DATA LDXNAESA6IA2LBERB6
5310 DATA LDYNACSA4IA0KBCQB4
5320 DATA LSRH4AN4ES46K5EQ56
5330 DATA NOPGEA
5340 DATA ORAN0DS05I09K1DL19P01O11Q15
5350 DATA PHAG48,PHPG08,PLAG68,PLPG28
5390 DATA ROLH2AN2ES26K3EQ36
5400 DATA RORH6AN6ES66K7EQ76
5410 DATA RTIG40,RTSG60
5430 DATA SBCNEDSE5IE9KFDLF9PE1OF1QF5
```

```
5440 DATA SECG38,SEDGF8,SEIG78
5470 DATA STAN8DS85K9DL99P81091Q95
5480 DATA STXN8ES86R96
5490 DATA STYN8CS84Q94
5500 DATA TAXGAA,TAYGA8,TSXGBA,TXAG8A
5510 DATA TXSG9A,TYAG98
6000 AD=0
6005 Q$=LEFT$(OP$,1):IF Q$="$" OR Q$="%"
     {SPACE}OR (ASC(Q$)>64 AND ASC(Q$)<91
     )THEN6030
6010 IF ASC(Q$)>47 AND ASC(Q$)<58 THEN 60
     30
6020 OP$=RIGHT$(OP$,LEN(OP$)-1):GOTO 6000
6030 Q$=RIGHT$(OP$,1):Q1=ASC(Q$):IF (Q1>4
     7 ANDQ1<58)OR(Q1>64 AND Q1<91)THEN60
     50
6035 IF Q$="+" THEN 6050
6040 OP$=LEFT$(OP$,LEN(OP$)-1):GOTO 6030
6050 IF RIGHT$(OP$,2)=",X" THEN OP$=LEFT$
     (OP$,LEN(OP$)-2)
6052 IF RIGHT$(OP$,2)=",Y" THEN OP$=LEFT$
     (OP$,LEN(OP$)-2)
6053 IF RIGHT$(OP$,1)=")" THEN OP$=LEFT$(
     OP$,LEN(OP$)-1)
6055 IF LEFT$(OP$,1)="$" THEN N$=OP$:GOSU
     B 7000:NUMBER=V:GOTO 6100
6060 IF LEFT$(OP$,1)="%" THEN N$=OP$:GOSU
     B 8000:NUMBER=V:GOTO 6100
6070 IF ASC(LEFT$(OP$,1))<58 THEN NUMBER=
     VAL(OP$):GOTO 6100
6075 IF RIGHT$(OP$,1)="+" THEN AD=AD+1:OP
     $=LEFT$(OP$,LEN(OP$)-1):GOTO 6075
6080 FOR W1=1 TO M2:IF S$(W1)=OP$ THEN NU
     MBER=V(W1):W1=999
6090 NEXT W1:IF W1=M2+1 THEN PRINT"{RVS}U
     NDEFINED SYMBOL ERROR":GOTO 300
6100 NU=NU+AD:RETURN
7000 IF LEFT$(N$,1)="$" THEN N$=RIGHT$(N$
     ,LEN(N$)-1)
7010 V=0:IF LEN(N$)=4 THEN 7030
7020 N$=LEFT$("0000",4-LEN(N$))+N$
7030 FOR R2=1 TO 4:D$=MID$(N$,R2,1):TV=AS
     C(D$)-48:IF TV>9 THEN TV=TV-7
7040 V=TV*16↑(4-R2)+V:NEXT R2:RETURN
8000 IF LEFT$(N$,1)="%" THEN N$=RIGHT$(N$
     ,LEN(N$)-1)
8010 V=0:FOR Z=LEN(N$) TO 1 STEP -1:V=V+V
     AL(MID$(N$,Z,1))*2↑(LEN(N$)-Z):NEXT
     {SPACE}Z
```

204

```
8020 RETURN
9000 FD=INT(N/4096):N=(N/4096-FD)*4096:SD
     =INT(N/256):N=(N/256-SD)*256
9010 TD=INT(N/16):N=INT((N/16-TD)*16):R$=
     MID$(H$,FD+1,1)+MID$(H$,SD+1,1)
9020 R$=R$+MID$(H$,TD+1,1)+MID$(H$,N+1,1)
     :RETURN
10000 IF A$(T)="" THEN OC$="":LB$="":GOTO
      10100
10005 LI(1)=0:LI(2)=0:LI(3)=0:LI=0
10010 FOR R2=1 TO LEN(A$(T)):IF MID$(A$(T
      ),R2,1)=" " THEN LI=LI+1:LI(LI)=R2
10020 NEXT R2:IF LI(3)=0 THEN LI(3)=R2-1
10030 LB$=LEFT$(A$(T),LI(1)):OC$=MID$(A$(
      T),LI(1)+1,LI(2)-LI(1))
10040 OP$=RIGHT$(A$(T),LI(3)-LI(2)+1)
10050 IF LB$=" " THEN LB$="":GOTO 10070
10060 LB$=LEFT$(LB$,LEN(LB$)-1)
10070 OC$=LEFT$(OC$,LEN(OC$)-1)
10080 IF OP$=" " THEN OP$="":GOTO 10100
10090 OP$=RIGHT$(OP$,LEN(OP$)-1)
10100 RETURN
11000 PRINT"{CLR}":PRINT"{3 SPACES}THE AS
      SEMBLER STARTS WITH THE FIRST"
11010 PRINT"LINE OF THE MACHINE PROGRAM T
      O BE":PRINT"ENTERED."
11020 PRINT:PRINT"{3 SPACES}THIS IS INDIC
      ATED BY THE NUMBER 1,"
11030 PRINT"AND A WHITE CURSOR BESIDE IT.
      THIS"
11040 PRINT"MEANS THAT YOU ARE AT LINE 1
      {SPACE}AND IT IS"
11050 PRINT"WAITING FOR INPUT INTO THE LA
      BEL FIELD."
11060 PRINT:PRINT"{3 SPACES}IF YOU TYPE T
      O THE END OF THE FIELD,"
11070 PRINT"HIT {RVS}SPACE{OFF}, OR HIT
      {RVS}RETURN{OFF},YOU WILL JUMP"
11080 PRINT"TO THE NEXT FIELD.":PRINT
11090 PRINT"{3 SPACES}THE LENGTH OF THE
      {RVS}LABEL{OFF} FIELD IS"
11100 PRINT"{RVS}6{OFF} CHARACTERS, THE
      {RVS}OPCODE{OFF} FIELD IS {RVS}3
      {OFF},"
11110 PRINT"AND THE {RVS}OPERAND{OFF} FIE
      LD {RVS}10{OFF}."
11120 PRINT:PRINT"{3 SPACES}A {RVS}SPACE
      {OFF} OR {RVS}RETURN{OFF} IN THE
      {RVS}OPERAND{OFF}"
```

```
11130 PRINT"FIELD WILL PUT YOU AT THE BEG
      INING OF"
11140 PRINT"THE NEXT LINE."
11150 PRINT:PRINT"{RVS}TYPE ANY KEY TO CO
      NTINUE."
11160 GET Z$:IF Z$="" THEN 11160
11170 PRINT"{CLR}":PRINT"{3 SPACES}THERE
      {SPACE}ARE TWO SPECIAL COMMANDS YOU
      "
11180 PRINT"CAN TYPE WHILE IN THE {RVS}LA
      BEL FIELD{OFF} THESE"
11190 PRINT"ARE {RVS}FIX{OFF}, AND {RVS}E
      XIT{OFF}."
11200 PRINT:PRINT"{2 SPACES}{RVS}FIX{OFF}
      RETURNS YOU TO THE PREVIOUS LINE,"
11210 PRINT"SO THAT YOU CAN CORRECT ANY M
      ISTAKES.":PRINT
11220 PRINT"{2 SPACES}{RVS}EXIT{OFF} TAKE
      S YOU OUT OF THE INPUT"
11230 PRINT"MODE, AND INTO THE ASSEMBLY/E
      DIT MODE."
11240 PRINT:PRINT"{3 SPACES}WHEN IN THE
      {RVS}ASSEMBLY/EDIT{OFF} MODE A"
11250 PRINT"MENU WILL BE DISPLAYED. THE C
      OMMANDS":PRINT"ARE AS FOLLOWS:"
11260 PRINT:PRINT" C COMPACT THE LISTING
      {SPACE}(ELIMINATE":PRINT"{4 SPACES}
      EMPTY LINES)."
11270 PRINT" I INPUT MORE CODE (AFTER EDI
      TING)."
11280 PRINT"{4 SPACES}THIS ALSO ALLOWS YO
      U TO OVERWRITE"
11290 PRINT"{4 SPACES}PREVIOUS CODE."
11295 PRINT:PRINT"{RVS}TYPE ANY KEY TO CO
      NTINUE.{OFF}"
11296 GET Z$: IF Z$="" THEN 11296
11300 PRINT"{CLR}":PRINT" D DELETE CODE.
      {SPACE}YOU WILL BE ASKED FOR"
11310 PRINT"{4 SPACES}STARTING AND ENDING
      LINE NUMBERS."
11320 PRINT"{4 SPACES}EVERYTHING FROM THE
      FIRST LINE"
11330 PRINT"{4 SPACES}UP TO,BUT NOT INCLU
      DING THE LAST"
11340 PRINT"{4 SPACES}WILL BE DELETED. TO
      DELETE ONE"
11350 PRINT"{4 SPACES}LINE, TYPE IT'S NUM
      BER IN BOTH":PRINT"{4 SPACES}PLACES
      "
```

```
11360 PRINT" N INSERT CODE. YOU WILL BE A
      SKED THE"
11370 PRINT"{4 SPACES}INSERTION POINT AND
      THE # OF LINES"
11380 PRINT"{4 SPACES}TO BE INSERTED."
11390 PRINT" L LIST. YOU WILL BE ASKED FO
      R THE"
11400 PRINT"{4 SPACES}BEGINING AND ENDING
      LINE NUMBERS."
11402 PRINT" S SAVE. YOU WILL BE ASKED FO
      R THE"
11404 PRINT"{4 SPACES}FILENAME OF FILE TO
      BE SAVED."
11406 PRINT" O LOAD. YOU WILL BE ASKED FO
      R THE"
11408 PRINT"{4 SPACES}FILENAME OF FILE TO
      BE LOADED."
11410 PRINT" A ASSEMBLE. YOU WILL BE ASKE
      D TO PICK"
11420 PRINT"{4 SPACES}SCREEN OR PRINTER.
      {SPACE}AFTER ASSEMBLY"
11430 PRINT"{4 SPACES}THE CODE IS IN MEMO
      RY."
11440 PRINT" Q QUIT THE PROGRAM. IF HIT A
      CCIDENTALY"
11450 PRINT"{4 SPACES}YOU CAN RETURN TO P
      ROGRAM WITH"
11460 PRINT"{4 SPACES}{RVS}GOTO 300{OFF}.
      "
11465 PRINT:PRINT"{RVS}TYPE ANY KEY TO CO
      NTINUE.{OFF}"
11466 GET Z$: IF Z$="" THEN 11466
11470 PRINT"{CLR}":PRINT"{3 SPACES}VARIAB
      LES ARE DEFINED WITH THE"
11480 PRINT"VARIABLE NAME IN THE LABEL FI
      ELD, AN"
11490 PRINT"'=' IN THE OPCODE FIELD, AND
      {SPACE}THE MEMORY"
11500 PRINT"LOCATION OF THE VARIABLE IN T
      HE OPERAND":PRINT"FIELD."
11510 PRINT:PRINT"{3 SPACES}THE FIRST LIN
      E,AND ONLY THE FIRST"
11520 PRINT"LINE, SHOULD BE USED TO DEFIN
      E THE"
11530 PRINT"ORIGIN OF PROGRAM LOCATION. T
      HIS IS"
11540 PRINT"DONE WITH AN '*' IN THE LABEL
      FIELD,AND"
11545 PRINT"THE REST AS IN VARIABLES."
```

```
11550 PRINT:PRINT"{3 SPACES}THE FOLLOWING
      CONVENTIONS HOLD:":PRINT
11560 PRINT"{4 SPACES}# IMMEDIATE ADDRESS
      ING"
11570 PRINT"{4 SPACES}$ HEXADECIMAL NUMBE
      R (UP TO 4 CHAR)"
11580 PRINT"{4 SPACES}% BINARY (UP TO 9 C
      HAR)"
11590 PRINT"{4 SPACES}A ACCUMULATOR ADDRE
      SSING"
11600 PRINT:PRINT"{3 SPACES}DECIMAL ASSUM
      ED BY DEFAULT."
11605 PRINT:PRINT"{RVS}TYPE ANY KEY TO CO
      NTINUE.{OFF}"
11606 GET Z$: IF Z$="" THEN 11606
11610 PRINT"{CLR}":PRINT"{3 SPACES}A SYMB
      OL MUST BEGIN WITH A LETTER,"
11620 PRINT"AND CONTAIN ONLY LETTERS AND
      {SPACE}NUMBERS."
11630 PRINT:PRINT"{3 SPACES}BECAUSE 'A' I
      S USED IN ACCUMULATOR"
11640 PRINT"ADDRESSING, IT IS AN ILLEGAL
      {SPACE}SYMBOL. IT"
11650 PRINT"CAN BE USED WITH OTHER CHARS
      {SPACE}HOWEVER."
11660 PRINT:PRINT"{3 SPACES}ADDITION WITH
      IN THE OPERAND FIELD IS"
11670 PRINT"NON-STANDARD. ONLY SYMBOLS CA
      N BE ADDED"
11680 PRINT"TO. ADDITION IS DONE BY FOLLO
      WING THE"
11690 PRINT"SYMBOL WITH PLUS SIGN(S). THE
      NUMBER OF"
11700 PRINT"PLUS SIGNS EQUALS THE NUMBER
      {SPACE}TO BE":PRINT"ADDED."
11710 PRINT:PRINT"{3 SPACES}SELF-MODIFYIN
      G CODE SHOULD BE PLACED"
11720 PRINT"BEFORE THE CODE THAT MODIFIES
      IT."
11730 PRINT:PRINT"{3 SPACES}MEM=200 AND M
      2=100 CAN BE USED FOR"
11740 PRINT"LONGER PROGRAMS. HOWEVER THIS
      WILL TAKE"
11750 PRINT"VERY LONG. LARGER VALUES MAY
      {SPACE}RUN OUT OF"
11760 PRINT"MEMORY."
11770 PRINT:PRINT"{RVS}TYPE ANY KEY TO CO
      NTINUE.{OFF}"
11780 GET Z$: IF Z$="" THEN 11780
```

```
11790 PRINT"{CLR}":PRINT"{3 SPACES}THE
      {RVS}LOAD{OFF} AND {RVS}SAVE{OFF} C
      OMMANDS LOAD AND"
11800 PRINT"SAVE SOURCE CODE ONLY."
11810 PRINT:PRINT"{3 SPACES}TO USE THE MA
      CHINE CODE, FIRST LOAD"
11820 PRINT"THE SOURCE CODE, THEN ASSEMBL
      E IT,"
11830 PRINT"FINALLY TYPE 'NEW' (THIS WILL
       CLEAR THE"
11840 PRINT"BASIC PROGRAM) AND 'SYS' TO T
      HE START"
11850 PRINT"OF THE MACHINE CODE."
11860 PRINT:PRINT"{3 SPACES}A NEW BASIC P
      ROGRAM CAN ALSO THEN BE"
11870 PRINT"TYPED IN TO USE THE MACHINE C
      ODE."
11880 PRINT:PRINT"{RVS}TYPE ANY KEY TO CO
      NTINUE.{OFF}"
11890 GET Z$: IF Z$="" THEN 11890
11900 RETURN
12000 PRINT"LOADING NEW FILE WILL DESTROY
       OLD FILE.":PRINT"LOAD ? (Y/N)"
12003 GET Z$:IF Z$="" OR (Z$<>"Y" AND Z$<
      >"N") THEN 12003
12005 IF Z$="N" THEN GOTO 300
12010 INPUT"FILENAME ";FL$
12020 OPEN 1,1,0,FL$:REM FOR TAPE
12025 REM FOR DISK USE: OPEN 1,8,8,"0:"+F
      L$+"S,R"
12030 FOR T=1 TO MEM:A$(T)="":NEXT T
12040 FOR T=1 TO MEM
12050 GET# 1,IO$:IF IO$=CHR$(13) THEN 12070
12060 A$(T)=A$(T)+IO$:GOTO 12050
12070 NEXT T
12080 CLOSE 1
12090 GOTO 300
13000 PRINT"DO YOU WANT TO SAVE FILE ? (Y/N)"
13003 GET Z$:IF Z$="" OR (Z$<>"Y" AND Z$<
      >"N") THEN 13003
13005 IF Z$="N" THEN GOTO 300
13010 INPUT"FILENAME ";FL$
13020 OPEN 1,1,1,FL$:REM FOR TAPE
13025 REM FOR DISK USE: OPEN 1,8,8,"0:"+F
      L$+"S,W"
13030 FOR T=1 TO MEM
13040 PRINT# 1,A$(T);CHR$(13);
13050 NEXT T
13060 CLOSE 1
13070 GOTO 300
```

Decoding BASIC Statements

John Heilborn

Although most people who use BASIC have a fair understanding of how data is stored in the computer, few ever really get a clear idea of how the BASIC programs themselves are stored. A special part of the computer's operating system called the screen editor handles all the dirty work of inserting, deleting, and modifying BASIC program lines for you.

There are, however, some functions that are inaccessible through the screen editor, and utilizing them can make writing programs much easier.

The Mysterious Special Function Symbols

The special symbols provide you with some very powerful programming features. They can also leave you with some very hard-to-read listings when you have made extensive use of the cursor control or color control keys within your programs. For example, typing the SHIFT-CLEAR/HOME key combination will put an inverse video heart in your program line.

By searching your program lines directly in memory, it is possible to locate each of the special symbols. Once they are located, you can convert them into words that describe their actual functions. This will leave you with programs that are much easier to read and modify.

Where Is the Program?

BASIC can store programs in several different places in memory, but normally BASIC statements begin at memory location 2049. Since the program lines themselves are stored in the same format no matter where BASIC puts them, all of the examples in this article will begin at 2049.

The figure is a diagram of a BASIC statement. It represents the first line in a program.

As you can see from the figure, the BASIC line is broken up into sections. The first two bytes in the line contain the memory location of the beginning of the next program line. If you were to

PEEK those locations, you would find that they contain two separate numbers which combine to represent a hexadecimal number. Let's take a closer look at how this works and why it is done this way.

Structure of a BASIC Statement

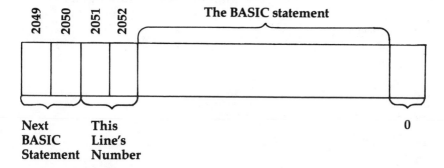

Hexadecimal Numbers

All of the numbers in the computer are actually stored as binary numbers. These are numbers that are made up of only ones and zeros. While this may seem like an impractical way to store numbers, it makes perfect sense to the computer because its circuits can operate in only one of two conditions — on or off. The ons are represented as ones and the offs are zeros.

The individual ones and zeros are called *bits* and the combined numbers they make (each of which contains eight bits) are called *bytes*. Because there are eight bits in each byte, each byte can represent any number between 0 and 255. Since program line numbers in BASIC can be greater than 255, it is necessary to use two bytes to represent the line numbers. Two bytes together can represent any number between 0 and 65535, but the largest line number BASIC allows is 63999.

Looking Ahead

To decode the hexadecimal number, multiply the value stored in the second byte (high byte) by 256 and add the result to the value in the first byte (low byte). Enter the following program line:

```
10 REM THIS IS A TEST
```

Now PEEK memory locations 2049 (low byte) and 2050 (high byte). You'll find that they contain the values 22 and 8. Multiply 8

by 256 (2048) and add 22 for a total of 2070. Therefore, the next program line will begin at memory location 2070.

Line Numbers

The next two memory locations (2051 and 2052) contain the program line number. The values you'll get by PEEKing these locations are 10 and 0. Once again, multiply the second number by 256 and add it to the first number. This time the result is 10 — our line number!

Now let's renumber this program. POKE location 2051 with the value 100:

POKE 2051, 100

and LIST the program. The line number should now be 100. POKEing 100 into location 2052 will cause the line number to jump to 25700.

Tokens

Every BASIC command has a corresponding *token*. The token is a single number that represents the command. For example, if you PEEK location 2053, the computer will display the tokenized value for the REM statement, 143. The table below contains all of the BASIC statements and their tokens.

BASIC Tokens

END	128	LOAD	147	FN	165	FRE	184
FOR	129	SAVE	148	SPC	166	POS	185
NEXT	130	VERIFY	149	THEN	167	SQR	186
DATA	131	DEF	150	NOT	168	RND	187
INPUT #	132	POKE	151	STEP	169	LOG	188
INPUT	133	PRINT #	152	+	170	EXP	189
DIM	134	PRINT	153	-	171	COS	190
READ	135	CONT	154	*	172	SIN	191
LET	136	LIST	155	/	173	TAN	192
GOTO	137	CLR	156	↑	174	ATN	193
RUN	138	CMD	157	AND	175	PEEK	194
IF	139	SYS	158	OR	176	LEN	195
RESTORE	140	OPEN	159	>	177	STR$	196
GOSUB	141	CLOSE	160	=	178	VAL	197
RETURN	142	GET	161	<	179	ASC	198
REM	143	GET #		SGN	180	CHR$	199
STOP	144	NEW	162	INT	181	LEFT$	200
ON	145	TAB (	163	ABS	182	RIGHT$	201
WAIT	146	TO	164	USR	183	MID$	202

GET # has no separate token.

Changing the value in location 2053 can modify the BASIC statement. Change the value in 2053 to 153 with:

POKE 2053, 153

Now LIST the program. You have changed the REM statement into a PRINT statement! RUN the program to show that the change is genuine.

Special Function Codes

The special function codes enable you to use some of the keyboard control functions that are ordinarily accessible only in immediate mode. For example, pressing the key marked CTRL and one of the number keys at the top of the keyboard will change the color of the characters as they are printed on the screen. By using the CHR$ code for that function within a program line, you can use the same feature within a program. Enter this line:

```
10 PRINT "{RVS}{RED}RED,{WHT} WHITE,
   {OFF}AND{RVS}{7}BLUE"
```

For a complete table of all the special function codes, look at the *Commodore 64 User's Guide* that came with your computer. The special function codes are listed with the rest of the CHR$ functions in Appendix F.

ASCII Data

The rest of the information in your programs is stored as ASCII data. In other words, if you PEEK a location that has a standard character stored in it, it will contain the number that is the ASCII value of that character. Enter these lines:

```
10 PRINT "THIS IS TEXT"
20 FOR R=2054 TO 2069
30 PRINTR;PEEK(R);CHR$(PEEK(R))
40 NEXT
```

This routine displays the data as it would normally be printed and then displays the data by memory location, ASCII value, and CHR$ code. With this display, it is easy to see that changing a value in one of the memory locations between 2056 and 2067 will allow you to modify the text directly.

Zero as a Marker

Each BASIC statement stored in memory ends with a zero (see the figure), which serves as an "end of statement" marker. Note

that the marker is a byte with the value of zero, whereas zeroes *within* the statement — for example, the two zeroes in the statement GOTO 100 — are stored as the ASCII representation of zero, which is 48.

The zero byte has two other uses in BASIC. The first byte in the BASIC RAM area (before the first BASIC statement) must contain a zero. Try a PEEK(2048) to check this. Also, two zero bytes as the address of the next program line indicate that the end of the BASIC program has been reached, so BASIC programs always end with three zero bytes in a row.

Easy Lister

BASIC program listings as they normally appear on the screen can be hard to understand. It's difficult to remember what all the special characters appearing as inverse video symbols are supposed to represent. The following program makes listings much easier to read. It goes through the BASIC program in memory byte by byte and interprets each BASIC token, special symbol, or graphics character.

To display all of the special symbols and characters, you need to generate two tables in memory that contain all the possible codes that can appear in a program line. In the program below, these are called table A$ and table B$. Table A$ contains the tokenized BASIC commands and table B$ contains the CHR$ codes for the graphics characters and the descriptions of the special functions.

To use the program, type it in carefully and SAVE it to tape or disk. You can test the program by having it list itself if you temporarily omit line 62040 and type RUN. When you wish to make a listing, follow these steps to append the Easy Lister program to the program you wish to list:

1. Tell the computer where the end of your current program is by typing:

`POKE 43,PEEK(45)-2:POKE 44,PEEK(46)`

2. LOAD the Easy Lister program from tape or disk.

3. Restore BASIC to its normal starting condition by typing:

`POKE 43,1:POKE 44,8`

When you LIST the program now you should see your original program with the lister program added to the end. Activate the lister by typing:

RUN 61000

The program as presented assumes that your printer is connected as device 4, which is standard for Commodore printers. If you are using an RS-232 printer connected as device 2, delete line 62010 and replace line 61000 with:

```
61000 OPEN 1,2,0
```

An OPEN statement for device 2 should come before the string arrays A$ and B$ are defined because OPENing an RS-232 channel allocates memory for input and output buffers which can cause a loss of data in string variables. If you wish to list to the screen instead of a printer, simply delete line 62010 and change the PRINT#1, statements in lines 62050, 62080, 62110, and 62120 to PRINT.

Creating Tables in Memory

```
61000 REM ---- SET UP 'A' TABLE ----
61010 DIMA$(255),B$(255):FOR R=1 TO 31
61020 A$(R)="CHR$("+RIGHT$(STR$(R),LEN(ST
      R$(R))-1)+")":NEXT
61030 FOR R=32 TO 90
61040 A$(R)=CHR$(R):NEXT
61050 FOR R=91 TO 127
61060 A$(R)="CHR$("+RIGHT$(STR$(R),LEN(ST
      R$(R))-1)+")":NEXT
61070 DATA END,FOR,NEXT,DATA,INPUT#,INPUT
      ,DIM,READ,LET,GOTO,RUN,IF,RESTORE
61080 DATA GOSUB,RETURN,REM,STOP,ON,WAIT,
      LOAD,SAVE,VERIFY,DEF,POKE
61090 DATA PRINT#,PRINT,CONT,LIST,CLR,CMD
      ,SYS,OPEN,CLOSE,GET,NEW,TAB(,TO,FN,
      SPC
61100 DATA THEN,NOT,STEP,+,-,*,/,↑,AND,OR
      ,>,=,<,SGN,INT,ABS,USR,FRE,POS,SQR,
      RND
61110 DATA LOG,EXP,COS,SIN,TAN,ATN,PEEK,L
      EN,STR$,VAL,ASC,CHR$,LEFT$,RIGHT$,M
      ID$
61120 FOR R=128 TO 202
61130 READ A$(R): NEXT
61140 FOR R=203 TO 255
61150 A$(R)="CHR$("+RIGHT$(STR$(R),LEN(ST
      R$(R))-1)+")":NEXT
61160 REM ---- SET UP 'B' TABLE ----
61170 DATA 5,WHITE,17,CURSOR DOWN,18,REVE
      RSE ON,19,HOME,20,DELETE,28,RED,29
```

```
61180 DATA CURSOR RIGHT,30,GREEN,31,BLUE,
      999
61190 READ X:IF X=999 THEN 61210
61200 READ X$:B$(X)=CHR$(91)+X$+CHR$(93):
      GOTO 61190
61210 FOR R=32 TO 128: B$(R)=A$(R):NEXT
61220 DATA 129,ORANGE,133,F1,134,F3,135,F
      5,136,F7,137,F2,138,F4,139,F6,140,F
      8
61230 DATA 144,BLACK,145,CURSOR UP,146,RE
      VERSE OFF,147,CLEAR HOME,148,INSERT
61240 DATA 149,BROWN,150,LIGHT RED,151,GR
      EY 1,152,GREY 2,153,LIGHT GREEN,154
61250 DATA LIGHT BLUE,155,GREY 3,156,PURP
      LE,157,CURSOR LEFT,158,YELLOW,159,C
      YAN
61260 DATA 999
61270 READ X: IF X=999 THEN 61290
61280 READ X$:B$(X)=CHR$(91)+X$+CHR$(93):
      GOTO 61270
61290 FOR R=160 TO 255:B$(R)="CHR$("+RIGH
      T$(STR$(R),LEN(STR$(R))-1)+")":NEXT
62000 REM --- READ BASIC STATEMENTS ---
62010 OPEN 1,4
62020 A=2051:C=1
62030 R=PEEK(A)+((PEEK(A+1))*256)
62040 IF R>=61000 THEN 62130
62050 PRINT#1,RIGHT$(STR$(R),LEN(STR$(R))
      -1);" ";
62060 A=A+2:GOTO62090
62070 IF(PEEK(A)=0)AND(PEEK(A+1)=0)THEN 6
      2130
62080 IF PEEK(A)=0 THEN A=A+3:PRINT#1:GOT
      O 62030
62090 IF PEEK(A)=34 THEN C=C*-1
62100 IF C=-1 THEN 62120
62110 PRINT#1,A$(PEEK(A));:A=A+1:GOTO6207
      0
62120 PRINT#1,B$(PEEK(A));:A=A+1:GOTO6207
      0
62130 CLOSE 1:END
```

Micromon-64

Bill Yee

A machine language monitor is an essential tool for developing and debugging assembly language programs. It is especially useful on the Commodore 64 as it provides a much more powerful way to explore the inner workings of the computer. Micromon-64 is just such a monitor. It is based on my version of Micromon for the VIC-20.

Commands

What follows is a listing of all the commands available with Micromon-64. The listing includes a short explanation and the format needed.

Assembler

.A	401F	AD	14	03	LDA	$0314	: CHECK IRQ VECTOR
.A	4022	AE	15	03	LDX	$0315	
.A	4025	C9	91		CMP	#$91	
.A	4027	D0	04		BNE	$402D	
.A	4029						

The initial input of this command requires a starting address in hexadecimal. Once you have input one line, the assembler outputs the command letter A followed by the address of the next instruction. Assembler instructions are all 3-character mnemonics followed by an optional operand field. Operand data is taken to be hexadecimal and must be prefixed with a $. Immediate data must be further prefixed with a #. All address references are specified in hexadecimal and are absolute. Relative branches are calculated by the assembler by using the difference between the target and the current addresses of the branch. A colon (:) can be used to terminate a line so that comments can follow. To exit the assembler, hit the RETURN key after the address prompt.

Break Set

.B   2000   0010

Break Set allows you to break execution of code after a specified address has occurred for a specified number of times. Code execution must be started with the Quick trace command. If no

count is specified, execution stops at first occurrence of the specified address. For the example, execution breaks on the sixteenth time the instruction at location $2000 is executed.

Compare Memory

.C   2000   2FFF   C000

Comparison of two memory blocks is done with output of addresses of the locations in the first block that have data bytes mismatching data bytes in corresponding relative locations in the second block. The command requires that the low and high addresses of the first block be specified followed by the low address of the second block. For the example, the first memory block from $2000 to $2FFF is compared to the second memory block from $C000 to $CFFF. Compare can be stopped by hitting the RUN/STOP key during output of mismatched data location addresses.

Disassembler

.D	4015	401C				
.,	4015	A9	DF		LDA	#$DF
.,	4017	A2	45		LDX	#$45
.,	4019	8D	16	03	STA	$0316
.,	401C	8E	17	03	STX	$0317

A block of code can be disassembled and printed by specifying the low and high addresses for the block. The RUN/STOP key can be used to halt output. If only one address is specified, then only the instruction at that address is disassembled.

.D	4001					
.,	4001	4C	15	40	JMP	$4015

Machine code can be edited by using the CRSR keys to move to and modify the bytes. Hit the RETURN key to enter the changes into memory. The new code is disassembled and redisplayed on the same line. Also, the address of the next instruction is displayed on the following line to assist you in making further changes. However, if you disassemble a block of code and then make a change in the middle of the block on the screen, take care you don't overwrite more than you intended by hitting the RETURN key too many times. In other words, don't hit RETURN while the cursor is sitting on a line beginning with a comma followed by an address plus one or more data bytes unless you want to change and disassemble that instruction. The comma is a "hidden" command which you can use to enter hexadecimal data into memory with disassembly of the data as you enter it. Hitting RETURN with no data after the address gets you out of the command. Moving the cursor to the top or bottom of the screen with one or more disassembled lines displayed causes disassembly down or up in memory respectively.

Exit Micromon

.E

Restore the IRQ and BRK interrupt vectors, reset the tape buffer to $033C, and then exit to the BASIC environment. The E command should be used to exit Micromon when the normal LOAD, SAVE, and VERIFY commands are to be used in the BASIC environment. Always use SYS49152 to access or reenter Micromon-64 located at $C000.

Fill Memory

```
.F    2000    3FFF    00
.F    4000    47FF    FF
```

Fill a block of memory with the data byte specified. Memory is written from low to high, and no check is made on the writes. For the first example, memory area from $2000 to $3FFF is zeroed. For the second example, memory area from 14000 to $47FF has the bits set to all ones.

Go Run

```
.G
.G    2000
```

The register image shown by the register display command is set into the microprocessor registers prior to execution of machine language code at full speed. For the first example, execution begins at the address given for PC (Program Counter) in the register display. For the second example, execution begins at the address specified, which is $2000.

You should have a BRK instruction (value 00) in your code to generate a breakpoint for software interrupt back into Micromon. On BRK, the register image is saved and displayed. Also, the address of the instruction following the BRK is saved in PC for execution continuation later if another Go Run command is given. If a BRK is never executed, you cannot get back into Micromon. The RUN/STOP and RESTORE keys can be used to

halt execution. A NMI (Non-Maskable Interrupt) is generated which puts you into the BASIC environment. A SYS49152 is needed to reenter Micromon at $C000.

Hunt Memory

```
.H   1000   5FFF   'ASCII CHARACTER STRING
.H   0000   1000   01   02   03   04   05   06
```

A block of memory specified by a low and a high address is scanned from low to high for a maximum of 32 characters or bytes of data. The address of each occurrence is printed out. During address output, the hunt can be stopped with the RUN/STOP key. For the examples shown, the first is for characters and the second is a data byte sequence. A match is always found at $0365, as that is where the match characters or data are stored.

Jump to Micromon Subroutine

```
.J   3000
```

The machine language subroutine at location $3000 is called while remaining in the Micromon environment. The subroutine must exit by using a RTS (ReTurn from Subroutine) instruction which causes a return to the command input section of Micromon. The machine image as shown by the register display command is not used, nor is it disturbed when the subroutine returns to Micromon.

LOAD Memory from Device

```
.L   4000   "TEST FILE"   08
```

Search for and, if found, load into memory starting at $4000 the data file on device #8 named TEST FILE. Device #8 is the 1541 floppy disk which requires that a filename be specified. If the device number is not specified, it defaults to device #1, which is the cassette tape. For tape, if no filename is specified, the first file found is loaded. The last address loaded is determined by the length of the data file. The BASIC memory pointers are not affected by this load. When loading from tape, the original memory addresses and name of the last file read can be inspected by doing a memory display of the tape buffer, which is located at $0375 for Micromon.

Memory Display

```
.M   4E70   4E80
.:   4E70   49   43   32   30   20   4D   49   43   IC20 MIC
.:   4E78   52   4F   4D   4F   4E   20   56   31   ROMON V1
.:   4E80   2E   30   20   20   20   42   49   4C   .0 BIL

.M   4E88
.:   4E88   4C   20   59   45   45   20   32   32   L YEE 22
```

Display memory in eight-byte segments followed by ASCII translation. The bytes following the address may be modified by moving the cursor over the data and overstriking with the new data. Changes are entered into memory when RETURN is hit. As with the comma disassembly command, the address of the next memory area is output to assist in further changes. The colon is also a "hidden" command you can use by inputting colon plus address and hexadecimal data. If one or more memory display lines are on the screen, moving the cursor to the top or bottom of the screen causes scrolling and display of the next segment of eight bytes down or up in memory.

New Locater

```
.N   2000   2003   6000   C000   CFFF
.N   2FB5   2FFE   6000   C000   CFFF W
```

The first example fixes all three-byte instructions in the memory area from $2000 to $2003 by adding $6000 to the absolute address in the two bytes following the instruction opcode. Any absolute addresses found that are outside the range from $C000 to $CFFF are not adjusted. Also, if a bad opcode is encountered, the processing stops with a disassembly and display of the bad opcode. The second example searches for two-byte or word addresses, and those found in the range from $C000 to $CFFF are adjusted by having $6000 added to their value.

Offset or Branch Calculate

```
.0   1004   1000   FA
```

Calculate the offset for branch instructions. The first address is for the location containing the branch opcode, and the second address is the branch target address. Addresses and the resulting displayed offset byte are in hexadecimal.

Print Switcher

.P

If the output is to the screen, then switch the output to the RS-232 channel (device #2). If the output is not to the screen, restore the output to the screen with the RS-232 channel left active until the RS-232 output buffer is drained. Note that opening the RS-232 channel grabs 512 bytes for I/O buffering from the top of BASIC memory.

.P   0000

Regardless of the output, clear the RS-232 channel and set output to the screen.

.P   CCBB

If the output is to the screen, set CC into the RS-232 command register at $0294 and BB into the RS-232 control register at $0293. This command is invalid if output is not currently to the screen.

If you have a VIC printer on the serial I/O port, don't use this command for printing. Instead, use the CMD statement in the BASIC environment to redirect screen output to the VIC printer prior to entering Micromon as follows:

OPEN4,4:CMD4:SYS49152:PRINT#4:CLOSE4

This line causes all screen output to go to the VIC printer until you exit Micromon with either the E or X command. The SYS49152 is used to access Micromon at $C000.

Quick Trace

.Q
.Q   4000

Each instruction is executed as in the Walk command, but no output occurs. The address specified in the Break Set command is checked for the break on the Nth occurrence. Execution is not at full speed. Hitting the RUN/STOP key will break execution which displays S* followed by the register image saved. For the first example, begin trace at the address in PC of the register display. For the second example, begin trace at location $4000.

Register Display

.R

	PC	IRQ	SR	AC	XR	YR	SP
.;	C04E	C391	32	32	00	1C	F7

The machine image saved is initialized by execution of a BRK instruction when Micromon is first entered. This image can be modified by positioning the cursor over the register values to be changed and overstriking with the new values. The changes are entered into the saved image when you hit the RETURN key. The semicolon is also a "hidden" command you can use directly.

Save Memory to Device

.S   4000   5000   "TEST FILE"   08

Save memory from $4000 up to, but *not including,* $5000 onto device #8, which is the 1541 floppy disk. If the device number is not specified, it defaults to device #1, which is the cassette tape. The name TEST FILE is placed in the tape file header or in the disk directory for the file saved. Note that files saved on tape or disk with the Micromon Save command can be loaded back into the original memory area while in the BASIC environment. The non-relocating form of the Load command in BASIC must be used. For the file saved in the example, executing the line

LOAD "TEST FILE",8,1

while in BASIC will load the data in TEST FILE back to the $4000 to $4FFF memory area. The BASIC memory pointers will be disturbed, so a New command should be executed to reset these pointers. Note that the BASIC memory pointers are *not* disturbed by the Micromon Load, Save, or Verify commands.

Transfer Memory

.T   4000   4FFF   6000

Transfer a copy of the data from the memory block at $4000 to $4FFF into the memory block at $6000 to $6FFF. Transfer begins at the high location of each block. For the example shown, the first byte copied is from $4FFF into $6FFF. The last byte copied is from $4000 into $6000. This is an important consideration when the source and destination memory blocks overlap.

Verify Memory from Device

.V   4000   "TEST FILE"   08

Search for and, if found, verify against memory starting at $4000 the data file on device #8 named TEST FILE. Device #8 is the 1541 floppy disk which requires that a filename be specified. If the device number is not specified, it defaults to device #1, which is the

223

cassette tape. For tape, if no filename is specified, the first file found is verified. When verifying from tape, the original memory addresses and name of the last file verified can be inspected by doing a memory display of the tape buffer which is located at $0375 for Micromon.

Walk Code

.W
.W   4000

The walk begins by setting microprocessor registers to the machine image shown in the register display. A single instruction is executed, an IRQ is generated, and the new machine image is saved and displayed as SR, AC, XR, YR, SP, followed by address, machine language, and disassembly of the next instruction to be executed. Hitting the RUN/STOP key stops walking. Hitting the J key while walking finishes execution of a subroutine at full speed. You can hit J when the next instruction to be executed is the JSR to the subroutine to be run at full speed. Or you can hit J when you are actually within the subroutine. Walk resumes on return from the subroutine. Hitting any other key during walking causes execution of the next instruction. Caution: Hitting J when you are walking in mainline code will probably cause unpredictable results. The most likely result is an attempted return to BASIC as Micromon is accessed by a SYS command and the return address is in the stack. For the examples shown, the first begins the walking at the address given by PC of the register display. The second begins the walking at a specified address, which is $4000.

Exit to BASIC

.X

Exit to the BASIC environment while leaving the Micromon vectors in the IRQ and BRK interrupt vector locations. The tape buffer is also left at $0375. This command allows you to operate in the BASIC environment but still trap execution of a BRK instruction via Micromon's breakpoint or software interrupt handler. However, in addition, certain IRQ interrupt conditions such as the moving of the cursor to the top or bottom of the screen with output from a D, M, or $ command displayed will cause scrolling and reentry into Micromon via its IRQ interrupt handler.

ASCII Conversion

. "B   42   66   0100   0010

An ASCII, graphics, or control character is input to obtain the hexadecimal, decimal, or binary values for the character.

Decimal Conversion

. # 16706   4142   A   B   0100   0001   0100   0010

A decimal number is input to obtain the hexadecimal, ASCII characters of the two bytes, and binary values for the decimal number.

Hexadecimal Conversion

.$4142   16706   A   B   0100   0001   0100   0010

A hexadecimal number is input to obtain the decimal, ASCII characters for the two bytes, and binary values for the hexadecimal number. The up/down CRSR key can be used to scroll the screen to get decreasing/increasing hexadecimal numbers converted once you have entered one number with this command.

Binary Conversion

.%0100000101000010   4142   16706   A   B

A binary number is input to obtain the hexadecimal, decimal, and ASCII characters of the two bytes for the binary number.

Checksum Memory

.&   C000   CFFF   A500

The data for the memory block from $C000 to $CFFF inclusive is byte-summed and displayed.

Command End Tone

.(

Enable the command end tone. A continuous tone will be generated at the end of execution of the next command. The tone can be turned off but still be enabled by just hitting the RETURN key. No tone is generated if there is an error while inputting the next command. This command is handy whenever you want to start a task that takes a long time to execute in Micromon but do not

want to continually watch the screen for task completion. Examples are saves and loads of large files to and from the cassette tape.

.)

Disable the command end tone.

Addition

.+ 1111 2222 3333

Two hexadecimal numbers are input to obtain their modulo 16 sum.

Subtraction

.- 3333 1111 2222

Two hexadecimal numbers are input, and the second is subtracted from the first to obtain their difference. Subtraction is done with twos complement arithmetic.

Disk Directory

```
.>0   "BILL YEE VICDSK1"      BY 2A
17    "COMM-64 MICROMON"      PRG
8     "V1.3 BOOTSTRAP"        PRG
639   BLOCKS FREE.
```

Input of > followed by RETURN interrogates and displays the 1541 floppy disk directory on the screen. Output can be halted by hitting the RUN/STOP key. The space bar causes output to wait.

Typing in Micromon-64

In order to enter Micromon-64 you must use the "Machine Language Editor (MLX)" program found in Appendix A and the DATA listing found at the end of this article. It is important to read the article that accompanies the MLX program. It may seem like extra work at first to have to type in two programs, but you'll save time later when you end up with a virtually error-free program.

In order to use MLX you must know the starting and ending addresses of Micromon-64.

The starting address is 49152.
The ending address is 53247.
Enter these addresses when prompted by MLX.

Table 1. Summary of Micromon-64 Instruction Commands

Micromon-64 Instruction	Command
Assembler	A
Break Set	B
Compare Memory	C
Disassembler	D
Exit Micromon	E
Fill Memory	F
Go Run	G
Hunt Memory	H
Jump to Micromon Subroutine	J
Load Memory from Device	L
Memory Display	M
New Locater	N
Offset or Branch Calculate	O
Print Switcher	P
Quick Trace	Q
Register Display	R
Save Memory to Device	S
Transfer Memory	T
Verify Memory from Device	V
Walk Code	W
Exit to BASIC	X
ASCII Conversion	"
Decimal Conversion	#
Hexadecimal Conversion	$
Binary Conversion	%
Checksum Memory	&
Command End Tone Enable	(
Command End Tone Disable	)
Addition	+
Subtraction	-
Disk Directory	>
Modify Machine Code and Disassemble	,
Modify Up to 8 Data Bytes In Hexadecimal	:
Modify Image Shown by Register Display	;

Loading Micromon from Disk or Tape

Once you have SAVEd Micromon-64 to disk or tape using the Machine Language Editor, you will want to LOAD it back into memory for future use. Follow these steps to LOAD from BASIC:

1. Type NEW and press RETURN.
2. Type CLR and press RETURN.

3. LOAD Micromon-64
Tape type LOAD "MICROMON-64",1,1
Disk type LOAD "MICROMON-64",8,1
Press RETURN
4. Once Micromon-64 is in memory, type NEW and press
RETURN.
5. Type CLR and press RETURN.
6. Type SYS49152 and press RETURN.

Relocation

I located Micromon-64 in the 4K byte address space from $C000 to
$CFFF. This space is above the BASIC ROM area and so is not in-
cluded with the contiguous area defined for BASIC RAM. However, you may still want to relocate Micromon-64 elsewhere, and
as with VIC Micromon, this version can be relocated with its own
commands. For example, to relocate it into the $2000 to $2FFF
memory area, use the following sequence of operations.

.T   C000   CFFF   2000

The Micromon code at $C000 to $CFFF is copied into the memory
area from $2000 to $2FFF.

.-   2000   C000

The difference is $6000. This value must be added to all absolute
address references in Micromon to convert from the $C000 to
$CFFF range into the $2000 to $2FFF range. The New Locater
command is used to do this conversion as follows.

.N   2000   2003   6000   C000   CFFF
.N   2012   2E6D   6000   C000   CFFF

The Micromon machine language code at $2000 to $2FFF and
$2012 to $2E6D is scanned for absolute address references. Those
found with values in the range from $C000 to $CFFF are adjusted
by adding $6000 to give new absolute addresses. These new
addresses allow the code at $2000 to $2FFF to execute properly in
that address space.

.N   2FB5   2FFE   6000   C000   CFFF   W

The Micromon command vector table at $2FB5 to $2FFE is
scanned for two-byte or word addresses. Those found with
values in the range from $C000 to $CFFF are adjusted by adding
$6000 to give new absolute addresses. The result is a new set of
address vectors to allow the Micromon command handler to
access the command routines in the $2000 to $2FFF address
space.

Finally, there are seven locations which must be changed directly. Use the memory display command to display these locations. Change the values by moving the cursor over the old value, entering the new value, and hitting the RETURN key to enter the changes into memory. If you don't wish to display the current contents, you can input the colon command followed by the address and new data byte in hexadecimal. Hit RETURN to enter the data into memory.

Table 2. Memory Locations Requiring Direct Change

Location	Old Value	New Value
2018	C5	25
202A	C3	23
2322	CF	2F
2392	CC	2C
2649	C5	25
2701	C5	25
28A7	C3	23

After you have completed all of the operations shown, you can save the relocated Micromon code to tape or disk with the Micromon SAVE command as follows.

For tape:

.S   2000   3000   "NEW FILENAME"

For disk:

.S   2000   3000   "NEW FILENAME"   08

You should leave the original Micromon code for $C000 to $CFFF on disk or tape as a permanent backup. The relocated Micromon at $2000 to $2FFF can be tested by first exiting Micromon at $C000 with the E command. Then, from BASIC environment use SYS8192 to enter the relocated COMM-64 Micromon code at $2000. To insure that there are no addresses in the relocated code still having a value from $C000 to $CFFF, you can zap the Micromon code at $C000 to $CFFF with the Fill Memory command as follows.

.F   C000   CFFF   00

Successful execution of this command and subsequent successful exercising of most of the other Micromon commands verify that the code has been relocated properly. As a further check, for the version given in this article, relocation to the

memory area from $2000 to $2FFF should include a change of the
last byte at location $2FFF from $A9 to $E9. This should result in a
$2000 to $2FFF checksum of $9800 using Micromon's checksum
memory command. Checksum for Micromon-64 V1.3 at $C000 to
$CFFF is $8E00.

Micromon-64

```
49152 :120,076,021,192,169,018,084
49158 :032,210,255,169,157,032,093
49164 :210,255,096,032,021,253,111
49170 :032,024,229,169,223,162,089
49176 :197,141,022,003,142,023,040
49182 :003,173,020,003,174,021,168
49188 :003,201,145,208,004,224,053
49194 :195,240,009,141,096,003,214
49200 :142,097,003,032,164,200,174
49206 :169,117,133,178,169,128,180
49212 :141,138,002,133,157,162,025
49218 :215,032,096,206,142,072,061
49224 :003,142,100,003,088,000,152
49230 :206,061,003,208,003,206,253
49236 :060,003,032,163,197,162,189
49242 :066,169,042,076,077,201,209
49248 :169,063,032,210,255,169,226
49254 :000,044,169,017,141,004,221
49260 :212,032,163,197,169,046,159
49266 :032,210,255,169,000,141,153
49272 :078,003,141,086,003,141,060
49278 :100,003,162,127,154,032,192
49284 :156,200,201,046,240,249,200
49290 :201,032,240,245,162,036,030
49296 :221,144,207,208,019,141,060
49302 :073,003,138,010,170,189,221
49308 :181,207,133,251,189,182,019
49314 :207,133,252,108,251,000,089
49320 :202,016,229,076,096,192,211
49326 :162,002,208,002,162,000,198
49332 :180,251,208,009,180,252,236
49338 :208,003,238,086,003,214,170
49344 :252,214,251,096,169,000,150
49350 :141,078,003,032,019,194,153
49356 :162,009,032,072,201,202,114
49362 :208,250,096,162,002,181,085
49368 :250,072,189,083,003,149,194
49374 :250,104,157,083,003,202,253
49380 :208,241,096,173,084,003,009
49386 :172,085,003,076,244,192,238
49392 :165,253,164,254,056,229,081
```

```
49398 :251,141,083,003,152,229,081
49404 :252,168,013,083,003,096,099
49410 :169,000,240,002,169,001,071
49416 :141,087,003,032,219,199,177
49422 :032,163,197,032,240,192,102
49428 :032,049,200,144,024,032,245
49434 :231,192,144,127,032,089,073
49440 :193,230,253,208,002,230,124
49446 :254,032,047,201,172,086,062
49452 :003,208,110,240,232,032,101
49458 :231,192,024,173,083,003,244
49464 :101,253,133,253,152,101,025
49470 :254,133,254,032,213,192,116
49476 :032,089,193,032,231,192,069
49482 :176,081,032,174,192,032,249
49488 :178,192,172,086,003,208,151
49494 :070,240,235,162,000,161,186
49500 :251,172,087,003,240,002,079
49506 :129,253,193,253,240,011,153
49512 :032,008,200,032,072,201,137
49518 :032,225,255,240,042,096,232
49524 :032,246,199,032,177,201,235
49530 :240,030,174,086,003,208,095
49536 :028,032,240,192,144,023,019
49542 :096,032,100,200,141,075,010
49548 :003,032,124,193,173,075,228
49554 :003,129,251,032,047,201,041
49560 :208,243,076,096,192,076,019
49566 :104,192,032,116,193,032,059
49572 :156,200,201,039,208,018,218
49578 :032,156,200,157,101,003,051
49584 :232,032,180,201,240,032,069
49590 :224,032,208,243,240,026,131
49596 :142,089,003,032,111,200,253
49602 :144,214,157,101,003,232,021
49608 :032,180,201,240,009,032,126
49614 :103,200,144,200,224,032,085
49620 :208,238,142,074,003,032,141
49626 :163,197,162,000,160,000,132
49632 :177,251,221,101,003,208,161
49638 :010,200,232,236,074,003,217
49644 :208,242,032,104,193,032,023
49650 :047,201,032,124,193,176,247
49656 :227,032,032,196,032,240,239
49662 :192,144,013,160,044,032,071
49668 :196,192,032,111,194,032,249
49674 :225,255,208,238,032,171,115
49680 :197,208,138,032,061,201,085
49686 :032,008,200,032,072,201,055
```

```
49692 :032,201,205,072,032,207,009
49698 :194,104,032,230,194,162,182
49704 :006,224,003,208,020,172,161
49710 :077,003,240,015,173,088,130
49716 :003,201,232,177,251,176,068
49722 :029,032,101,194,136,208,246
49728 :241,014,088,003,144,014,056
49734 :189,233,206,032,142,197,045
49740 :189,239,206,240,003,032,217
49746 :142,197,202,208,210,096,113
49752 :032,123,194,170,232,208,023
49758 :001,200,152,032,101,194,006
49764 :138,142,074,003,032,015,248
49770 :200,174,074,003,096,173,058
49776 :077,003,032,122,194,133,161
49782 :251,132,252,096,056,164,045
49788 :252,170,016,001,136,101,032
49794 :251,144,001,200,096,168,222
49800 :074,144,011,074,176,023,126
49806 :201,034,240,019,041,007,172
49812 :009,128,074,170,189,152,102
49818 :206,176,004,074,074,074,250
49824 :074,041,015,208,004,160,150
49830 :128,169,000,170,189,220,018
49836 :206,141,088,003,041,003,142
49842 :141,077,003,152,041,143,223
49848 :170,152,160,003,224,138,007
49854 :240,011,074,144,008,074,229
49860 :074,009,032,136,208,250,137
49866 :200,136,208,242,096,177,237
49872 :251,032,101,194,162,001,181
49878 :032,206,192,204,077,003,160
49884 :200,144,240,162,003,192,137
49890 :003,144,241,096,168,185,039
49896 :246,206,141,084,003,185,073
49902 :054,207,141,085,003,169,129
49908 :000,160,005,014,085,003,255
49914 :046,084,003,042,136,208,001
49920 :246,105,063,032,210,255,143
49926 :202,208,234,076,072,201,231
49932 :032,246,199,169,003,032,181
49938 :158,195,160,044,076,049,188
49944 :197,169,008,133,186,169,118
49950 :001,162,165,160,207,032,245
49956 :189,255,169,096,133,185,039
49962 :032,213,243,165,186,032,145
49968 :180,255,165,185,032,150,247
49974 :255,169,000,133,144,160,147
49980 :003,132,183,032,165,255,062
```

```
49986 :133,195,032,165,255,133,211
49992 :196,164,144,208,062,164,242
49998 :183,136,208,235,166,195,177
50004 :165,196,032,205,189,169,016
50010 :032,032,022,231,032,165,092
50016 :255,166,144,208,038,201,084
50022 :000,240,024,032,022,231,139
50028 :032,225,255,240,026,032,150
50034 :228,255,240,232,201,032,022
50040 :208,228,032,228,255,240,031
50046 :251,208,221,169,013,032,252
50052 :022,231,160,002,076,061,172
50058 :195,032,066,246,076,104,089
50064 :192,169,204,072,169,119,045
50070 :072,008,072,072,072,108,042
50076 :096,003,141,075,003,072,034
50082 :032,156,200,032,016,201,031
50088 :208,248,104,073,255,076,108
50094 :114,194,032,032,196,174,148
50100 :086,003,208,013,032,240,250
50106 :192,144,008,032,200,195,189
50112 :032,225,255,208,238,076,202
50118 :014,194,032,163,197,162,192
50124 :046,169,058,032,030,200,227
50130 :032,072,201,032,008,200,243
50136 :169,008,032,250,200,169,020
50142 :008,032,171,195,032,072,220
50148 :201,032,004,192,234,234,101
50154 :160,008,162,000,161,251,208
50160 :072,041,127,201,032,104,049
50166 :176,002,169,046,032,210,113
50172 :255,169,000,133,212,032,029
50178 :047,201,136,208,231,076,133
50184 :229,202,032,246,199,169,061
50190 :008,032,158,195,032,171,098
50196 :197,032,200,195,169,058,103
50202 :141,119,002,076,061,197,110
50208 :032,246,199,133,253,134,005
50214 :254,032,180,201,240,003,180
50220 :032,251,199,076,163,197,194
50226 :032,065,200,133,253,134,099
50232 :254,162,000,142,102,003,207
50238 :032,156,200,201,032,240,155
50244 :244,157,079,003,232,224,239
50250 :003,208,241,202,048,020,028
50256 :189,079,003,056,233,063,191
50262 :160,005,074,110,102,003,028
50268 :110,101,003,136,208,246,128
50274 :240,233,162,002,032,180,179
```

```
50280 :201,240,034,201,058,240,054
50286 :030,201,032,240,243,032,120
50292 :133,197,176,015,032,124,025
50298 :200,164,251,132,252,133,230
50304 :251,169,048,157,101,003,089
50310 :232,157,101,003,232,208,043
50316 :217,142,084,003,162,000,236
50322 :142,086,003,162,000,142,169
50328 :075,003,173,086,003,032,012
50334 :135,194,174,088,003,142,126
50340 :085,003,170,189,054,207,104
50346 :032,101,197,189,246,206,117
50352 :032,101,197,162,006,224,130
50358 :003,208,020,172,077,003,153
50364 :240,015,173,088,003,201,140
50370 :232,169,048,176,030,032,113
50376 :098,197,136,208,241,014,070
50382 :088,003,144,014,189,233,109
50388 :206,032,101,197,189,239,152
50394 :206,240,003,032,101,197,229
50400 :202,208,210,240,006,032,098
50406 :098,197,032,098,197,173,001
50412 :084,003,205,075,003,208,046
50418 :127,032,049,200,172,077,131
50424 :003,240,047,173,085,003,031
50430 :201,157,208,032,032,240,100
50436 :192,144,001,136,200,208,117
50442 :111,152,042,174,083,003,063
50448 :224,130,168,208,003,176,157
50454 :003,056,176,096,202,202,245
50460 :138,172,077,003,208,003,117
50466 :185,252,000,145,251,136,235
50472 :208,248,173,086,003,145,135
50478 :251,160,065,140,119,002,015
50484 :032,171,197,032,196,192,104
50490 :032,111,194,169,032,141,225
50496 :120,002,141,125,002,165,107
50502 :252,032,148,197,142,121,194
50508 :002,141,122,002,165,251,247
50514 :032,148,197,142,123,002,214
50520 :141,124,002,169,007,133,152
50526 :198,076,104,192,032,101,029
50532 :197,142,074,003,174,075,253
50538 :003,221,101,003,240,013,175
50544 :104,104,238,086,003,240,119
50550 :003,076,149,196,076,096,202
50556 :192,232,142,075,003,174,174
50562 :074,003,096,201,048,144,184
50568 :003,201,071,096,056,096,147
```

```
50574  :205,078,003,208,026,096,246
50580  :072,074,074,074,074,032,036
50586  :039,200,170,104,041,015,211
50592  :076,039,200,169,013,032,177
50598  :210,255,169,010,044,169,255
50604  :145,032,210,255,173,017,236
50610  :208,009,016,141,017,208,009
50616  :096,234,234,141,063,003,187
50622  :008,104,041,239,141,062,017
50628  :003,142,064,003,140,065,101
50634  :003,104,024,105,001,141,068
50640  :061,003,104,105,000,141,110
50646  :060,003,169,128,141,072,019
50652  :003,208,031,032,164,200,090
50658  :032,221,253,216,104,141,169
50664  :065,003,104,141,064,003,100
50670  :104,141,063,003,104,141,026
50676  :062,003,104,141,061,003,106
50682  :104,141,060,003,173,020,239
50688  :003,141,068,003,173,021,153
50694  :003,141,067,003,186,142,036
50700  :066,003,088,173,062,003,151
50706  :041,016,240,003,076,078,216
50712  :192,044,072,003,080,031,190
50718  :173,060,003,205,091,003,053
50724  :208,107,173,061,003,205,025
50730  :090,003,208,099,173,094,197
50736  :003,208,091,173,095,003,109
50742  :208,083,169,128,141,072,087
50748  :003,048,018,078,072,003,026
50754  :144,210,174,066,003,154,049
50760  :169,197,072,169,186,072,169
50766  :076,022,199,032,163,197,255
50772  :032,036,201,141,075,003,060
50778  :160,000,032,002,201,173,146
50784  :061,003,174,060,003,133,018
50790  :251,134,252,032,072,201,020
50796  :169,036,141,078,003,032,055
50802  :022,194,032,228,255,240,061
50808  :251,201,003,208,003,076,094
50814  :104,192,201,074,208,077,214
50820  :169,001,141,072,003,208,214
50826  :070,206,095,003,206,094,044
50832  :003,165,145,201,127,208,225
50838  :058,162,083,076,091,192,044
50844  :169,000,240,018,173,092,080
50850  :003,174,093,003,141,094,158
50856  :003,142,095,003,169,064,132
50862  :208,002,169,128,141,072,126
```

```
50868 :003,032,180,201,240,015,083
50874 :201,032,208,110,032,085,086
50880 :200,032,243,200,032,180,055
50886 :201,208,099,032,163,197,074
50892 :173,072,003,240,055,162,141
50898 :000,173,017,208,168,041,049
50904 :016,240,016,152,041,239,152
50910 :141,017,208,234,234,160,192
50916 :012,202,208,253,136,208,223
50922 :250,120,169,084,141,004,234
50928 :220,142,005,220,173,014,246
50934 :220,041,128,009,017,141,034
50940 :014,220,169,223,162,197,213
50946 :141,068,003,142,067,003,170
50952 :174,066,003,154,120,173,186
50958 :068,003,174,067,003,032,105
50964 :168,200,173,060,003,072,184
50970 :173,061,003,072,173,062,058
50976 :003,072,173,063,003,174,008
50982 :064,003,172,065,003,064,153
50988 :076,096,192,032,065,200,193
50994 :141,090,003,142,091,003,008
51000 :169,000,141,092,003,141,090
51006 :093,003,032,082,200,141,101
51012 :092,003,142,093,003,076,221
51018 :104,192,032,219,199,141,193
51024 :098,003,142,099,003,032,201
51030 :082,200,141,079,003,142,221
51036 :080,003,032,082,200,141,118
51042 :081,003,142,082,003,032,185
51048 :180,201,240,010,032,207,206
51054 :255,201,087,208,003,238,078
51060 :078,003,032,049,200,174,140
51066 :086,003,208,024,032,231,194
51072 :192,144,019,172,078,003,224
51078 :208,026,177,251,032,135,195
51084 :194,170,189,246,206,208,073
51090 :006,032,196,192,076,104,240
51096 :192,172,077,003,192,002,022
51102 :208,051,240,003,140,077,109
51108 :003,136,056,177,251,170,189
51114 :237,079,003,200,177,251,093
51120 :237,080,003,144,030,136,038
51126 :173,081,003,241,251,200,107
51132 :173,082,003,241,251,144,058
51138 :016,136,024,138,109,098,203
51144 :003,145,251,200,177,251,203
51150 :109,099,003,145,251,032,077
51156 :047,201,136,016,250,048,142
```

```
51162 :158,032,065,200,133,253,035
51168 :134,254,032,082,200,141,043
51174 :084,003,142,085,003,032,067
51180 :156,200,032,085,200,133,018
51186 :251,134,252,096,032,065,048
51192 :200,176,246,032,085,200,163
51198 :176,003,032,082,200,133,112
51204 :253,134,254,096,165,252,134
51210 :032,015,200,165,251,072,233
51216 :074,074,074,074,032,039,127
51222 :200,170,104,041,015,032,072
51228 :039,200,072,138,032,210,207
51234 :255,104,076,210,255,024,190
51240 :105,246,144,002,105,006,136
51246 :105,058,096,162,002,181,138
51252 :250,072,181,252,149,250,182
51258 :104,149,252,202,208,243,192
51264 :096,169,000,141,089,003,050
51270 :032,156,200,201,032,240,163
51276 :249,032,124,200,176,008,097
51282 :032,156,200,032,103,200,037
51288 :144,007,170,032,103,200,232
51294 :144,001,096,076,096,192,187
51300 :032,116,193,169,000,141,239
51306 :089,003,032,156,200,201,019
51312 :032,208,009,032,156,200,237
51318 :201,032,208,015,024,096,182
51324 :032,145,200,010,010,010,019
51330 :010,141,089,003,032,156,049
51336 :200,032,145,200,013,089,047
51342 :003,056,096,201,058,008,052
51348 :041,015,040,144,002,105,239
51354 :008,096,032,180,201,208,111
51360 :250,076,101,192,169,145,069
51366 :162,195,141,020,003,142,061
51372 :021,003,096,032,180,201,193
51378 :240,055,032,246,199,165,091
51384 :251,005,252,240,034,165,107
51390 :154,201,003,208,158,165,055
51396 :251,141,147,002,165,252,130
51402 :141,148,002,169,002,170,066
51408 :168,032,186,255,032,192,049
51414 :255,162,002,032,201,255,097
51420 :076,117,192,169,000,032,040
51426 :195,255,169,003,133,154,111
51432 :076,104,192,165,154,201,100
51438 :003,240,220,208,241,141,011
51444 :061,003,142,060,003,096,097
51450 :141,075,003,160,000,032,149
```

```
51456 :072,201,177,251,032,015,236
51462 :200,032,047,201,206,075,255
51468 :003,208,240,096,032,103,182
51474 :200,144,008,162,000,129,149
51480 :251,193,251,208,105,032,040
51486 :047,201,206,075,003,096,146
51492 :169,062,133,251,169,003,055
51498 :133,252,169,005,096,230,159
51504 :251,208,009,230,255,230,207
51510 :252,208,003,238,086,003,076
51516 :096,152,072,032,163,197,004
51522 :104,162,046,032,030,200,128
51528 :169,032,076,210,255,032,078
51534 :030,200,162,000,189,118,009
51540 :207,032,210,255,232,224,220
51546 :028,208,245,160,059,032,054
51552 :061,201,173,060,003,032,114
51558 :015,200,173,061,003,032,074
51564 :015,200,032,072,201,173,033
51570 :067,003,032,015,200,173,092
51576 :068,003,032,015,200,032,214
51582 :036,201,032,250,200,076,153
51588 :104,192,076,096,192,032,056
51594 :065,200,032,243,200,032,142
51600 :082,200,141,068,003,142,012
51606 :067,003,032,036,201,141,118
51612 :075,003,032,156,200,032,142
51618 :016,201,208,248,240,219,014
51624 :032,207,255,201,032,240,111
51630 :249,208,006,032,000,200,101
51636 :032,207,255,201,013,096,216
51642 :160,001,132,186,169,000,066
51648 :162,101,160,003,032,189,071
51654 :255,168,032,246,199,173,247
51660 :073,003,201,083,208,008,012
51666 :032,180,201,240,175,032,046
51672 :251,199,032,168,201,240,027
51678 :041,201,034,208,163,032,133
51684 :207,255,201,034,240,011,152
51690 :145,187,230,183,200,192,091
51696 :081,144,240,176,145,032,034
51702 :180,201,240,014,032,103,248
51708 :200,041,031,240,133,133,006
51714 :186,032,168,201,208,217,246
51720 :169,000,133,185,173,073,229
51726 :003,201,083,208,012,169,178
51732 :251,166,253,164,254,032,116
51738 :216,255,076,104,192,073,174
51744 :076,240,002,169,001,166,174
```

```
51750 :251,164,252,032,213,255,181
51756 :165,144,041,016,240,234,116
51762 :169,105,160,163,032,030,197
51768 :171,076,096,192,032,246,101
51774 :199,032,165,192,076,104,062
51780 :192,032,246,199,032,047,048
51786 :201,032,047,201,032,000,075
51792 :200,032,072,201,032,240,089
51798 :192,144,010,152,208,021,045
51804 :173,083,003,048,016,016,175
51810 :008,200,208,011,173,083,013
51816 :003,016,006,032,015,200,120
51822 :076,104,192,076,096,192,078
51828 :032,246,199,032,138,202,197
51834 :076,104,192,032,163,197,118
51840 :162,046,169,036,032,030,091
51846 :200,032,008,200,032,234,072
51852 :202,032,176,202,032,072,088
51858 :201,032,150,202,032,153,148
51864 :202,032,072,201,162,004,057
51870 :169,048,024,014,084,003,244
51876 :046,085,003,105,000,032,179
51882 :210,255,202,208,239,096,100
51888 :165,252,166,251,141,085,212
51894 :003,142,084,003,032,072,006
51900 :201,165,252,032,196,202,212
51906 :165,251,170,032,072,201,061
51912 :138,041,127,201,032,008,235
51918 :176,010,169,018,032,210,053
51924 :255,138,024,105,064,170,200
51930 :138,032,210,255,169,000,254
51936 :133,212,040,176,202,169,132
51942 :146,076,210,255,032,072,253
51948 :201,166,251,165,252,076,067
51954 :205,189,032,005,203,176,028
51960 :065,032,072,201,032,008,146
51966 :200,032,141,202,076,104,241
51972 :192,162,004,169,000,133,152
51978 :252,032,194,203,032,043,254
51984 :203,133,251,032,034,203,104
51990 :032,061,203,202,208,247,207
51996 :008,032,072,201,040,096,221
52002 :032,180,201,240,015,201,135
52008 :032,240,011,201,048,144,204
52014 :011,201,058,176,007,041,028
52020 :015,096,104,104,024,096,235
52026 :076,096,192,133,254,165,206
52032 :252,072,165,251,072,006,114
52038 :251,038,252,006,251,038,138
```

```
52044 :252,104,101,251,133,251,144
52050 :104,101,252,133,252,006,162
52056 :251,038,252,165,254,101,125
52062 :251,133,251,169,000,101,231
52068 :252,133,252,096,032,194,035
52074 :203,141,085,003,072,072,170
52080 :032,072,201,032,072,201,210
52086 :104,032,015,200,032,072,061
52092 :201,104,170,169,000,032,032
52098 :241,202,032,072,201,032,142
52104 :150,202,076,104,192,032,124
52110 :159,203,032,072,201,032,073
52116 :008,200,032,234,202,032,088
52122 :176,202,076,104,192,162,042
52128 :015,169,000,133,251,133,093
52134 :252,032,194,203,032,043,154
52140 :203,032,188,203,032,034,096
52146 :203,032,188,203,202,208,190
52152 :247,076,072,201,074,038,124
52158 :251,038,252,096,032,156,247
52164 :200,201,032,240,249,096,190
52170 :169,015,141,024,212,169,164
52176 :000,141,005,212,169,240,207
52182 :162,068,160,149,141,006,132
52188 :212,142,001,212,140,000,159
52194 :212,076,101,192,000,032,071
52200 :000,200,076,235,199,032,206
52206 :231,203,024,165,251,101,189
52212 :253,133,251,165,252,101,119
52218 :254,133,252,076,013,204,158
52224 :032,231,203,032,240,192,162
52230 :132,252,173,083,003,133,014
52236 :251,032,072,201,032,008,096
52242 :200,076,104,192,169,000,247
52248 :170,168,141,024,212,076,047
52254 :218,203,000,120,032,021,112
52260 :253,088,169,060,133,178,149
52266 :174,066,003,154,165,115,207
52272 :201,230,240,149,108,000,208
52278 :160,032,231,203,032,049,249
52284 :200,032,072,201,160,000,213
52290 :140,084,003,140,085,003,009
52296 :032,240,192,144,027,172,111
52302 :086,003,208,022,024,177,086
52308 :251,109,084,003,141,084,244
52314 :003,152,109,085,003,141,071
52320 :085,003,032,047,201,076,028
52326 :072,204,173,085,003,032,159
52332 :015,200,173,084,003,032,103
```

```
52338 :015,200,076,104,192,173,106
52344 :100,003,208,004,165,198,030
52350 :208,003,076,129,234,173,181
52356 :119,002,201,017,208,125,036
52362 :165,214,201,024,208,240,166
52368 :165,209,133,253,165,210,255
52374 :133,254,169,025,141,094,198
52380 :003,160,001,032,084,206,130
52386 :201,058,240,026,201,044,164
52392 :240,022,201,036,240,018,157
52398 :206,094,003,240,205,056,210
52404 :165,253,233,040,133,253,233
52410 :176,225,198,254,208,221,188
52416 :141,073,003,032,013,206,148
52422 :176,184,173,073,003,201,240
52428 :058,208,017,024,165,251,159
52434 :105,008,133,251,144,002,085
52440 :230,252,032,200,195,076,177
52446 :244,204,201,036,240,026,149
52452 :032,201,205,032,111,194,235
52458 :169,000,141,078,003,160,017
52464 :044,032,019,194,169,000,186
52470 :133,198,076,014,194,076,169
52476 :129,234,032,047,201,032,159
52482 :125,202,076,244,204,201,030
52488 :145,208,240,165,214,208,164
52494 :236,165,209,133,253,165,151
52500 :210,133,254,169,025,141,184
52506 :094,003,160,001,032,084,144
52512 :206,201,058,240,026,201,196
52518 :044,240,022,201,036,240,053
52524 :018,206,094,003,240,021,114
52530 :024,165,253,105,040,133,002
52536 :253,144,225,230,254,208,090
52542 :221,141,073,003,032,013,033
52548 :206,144,003,076,129,234,092
52554 :173,073,003,201,058,240,054
52560 :006,201,036,240,029,208,032
52566 :039,032,208,205,056,165,023
52572 :251,233,008,133,251,176,120
52578 :002,198,252,032,203,195,212
52584 :169,000,133,198,032,008,132
52590 :206,076,112,192,032,208,168
52596 :205,032,178,192,032,128,115
52602 :202,076,104,205,032,208,181
52608 :205,165,251,166,252,133,020
52614 :253,134,254,169,016,141,077
52620 :094,003,056,165,253,237,180
52626 :094,003,133,251,165,254,022
```

```
52632 :233,000,133,252,032,201,235
52638 :205,032,111,194,032,240,204
52644 :192,240,007,176,243,206,204
52650 :094,003,208,224,238,077,246
52656 :003,173,077,003,032,171,123
52662 :195,162,000,161,251,142,069
52668 :078,003,169,044,032,067,069
52674 :201,032,022,194,076,104,055
52680 :205,162,000,161,251,076,031
52686 :135,194,166,210,032,215,134
52692 :205,166,244,232,232,232,243
52698 :134,173,134,254,162,000,051
52704 :134,172,169,040,133,253,101
52710 :160,192,162,003,136,177,036
52716 :172,145,253,152,208,248,134
52722 :198,173,198,254,202,016,003
52728 :241,169,032,166,210,134,176
52734 :254,132,253,160,039,145,213
52740 :253,136,016,251,169,019,080
52746 :076,210,255,192,040,208,223
52752 :002,056,096,032,084,206,236
52758 :201,032,240,243,136,032,138
52764 :061,206,170,032,061,206,252
52770 :133,251,134,252,169,255,204
52776 :141,100,003,133,204,165,018
52782 :207,240,010,165,206,164,014
52788 :211,145,209,169,000,133,151
52794 :207,024,096,032,084,206,195
52800 :032,145,200,010,010,010,215
52806 :010,141,089,003,032,084,173
52812 :206,032,145,200,013,089,249
52818 :003,096,177,253,200,041,084
52824 :127,201,032,176,002,009,123
52830 :064,096,189,152,205,032,064
52836 :210,255,232,208,247,096,068
52842 :000,000,000,000,000,147,253
52848 :017,032,032,018,032,032,019
52854 :032,032,077,073,067,082,225
52860 :079,077,079,078,045,054,024
52866 :052,032,032,067,079,077,213
52872 :080,085,084,069,033,032,007
52878 :032,066,079,079,075,083,044
52884 :032,032,032,032,064,002,086
52890 :069,003,208,008,064,009,003
52896 :048,034,069,051,208,008,066
52902 :064,009,064,002,069,051,169
52908 :208,008,064,009,064,002,015
52914 :069,179,208,008,064,009,203
52920 :000,034,068,051,208,140,173
```

```
52926  :068,000,017,034,068,051,172
52932  :208,140,068,154,016,034,048
52938  :068,051,208,008,064,009,098
52944  :016,034,068,051,208,008,081
52950  :064,009,098,019,120,169,181
52956  :000,033,129,130,000,000,000
52962  :089,077,145,146,134,074,123
52968  :133,157,044,041,044,035,174
52974  :040,036,089,000,088,036,015
52980  :036,000,028,138,028,035,253
52986  :093,139,027,161,157,138,197
52992  :029,035,157,139,029,161,038
52998  :000,041,025,174,105,168,007
53004  :025,035,036,083,027,035,253
53010  :036,083,025,161,000,026,093
53016  :091,091,165,105,036,036,036
53022  :174,174,168,173,041,000,248
53028  :124,000,021,156,109,156,090
53034  :165,105,041,083,132,019,075
53040  :052,017,165,105,035,160,070
53046  :216,098,090,072,038,098,154
53052  :148,136,084,068,200,084,012
53058  :104,068,232,148,000,180,030
53064  :008,132,116,180,040,110,146
53070  :116,244,204,074,114,242,048
53076  :164,138,000,170,162,162,112
53082  :116,116,116,114,068,104,212
53088  :178,050,178,000,034,000,024
53094  :026,026,038,038,114,114,202
53100  :136,200,196,202,038,072,184
53106  :068,068,162,200,013,032,145
53112  :032,032,032,080,067,032,139
53118  :032,073,082,081,032,032,202
53124  :083,082,032,065,067,032,237
53130  :088,082,032,089,082,032,031
53136  :083,080,065,066,067,068,061
53142  :070,071,072,076,077,078,082
53148  :081,082,040,084,087,088,106
53154  :044,058,059,036,035,034,172
53160  :043,045,079,073,074,037,007
53166  :038,069,086,041,062,255,213
53172  :255,186,201,175,200,050,223
53178  :196,047,199,002,193,249,048
53184  :193,135,193,156,198,160,203
53190  :193,186,201,176,195,076,201
53196  :199,160,198,080,201,202,220
53202  :203,006,193,176,198,042,004
53208  :204,012,195,010,196,137,202
53214  :201,116,202,244,202,104,011
```

```
53220  :203,237,203,000,204,069,120
53226  :202,096,192,060,202,141,103
53232  :203,055,204,033,204,186,101
53238  :201,022,204,025,195,096,221
53244  :192,096,192,255,000,000,219
```

Appendix A

Using the Machine Language Editor: MLX

Using the Machine Language Editor: MLX

Charles Brannon

Remember the last time you typed in the BASIC loader for a long machine language program? You typed in hundreds of numbers and commas. Even then, you couldn't be sure if you typed it in right. So you went back, proofread, tried to run the program, crashed, went back and proofread again, corrected a few typing errors, ran again, crashed again, rechecked your typing ... Frustrating, wasn't it?

Until now, though, that has been the best way to get machine language into your computer. Unless you happen to have an assembler and are willing to wrangle with machine language on the assembly level, it is much easier to enter a BASIC program that reads DATA statements and POKEs the numbers into memory.

Some of these "BASIC loaders" will use a *checksum* to see if you've typed the numbers correctly. The simplest checksum is just the sum of all the numbers in the DATA statements. If you make an error, your checksum will not match up with the total. Some programmers make your task easier by including checksums every few lines, so you can locate your errors more easily.

Now, MLX comes to the rescue. MLX is a great way to enter all those long machine language programs with a minimum of fuss. MLX lets you enter the numbers from a special list that looks similar to DATA statements. It checks your typing on a line-by-line basis. It won't let you enter illegal characters when you should be typing numbers. It won't let you enter numbers greater than 255.

247

It will prevent you from entering the numbers on the wrong line. In short, MLX will make proofreading obsolete.

Tape or Disk Copies

In addition, MLX will generate a ready-to-use copy of your machine language program on tape or disk. You can then use the LOAD command to read the program into the computer, just like a BASIC program. Specifically, you enter:

LOAD "program name",1,1 (for tape)
or
LOAD "program name",8,1 (for disk)

To start the program, you need to enter a SYS command that transfers control from BASIC to your machine language program. The starting SYS will always be given in the article which presents the machine language program in MLX format.

Using MLX

Type in and SAVE MLX (you'll want to use it in the future). When you're ready to type in the machine language program, RUN MLX. MLX will ask you for two numbers: the starting address and the ending address. For Micromon-64, these numbers should be: 49152 and 53247 respectively.

You'll then get a prompt showing the specified starting address. (For Micromon-64, the prompt will be: 49152)

The prompt is the current line you are entering from the MLX-format listing. Each line is six numbers plus a checksum. If you enter any of the six numbers wrong, or enter the checksum wrong, the 64 will sound a buzzer and prompt you to reenter the entire line. If you enter the line correctly, a pleasant bell tone will sound and you may go on to enter the next line.

A Special Editor

You are not using the normal Commodore 64 BASIC editor with MLX. For example, it will only accept numbers as input. If you need to make a correction, press the INST/DEL key; the entire number is deleted. You can press it as many times as necessary, back to the start of the line. If you enter three-digit numbers as listed, the computer will automatically print the comma and go on to accept the next number in the line. If you enter less than three digits, you can press either the comma, space bar, or RETURN key to advance to the next number. The checksum will automatically appear in inverse video; don't worry — it's high-lighted for emphasis.

When testing it, I've found MLX to be an extremely easy way to enter long listings. With the audio cues provided, you don't even have to look at the screen if you're a touch-typist.

Done at Last!

When you get through typing, assuming you type your machine language program all in one session, you can then save the completed and bug-free program to tape or disk. Follow the instructions displayed on the screen. If you get any error messages while saving, you probably have a bad disk, or the disk was full, or you made a typo when entering the MLX program. (Sorry, MLX can't check itself!)

Command Control

What if you don't want to enter the whole program in one sitting? MLX lets you enter as much as you want, save the completed portion, and then reload your work from tape or disk when you want to continue. MLX recognizes these few commands:

SHIFT-S: Save
SHIFT-L: Load
SHIFT-N: New Address
SHIFT-D: Display

Hold down SHIFT while you press the appropriate key. You will jump out of the line you've been typing, so I recommend you do it at a new prompt. Use the Save command to store what you've been working on. It will write the tape or disk file as if you've finished. Remember what address you stop on. The next time you RUN MLX, answer all the prompts as you did before, then insert the disk or tape containing the stored file. When you get to the entry prompt (49152: for Micromon-64), press SHIFT-L to reload the file into memory. You'll then use the New Address command (SHIFT-N) to resume typing.

New Address and Display

After you press SHIFT-N, enter the address where you previously stopped. The prompt will change, and you can then continue typing. Always enter a New Address that matches up with one of the line numbers in the special listing, or else the checksums won't match up. You can use the Display command to display a section of your typing. After you press SHIFT-D, enter two addresses within the line number range of the listing. You can stop the display by pressing any key.

Tricky Stuff

The special commands may seem a little confusing, but as you work with MLX, they will become valuable. For example, what if you forgot where you stopped typing? Use the Display command to scan memory from the beginning to the end of the program. When you see a bunch of 170's, stop the listing (press a key) and continue typing where the 170's start. Some programs contain many sections of 170's. To avoid typing them, you can use the New Address command to skip over the blocks of 170's. Be careful, though; you don't want to skip over anything you *should* type.

You can use the Save and Load commands to make copies of the completed machine language program. Use Load command to reload the tape or disk, then insert a new tape or disk and use the Save command to create a new copy.

One quirk about tapes made with the MLX Save command: when you load them, the message "FOUND program" may appear twice. The tape will load just fine, however.

Programmers will find MLX to be an interesting program which protects the user from most typing mistakes. Some screen formatting techniques are also used. Most interesting is the use of ROM Kernal routines for LOADing and SAVEing blocks of memory. To use these routines, just POKE in the starting address (low byte/high byte) into memory locations 251 and 252 and POKE the ending address into locations 254 and 255. Any error code for the SAVE or LOAD can be found in location 253 (an error would be a code less than ten).

I hope you will find MLX to be a true labor-saving program. Since it has been tested by entering actual programs, you can count on it as an aid for generating bug-free machine language. Be sure to save MLX; it will be used for future applications in *COMPUTE!* Magazine, *COMPUTE!'s Gazette* and COMPUTE! Books.

Machine Language Editor (MLX)

```
100 PRINT"{CLR}{RED}";CHR$(142);CHR$(8);:
    POKE53281,1:POKE53280,1
101 POKE 788,52:REM DISABLE RUN/STOP
110 PRINT"{RVS}{40 SPACES}";
120 PRINT"{RVS}{15 SPACES}{RIGHT}{OFF}
    {*}£{RVS}{RIGHT} {RIGHT}{2 SPACES}
    {*}{OFF}{*}£{RVS}£{RVS}
    {13 SPACES}";
```

```
130 PRINT"{RVS}{15 SPACES}{RIGHT} {G}
    {RIGHT} {2 RIGHT} {OFF}£{RVS}£{*}
    {OFF}{*}{RVS}{13 SPACES}";
140 PRINT"{RVS}{40 SPACES}"
150 V=53248:POKE2040,13:POKE2041,13:FORI=
    832TO894:POKEI,255:NEXT:POKEV+27,3
160 POKEV+21,3:POKEV+39,2:POKEV+40,2:POKE
    V,144:POKEV+1,54:POKEV+2,192:POKEV+3,
    54
170 POKEV+29,3
180 FORI=0TO23:READA:POKE679+I,A:POKEV+39
    ,A:POKEV+40,A:NEXT
185 DATA169,251,166,254,164,255,32,216,25
    5,133,253,96
187 DATA169,0,166,251,164,252,32,213,255,
    133,253,96
190 POKEV+39,7:POKEV+40,7
200 PRINT"{2 DOWN}{PUR}{BLK}{3 SPACES}A F
    AILSAFE MACHINE LANGUAGE EDITOR
    {5 DOWN}"
210 PRINT"{5}{2 UP}STARTING ADDRESS?
    {8 SPACES}{9 LEFT}";:INPUTS:F=1-F:C$=
    CHR$(31+119*F)
220 IFS<256OR(S>4096OANDS<49152)ORS>53247
    THENGOSUB3000:GOTO210
225 PRINT:PRINT:PRINT
230 PRINT"{5}{2 UP}ENDING ADDRESS?
    {8 SPACES}{9 LEFT}";:INPUTE:F=1-F:C$=
    CHR$(31+119*F)
240 IFE<256OR(E>4096OANDE<49152)ORE>53247
    THENGOSUB3000:GOTO230
250 IFE<STHENPRINTC$;"{RVS}ENDING < START
    {2 SPACES}":GOSUB1000:GOTO 230
260 PRINT:PRINT:PRINT
300 PRINT"{CLR}";CHR$(14):AD=S:POKEV+21,0
310 PRINTRIGHT$("0000"+MID$(STR$(AD),2),5
    );":";:FORJ=1TO6
320 GOSUB570:IFN=-1THENJ=J+N:GOTO320
390 IFN=-211THEN 710
400 IFN=-204THEN 790
410 IFN=-206THENPRINT:INPUT"{DOWN}ENTER N
    EW ADDRESS";ZZ
415 IFN=-206THENIFZZ<SORZZ>ETHENPRINT"
    {RVS}OUT OF RANGE":GOSUB1000:GOTO410
417 IFN=-206THENAD=ZZ:PRINT:GOTO310
420 IF N<>-196 THEN 480
430 PRINT:INPUT"DISPLAY:FROM";F:PRINT,"TO
    ";:INPUTT
```

```
440 IFF<SORF>EORT<SORT>ETHENPRINT"AT LEAS
    T";S;"{LEFT}, NOT MORE THAN";E:GOTO43
    0
450 FORI=FTOTSTEP6:PRINT:PRINTRIGHT$("000
    0"+MID$(STR$(I),2),5);":";
451 FORK=0TO5:N=PEEK(I+K):PRINTRIGHT$("00
    "+MID$(STR$(N),2),3);",";
460 GETA$:IFA$>""THENPRINT:PRINT:GOTO310
470 NEXTK:PRINTCHR$(20);:NEXTI:PRINT:PRIN
    T:GOTO310
480 IFN<0 THEN PRINT:GOTO310
490 A(J)=N:NEXTJ
500 CKSUM=AD-INT(AD/256)*256:FORI=1TO6:CK
    SUM=(CKSUM+A(I))AND255:NEXT
510 PRINTCHR$(18);:GOSUB570:PRINTCHR$(20)
515 IFN=CKSUMTHEN530
520 PRINT:PRINT"LINE ENTERED WRONG : RE-E
    NTER":PRINT:GOSUB1000:GOTO310
530 GOSUB2000
540 FORI=1TO6:POKEAD+I-1,A(I):NEXT:POKE54
    272,0:POKE54273,0
550 AD=AD+6:IF AD<E THEN 310
560 GOTO 710
570 N=0:Z=0
580 PRINT"{+}";
581 GETA$:IFA$=""THEN581
585 PRINTCHR$(20);:A=ASC(A$):IFA=13ORA=44
    ORA=32THEN670
590 IFA>128THENN=-A:RETURN
600 IFA<>20 THEN 630
610 GOSUB690:IFI=1ANDT=44THENN=-1:PRINT"
    {LEFT} {LEFT}";:GOTO690
620 GOTO570
630 IFA<48ORA>57THEN580
640 PRINTA$;:N=N*10+A-48
650 IFN>255 THEN A=20:GOSUB1000:GOTO600
660 Z=Z+1:IFZ<3THEN580
670 IFZ=0THENGOSUB1000:GOTO570
680 PRINT",";:RETURN
690 S%=PEEK(209)+256*PEEK(210)+PEEK(211)
691 FORI=1TO3:T=PEEK(S%-I)
695 IFT<>44ANDT<>58THENPOKES%-I,32:NEXT
700 PRINTLEFT$("{3 LEFT}",I-1);:RETURN
710 PRINT"{CLR}{RVS}*** SAVE ***{3 DOWN}"
720 INPUT"{DOWN} FILENAME";F$
730 PRINT:PRINT"{2 DOWN}{RVS}T{OFF}APE OR
    {RVS}D{OFF}ISK: (T/D)"
740 GETA$:IFA$<>"T"ANDA$<>"D"THEN740
750 DV=1-7*(A$="D"):IFDV=8THENF$="0:"+F$
```

252

```
760 OPEN 1,DV,1,F$:POKE252,S/256:POKE251,
    S-PEEK(252)*256
765 POKE255,E/256:POKE254,E-PEEK(255)*256
770 POKE253,10:SYS 679:CLOSE1:IFPEEK(253)
    >9ORPEEK(253)=0THENPRINT"{DOWN}DONE."
    :END
780 PRINT"{DOWN}ERROR ON SAVE.{2 SPACES}T
    RY AGAIN.":IFDV=1THEN720
781 OPEN15,8,15:INPUT#15,DS,DS$:PRINTDS;D
    S$:CLOSE15:GOTO720
790 PRINT"{CLR}{RVS}*** LOAD ***{2 DOWN}"
800 INPUT"{2 DOWN} FILENAME";F$
810 PRINT:PRINT"{2 DOWN}{RVS}T{OFF}APE OR
    {RVS}D{OFF}ISK: (T/D)"
820 GETA$:IFA$<>"T"ANDA$<>"D"THEN820
830 DV=1-7*(A$="D"):IFDV=8THENF$="0:"+F$
840 OPEN 1,DV,0,F$:POKE252,S/256:POKE251,
    S-PEEK(252)*256
850 POKE253,10:SYS 691:CLOSE1
860 IFPEEK(253)>9 OR PEEK(253)=0 THEN PRI
    NT:PRINT:GOTO310
870 PRINT"{DOWN}ERROR ON LOAD.{2 SPACES}T
    RY AGAIN.{DOWN}":IFDV=1THEN800
880 OPEN15,8,15:INPUT#15,DS,DS$:PRINTDS;D
    S$:CLOSE15:GOTO800
1000 REM BUZZER
1001 POKE54296,15:POKE54277,45:POKE54278,
     165
1002 POKE54276,33:POKE 54273,6:POKE54272,
     5
1003 FORT=1TO200:NEXT:POKE54276,32:POKE54
     273,0:POKE54272,0:RETURN
2000 REM BELL SOUND
2001 POKE54296,15:POKE54277,0:POKE54278,2
     47
2002 POKE 54276,17:POKE54273,40:POKE54272
     ,0
2003 FORT=1TO100:NEXT:POKE54276,16:RETURN
3000 PRINTC$;"{RVS}NOT ZERO PAGE OR ROM":
     GOTO1000
```

Appendix B

A Beginner's Guide to Typing In Programs

A Beginner's Guide to Typing In Programs

What Is a Program?

A computer cannot perform any task by itself. Like a car without gas, a computer has *potential*, but without a program, it isn't going anywhere. Most of the programs in this book are written in a computer language called BASIC. BASIC is easy to learn and is built into all Commodore 64s.

BASIC Programs

Computers can be picky. Unlike the English language, which is full of ambiguities, BASIC usually has only one right way of stating something. Every letter, character, or number is significant. A common mistake is substituting a letter such as O for the numeral 0, a lowercase l for the numeral 1, or an uppercase B for the numeral 8. Also, you must enter all punctuation such as colons and commas just as they appear in the magazine. Spacing can be important. To be safe, type in the listings *exactly* as they appear.

Braces and Special Characters

The exception to this typing rule is when you see the braces, such as {DOWN}. Anything within a set of braces is a special character or characters that cannot easily be listed on a printer. When you come across such a special statement, refer to "How To Type In Programs."

About DATA Statements

Some programs contain a section or sections of DATA statements. These lines provide information needed by the program. Some DATA statements contain actual programs (called machine language); others contain graphics codes. These lines are especially sensitive to errors.

If a single number in any one DATA statement is mistyped, your machine could lock up, or crash. The keyboard and STOP key may seem dead, and the screen may go blank. Don't panic — no damage is done. To regain control, you have to turn off your computer, then turn it back on. This will erase whatever program was in memory, *so always SAVE a copy of your program before you RUN it.* If your computer crashes, you can LOAD the program and look for your mistake.

Sometimes a mistyped DATA statement will cause an error message when the program is RUN. The error message may refer to the program line that READs the data. *The error is still in the DATA statements, though.*

Get to Know Your Machine

You should familiarize yourself with your computer before attempting to type in a program. Learn the statements you use to store and retrieve programs from tape or disk. You'll want to save a copy of your program, so that you won't have to type it in every time you want to use it. Learn to use your machine's editing functions. How do you change a line if you made a mistake? You can always retype the line, but you at least need to know how to backspace. Do you know how to enter inverse video, lowercase, and control characters? It's all explained in your computer's manuals.

A Quick Review

1) Type in the program a line at a time, in order. Press RETURN at the end of each line. Use backspace or the back arrow to correct mistakes.

2) Check the line you've typed against the line in the printed listing. You can check the entire program again if you get an error when you RUN the program.

3) Make sure you've entered statements in brackets as the appropriate control key (see "How To Type Programs" elsewhere in the book).

Appendix C

How To Type In Programs

How To Type in Programs

Many of the programs which are listed in this book contain special control characters (cursor control, color keys, inverse video, etc.). To make it easy to know exactly what to type when entering one of these programs into your computer, we have established the following listing conventions.

Generally, any Commodore 64 program listings will contain words within braces which spell out any special characters: {DOWN} would mean to press the cursor down key. {5 SPACES} would mean to press the space bar five times.

To indicate that a key should be *shifted* (hold down the SHIFT key while pressing the other key), the key would be underlined in our listings. For example, S would mean to type the S key while holding the shift key. This would appear on your screen as a "heart" symbol. If you find an underlined key enclosed in braces (e.g., {10 N}), you should type the key as many times as indicated (in our example, you would enter ten shifted N's).

If a key is enclosed in special brackets, [< >], you should hold down the *Commodore key* while pressing the key inside the special brackets. (The Commodore key is the key in the lower-left corner of the keyboard.) Again, if the key is preceded by a number, you should press the key as many times as necessary.

Rarely, you'll see a solitary letter of the alphabet enclosed in braces. These characters can be entered on the Commodore 64 by holding down the CTRL key while typing the letter in braces. For example, {A} would indicate that you should press CTRL-A.

About the *quote mode:* you know that you can move the cursor around the screen with the CRSR keys. Sometimes a programmer will want to move the cursor under program control. That's why you see all the {LEFT}'s, {HOME}'s, and {BLU}'s in our programs. The only way the computer can tell the difference between direct and programmed cursor control is the quote mode.

Once you press the quote (the double quote, SHIFT-2), you are in the quote mode. If you type something and then try to change it by moving the cursor left, you'll only get a bunch of reverse-video lines. These are the symbols for cursor left. The only editing key that isn't programmable is the DEL key; you can still use DEL to back up and edit the line. Once you type another quote, you are out of quote mode.

You also go into quote mode when you INSerT spaces into a line. In any case, the easiest way to get out of quote mode is to just press RETURN. You'll then be out of quote mode, and you can cursor up to the mistyped line and fix it.

Use the following table when entering cursor and color control keys:

Listing Conventions

When You Read:	Press:		See:	When You Read:	Press:		See:
{CLEAR}	SHIFT	CLR/HOME		{GRN}	CTRL	6	
{HOME}		CLR/HOME		{BLU}	CTRL	7	
{UP}	SHIFT	CRSR		{YEL}	CTRL	8	
{DOWN}		CRSR		{F1}	f1		
{LEFT}	SHIFT	CRSR		{F2}	f2		
{RIGHT}		CRSR		{F3}	f3		
{RVS}	CTRL	9		{F4}	f4		
{OFF}	CTRL	0		{F5}	f5		
{BLK}	CTRL	1		{F6}	f6		
{WHT}	CTRL	2		{F7}	f7		
{RED}	CTRL	3		{F8}	f8		
{CYN}	CTRL	4		←	←		
{PUR}	CTRL	5		↑	SHIFT	↑	

Index

If you've enjoyed the articles in this book, you'll find the same style and quality in every monthly issue of **COMPUTE!** Magazine. Use this form to order your subscription to **COMPUTE!**.

For Fastest Service,
Call Our **Toll-Free** US Order Line
800-334-0868
In NC call 919-275-9809

COMPUTE!

P.O. Box 5406
Greensboro, NC 27403

My Computer Is:
☐ Commodore 64 ☐ TI-99/4A ☐ Timex/Sinclair ☐ VIC-20 ☐ PET
☐ Radio Shack Color Computer ☐ Apple ☐ Atari ☐ Other _____
☐ Don't yet have one...

☐ $24 One Year US Subscription
☐ $45 Two Year US Subscription
☐ $65 Three Year US Subscription

Subscription rates outside the US:

☐ $30 Canada
☐ $42 Europe, Australia, New Zealand/Air Delivery
☐ $52 Middle East, North Africa, Central America/Air Mail
☐ $72 Elsewhere/Air Mail
☐ $30 International Surface Mail (lengthy, unreliable delivery)

Name _____

Address _____

City _____ State _____ Zip _____

Country _____

Payment must be in US Funds drawn on a US Bank; International Money Order, or charge card.
☐ Payment Enclosed   ☐ VISA
☐ MasterCard   ☐ American Express
Acc t. No. _____ Expires _____ /

20-5

COMPUTE! Books

P.O. Box 5406   Greensboro, NC 27403

Ask your retailer for these **COMPUTE! Books**. If he or she has sold out, order directly from **COMPUTE!**

For Fastest Service
Call Our **TOLL FREE US Order Line**
800-334-0868
In NC call 919-275-9809

Quantity	Title	Price	Total
_____	Machine Language for Beginners	**$14.95**†	_____
_____	Home Energy Applications	**$14.95**†	_____
_____	COMPUTE!'s First Book of VIC	**$12.95**†	_____
_____	COMPUTE!'s Second Book of VIC	**$12.95**†	_____
_____	COMPUTE!'s First Book of VIC Games	**$12.95**†	_____
_____	COMPUTE!'s First Book of 64	**$12.95**†	_____
_____	COMPUTE!'s First Book of Atari	**$12.95**†	_____
_____	COMPUTE!'s Second Book of Atari	**$12.95**†	_____
_____	COMPUTE!'s First Book of Atari Graphics	**$12.95**†	_____
_____	COMPUTE!'s First Book of Atari Games	**$12.95**†	_____
_____	Mapping The Atari	**$14.95**†	_____
_____	Inside Atari DOS	**$19.95**†	_____
_____	The Atari BASIC Sourcebook	**$12.95**†	_____
_____	Programmer's Reference Guide for TI-99/4A	**$14.95**†	_____
_____	COMPUTE!'s First Book of TI Games	**$12.95**†	_____
_____	Every Kid's First Book of Robots and Computers	**$ 4.95***	_____
_____	The Beginner's Guide to Buying A Personal Computer	**$ 3.95***	_____

* Add $1 shipping and handling. Outside US add $5 air mail; $2 surface mail.
† Add $2 shipping and handling. Outside US add $5 air mail; $2 surface mail.

Please add shipping and handling for each book ordered.   _____

Total enclosed or to be charged.   _____

All orders must be prepaid (money order, check, or charge). All payments must be in US funds. NC residents add 4% sales tax.
☐ Payment enclosed   Please charge my: ☐ VISA   ☐ MasterCard
☐ American Express   Acc t. No.   Expires   /

Name

Address

City   State   Zip

Country
Allow 4-5 weeks for delivery.

20-5